News Production

Journalists often say they act out of instinct and experience. Yet how do we reconcile this with academic discussions of the effects of ownership, advertising, news frames, and other institutional and cultural constraints on news production?

News Production: Theory and practice bridges this gap between journalistic theory and practice. The book assesses existing sociological theories of journalism and changes to news production through case studies of news production settings and interviews with journalists, thus providing both students and working professionals with an invaluable real-life account of reporting in the context of the contemporary newsroom.

Chapters cover practical and theoretical concerns including:

- Reporting
- Propaganda
- Meeting deadlines
- Target audiences
- Ethics and values
- Sources
- Images
- Rise of marketing factors.

News Production: Theory and practice is key reading for journalism students and those wanting to break into the industry.

David Machin works in the Department of Media and Communications at Leicester University. He is author of *The Anglo-American Media Connection* (1999), *Ethnographic Research for Media Studies* (2002) and a range of journal publications focused on issues of journalism and media production.

Sarah Niblock trained at *Birkenhead News* and *Liverpool Echo*. She also wrote for *Cosmopolitan* and *Company* for several years. Sarah is the author of *Inside Journalism* (Routledge 1996) and numerous other academic works on journalism and visual culture. She leads the Masters programme in journalism at Brunel University.

News Production
Theory and practice

David Machin
and
Sarah Niblock

First published 2006
by Routledge
2 Park Square, Milton Park, Abingdon, Oxon OX14 4RN

Simultaneously published in the USA and Canada
by Routledge
270 Madison Ave, New York, NY 10016

Routledge is an imprint of the Taylor & Francis Group, an informa business

Typeset in Galliard by
Florence Production Ltd, Stoodleigh, Devon
Printed and bound in Great Britain by
MPG Books Ltd, Bodmin, Cornwall

British Library Cataloguing in Publication Data
A catalogue record for this book is available from the British Library

Library of Congress Cataloging in Publication Data
Machin, David.
News production: theory and practice/David Machin and
Sarah Niblock.
p. cm.
Includes bibliographical references.
1. Journalism. 2. Reporters and reporting. 3. Television
broadcasting of news. I. Niblock, Sarah. II. Title.
PN4731.M273 2006
070–dc22 2006018037

ISBN10: 0–415–37140–6 (hbk)
ISBN10: 0–415–37141–4 (pbk)

ISBN13: 978–0-415–37140–7 (hbk)
ISBN13: 978–0-415–37141–4 (pbk)

Contents

Acknowledgements

The aim of this book is to establish a closer dialogue between academics and journalists, to help enrich public understanding of this dynamic and often controversial industry. We are grateful for the generosity of the many journalists and educators we have met and worked with in the course of preparing the manuscript, and from whom we have learnt an enormous amount. We are indebted to the many news organisations and their staff, who patiently answered questions and took time to explain and reflect in the midst of deadlines and other pressures. These include Gary Bainbridge, Jonty Beavan, Colin Bickler, Jon Brooker, Simon Cadman, Jon Godel, Colin Hughes, Ann McFerran, Jim Maceda, Kevin Murphy, Malcolm Rees, Mary Rees, Zoe Smith, Lou Thomas, Chris Walker and Brian Walters. Also, we are grateful for the input and advice from Professor Ros Coward, Professor Richard Keeble, Professor Howard Tumber, and from our friends, colleagues and students at Brunel University, University of Leicester, City University and Cardiff University. This book could not have been realised without the encouragement and support of Natalie Foster, Aileen Storry, Rose James and Katherine Sheppard for Routledge.

1 News journalism

Bridging the 'theory–practice' divide

News journalists often describe their thinking as so instinctive that it defies explanation. Split-second decision-making, gut instinct, curiosity and a 'nose' for news are highly prized attributes of any reporter or editor working in a fast-paced news environment. The editor of a leading international news agency said that 'with experience that thought process happens in about one-and-a-half seconds' (Niblock 1996: 8). Other leading journalists, such as UK flagship news anchor John Humphrys, have publicly lamented the way the news industry of the twenty-first century has been professionalised, and has called for the return to the core values of simplicity and accessibility. After all, he claims, 'any five-year-old can do my job'. Yet it is evident that journalism has become increasingly a graduate, if not postgraduate, occupation. Fewer and fewer entrants to this dynamic sphere become journalists straight from school, as editors opt for university-educated trainees. Simultaneously, events on a global scale are being transmitted increasingly through the grainy footage of ordinary citizens captured on mobile telephone cameras. Digital technology is changing the staffing needs of newsrooms, the Internet is providing a greater variety of news voices and debate, and over the last two decades waves of deregulation of the market have placed news production under increased commercial pressures. There is an urgent need to examine and update our understanding of how news journalism functions and impacts on our society. If, as journalists claim, newsgathering and production is conducted not through intellectual tools but through experience, tenacity and gut feeling, how do we respond to countless theoretical discussions about news that have emerged since as early as the nineteenth century? Can we – should we – try to accommodate the notion of the 'thinking practitioner', the news journalist who reflects on what they do?

A rich, interdisciplinary body of scholarship into news journalism has raised critical concern about the industry. Since the earliest days of mass communication questions have been raised as to the implications of popular journalism, of concentrated ownership, of unacceptable practices, of sexism and racism, of sensationalism and bias, to list but a few. Libraries stock an ever-increasing volume of academic textbooks and research monographs on journalism from media studies, cultural studies, sociology, gender studies and philosophy and communication studies. Academics from these disciplines have joined forces to combine their intellectual approaches in an attempt to offer fresher insights into the rapidly changing journalism context. In-depth studies of the history, development and products and processes of journalism have been undertaken which, it must be said, have proffered ominous and negative conclusions about the nature and integrity of journalism and its millions of practitioners. Now, in the twenty-first century, we have a burgeoning, autonomous branch of scholarship known as journalism studies.

Journalism studies, like other related studies of popular culture such as film and media studies, is emerging out of academic publication and debate. At the time of writing, it has centred on historical and political economic models of journalism. It also incorporates important issues concerning technology, mass communication, political communication, health and science, faith, representation and many more areas. However, what distinguishes journalism studies from the other types of study of the media is its engagement with practitioners. With the proliferation of journalism education in universities and colleges, a growing number of journalism trainers have become part of the wider academic debate on theory. International forums have been created to bring scholars and trainers together, such as the European Journalism Training Association, Association of Journalism Educators in the UK and the Journalism Studies Interest Group in the US. For many who work in higher education, there is frustration expressed about the so-called 'theory–practice divide'. Practitioners and trainers argue that theoretical models are not produced by working journalists and are therefore not a reflection of the everyday dilemmas and pressures faced in newsrooms. Similarly, theoretical researchers regret that practitioners and trainers are overly resistant to scholarship and reflection. Given the rapid evolution of the news machine from parish pump to global infrastructure, how well have these academic theories kept pace with reality? Or, as one television journalism lecturer put it: 'You can't teach students how to "do a Marx" in the BBC newsroom.' (i.e., what is the point of abstract critical theory if it is not grounded in the everyday practical realities of news?).

A new breed of journalism scholar is arriving on the scene: one who is attempting to find an accommodation between these schools of thought. Journalism education and research are no longer seen as anathema to good practice, judging by the hundreds of fully trained mid-career news people moving into higher education departments on full- or part-time contracts. This, coupled with the growing media literacy of audiences and practitioners, is leading to new lines of scholarly research that foreground practice over theory. New and fascinating illuminations are also emerging from practitioners themselves on what it is like to be faced with challenging professional dilemmas. This is what is being called research into reflective practice.

This book aims to shed new light on the everyday reflective practices of news journalists, by comparing and contrasting real-life case studies with some of the most abiding theories about journalism. In doing so, we wish to explore the efficacy of these theories, identifying their strengths but also the questions they raise. The central, underlying theme of the book is that theory and practice cannot be separated – theory can help to explain practice and practice can help us explore theory. What is particularly original and reflective about our book is the way we engage the journalists from our case studies in our research and critical debate. For too long, researchers have relied on the *products* of news to assert far-reaching conclusions about the state of modern journalism and the integrity of its practitioners. In other words, they have arrived at conclusions about the nature of the industry not on the basis of an understanding of processes but by reading newspaper texts, or by recording news bulletins. It is our belief, based on conversations with, and employment within, the industry over many years that this has caused great suspicion about the nature and relevance of scholarly inquiry into journalism. How can a sociologist, however skilled and trained in their discipline, know what its like to be on a newsdesk at deadline time? How can the academic possibly comprehend the myriad pressures – institutional, professional, editorial, commercial, psychological – that find their nexus in that split-second news judgement decision? How useful is it to critique the newsmakers if it leads to a complete divorce from and rejection of scholarly activity on the part of the latter group?

We address these concerns directly with professional news journalists. One of the authors is an academic who has been studying the media and audiences for over a decade and has increasingly become concerned about the lack of engagement with practitioners within much scholarly work. The other is a fully trained experienced news journalist, who can understand first-hand the language, pace and decision-making of the journalists she encounters. Instead of looking *in* on the products of news journalism from the *outside*, we explore the practices and the people from *within*. In doing so, some startling, fresh and constructive insights emerge. That is not to say that we do not find areas of concern that require deep interrogation in terms of their implications – this is not intended to be a glowing uncritical endorsement of modern-day news journalism and a rejection of theory. It is quite the opposite. We intend to redress some of what we perceive is the elitist exclusion of real-life journalists from academic discussions about their own work. There are of course a few notable exceptions which we refer to through this study and to whom we are indebted and inspired, such as Howard Tumber, Wendy Bacon, Tony Harcup, Richard Keeble, Ros Coward and others.

Why is this project so very important? In Western societies we view news as invaluable for the operation of our participatory democratic systems. News informs us of issues of economics, social problems, threats to society etc., so that we come to know about the world that is outside our everyday experience. This permits us to make informed judgements about who we choose to vote for or what we choose to buy, for instance. What journalists report on therefore has real effects on people's lives. A report about a problem with the schooling system, a crime wave or a faulty drug will affect public opinion. This will then place pressure on government policy to change legislation. This may then effect a change on social processes which in turn can be monitored by journalists. What we can see from this is that we cannot have democracy without journalism. Journalism, in this model, carries a massive social responsibility. It is crucial that, especially with the pace of change in the news business, we have in-depth dialogue with journalists and a better understanding of their everyday practices and decision-making.

Exploring the context for the practice of news journalism

This book will investigate and illuminate the everyday decision-making and practices of journalists in context, enabling it to successfully evaluate the efficacy of journalism theories. By context, we mean that contemporary news journalism operates at the nexus of a myriad of factors, both internal and external, that impact upon the practices of the reporter or editor. The consensual view of the role of the journalist is a seeker of truth, the eyes and ears of the people. We find such views widely aired. Michael Grade, in his 2005 inaugural Hugh Cudlipp Lecture at the London College of Communications, said of the BBC: 'The BBC has a duty to set a gold standard in news reporting, in accuracy, in impartiality, in creating a better understanding' (Grade 2005). Kevin Marsh, editor of BBC Radio 4's *Today* programme, in a speech to the Society of Editors in Autumn 2004, said that some of the important characteristics of good journalism were: 'Curiosity. Persistence. Toughness. . . . Ruthlessness with fact.' Similarly, The American Project for Excellence in Journalism states on its web site, www.journalism.org, that journalism is 'a discipline of verification' whose 'first obligation is to the truth'.

In this model, journalism is about bravely finding the facts and delivering them to the public with neutrality so that the truth can be known. The public does not have the time or resources to be able to find out about why wars are fought, where there are current famines in the world, and what dangers lie outside the home. Reporters dig around to investigate and reveal on the public's behalf. They select the events that are most relevant to people, find ways to investigate them further and identify sources that can shed light on the central issues. Scholarly research into journalism has traditionally been highly critical of the news industry when it veers from this model of integrity. However, when talking with news professionals, it is immediately apparent that they themselves realise that it is difficult to describe their jobs in these idealistic terms. While we might

Table 1.1 Obstacles to impartial reporting

Intrinsic – procedural	*Extrinsic – historical*
Newsworthiness	Legislation
Ownership	Regulatory framework
Training/socialisation	Cultural expectations
Deadlines	Competition
Target audience	

hope that journalists are the eyes and ears of the public, upholding democracy, there are a range of quite simple constraints, which are a part of the practical everyday nature of news production. The criticism with which most are familiar is that bad journalism or bad news happens when there is bias. But this misses the point, and in fact is a criticism that helps to conceal the real obstacles to impartial reporting. Some of these factors are summarised in Table 1.1, and will be explored in more depth below and referred to throughout the book.

Of course this is not a neat model, just as journalism practice cannot be overly simplified or compartmentalised. The Intrinsic – procedural is inescapably historical in the sense that newsroom operations have developed over time through precedent, and continue to evolve in response to technological and commercial developments. In a similar fashion, the regulatory framework evolves in response to Intrinsic – procedural factors, as evidenced in, for example, the extension of ethical codes to Internet journalism.

Intrinsic factors

Newsworthiness

Of all the events that happen in the world everyday, journalists are only able to cover very few of them. Of those few, only a tiny minority will receive front page or top-of-the-bulletin status. Some scholars have criticised journalists themselves for taking a powerful, subjective gate-keeping role that prevents untold stories reaching the headlines. Other scholars claim what is reported is down to proprietorial influences. Journalists themselves say that it is professional routines, lack of space/airtime and sheer gut instinct that determines newsworthiness. This book will examine who is right.

Ownership

Globally commercial news media are concentrated in very few hands. Many journalism scholars view the trend towards media chains, brands and consolidation with concern. Fewer publishers and broadcasters may mean that there are fewer editorial perspectives. However, it may also be argued that large news organisations can cut the costs of production and distribution, offering a bigger share of the budget to newsgathering and presentation. In contrast, journalists may say the profits are top-sliced by the shareholders.

Training/socialisation

Ideas of truth and neutrality, as opposed to their opposites, bias and opinion, are part of the mythology of journalism and when most young journalists decide to move into the field it is these notions that inspire them. Trainee journalists have the impression that throughout their careers, through curiosity and persistence, they will ruthlessly dig out and verify the facts with complete impartiality and share them with the public. The kinds of journalist that are most celebrated in the journalist community are those where some kind of physical danger has lead to the revealing of the facts. Journalist heroes are seen reporting wearing armoured vests as bullets and bombs whizz overhead, as was the case in the invasion of Iraq. But in order for young journalists to make a positive impression on their first employer and progress their careers in this highly competitive and demanding sphere, they must recognise, adhere to and internalise company values. This book will explore the difficult relationship between theoretical notions of ideal journalistic values alongside the real-life concerns and career uncertainties of young journalists.

Deadlines

Production schedules ensure that process can drive content, rather than the other way round, in contemporary newsrooms. Waiting for the ideal source is a luxury as the clock ticks closer to the hour when the presses roll or the bulletin goes on air. Journalism scholars have been critical of the limited array of sources repeatedly featured in news, accusing journalists of opting for establishment, authority figures rather than seeking diverse views. In reality, journalists will find long sought-after quotes cut by sub-editors if there is a shortage of space. Additionally, the pressure to be first with the news, as opposed to the most in-depth, is ever more acute.

Target audience

In the context of fierce competition, journalists are working in ever tighter financial and time constraints and under a new business ethos where news must be designed for specific target audiences. Critics of journalism argue that news is being overly simplified in order to fit in with advertising demographics, to reach mass audiences. Conversely, senior editors claim they are finding new ways of telling stories to audiences and readers who had previously not been catered for.

Extrinsic limitations

Legislation

The legal framework within which journalists operate can both protect and hinder news reporting. Freedom of speech is enshrined in Western legislation, but is increasingly under threat. Recent criticism of media coverage centring on celebrity coverage has led to calls for the outlawing of certain journalism practices such as covert recording. Those with power and money are seeking to control the news media through the courts. Journalists argue, conversely, that the legal obstacles around freedom of information make it very difficult for reporters to investigate matters of great public interest.

Regulatory framework

In a similar way to the legislative framework, journalists work within a regulatory code that seeks to establish and maintain the moral and ethical standards of news reporting. Critics of journalism standards highlight breaches of ethical codes: these in turn damage the trust that the public has for journalists and their integrity. Journalism practitioners may counter that for journalism to be truly a watchdog on democracy, it may sometimes be more ethical to act outside consensual moral codes; that journalists should not be part of a system, but always on its margins.

Cultural expectations

While this book focuses on journalism within the context of Western democracies, it must not be forgotten that journalists operate within a range of cultural contexts that may foreclose opportunities for breadth and depth of coverage. Political controls may impact upon what journalists are allowed to report, which may sometimes be through threat of death. In Western capitalist society, there are still differences of opinion over what role journalists should play. Journalists have a difficult balancing act in terms of satisfying a diversity of expectations. It must also not be forgotten that journalists are not just national, as regional and local reporters have a remit to reflect very different concerns from those based in capital cities. Many argue that it is very hard for them to always reflect their public's opinions, and that that public is diverse, demanding and ever-changing.

Competition

All journalism is to some extent reliant for its existence on a strong market position. Even public service broadcasting relies on satisfying its licence-payers that it provides best value for money. Academic approaches to journalism have been concerned with an over-emphasis on market concerns in the drive to offer news faster and most attractively. For editors, it is a case of fighting for the survival of their outlet in the competitive marketplace. This has been most evident in the attempts by the quality press to rebrand in order to stem reader losses to the mid-market and tabloid titles.

Sociologists' and historians' views of the news media are therefore often quite different from those of journalists themselves, though not always too far removed. This is not to say therefore that good journalism is not possible, only that a better journalist is aware of these things. This book is about knowing, understanding and working with these constraints, precisely for the reason of being a better journalist. Most seasoned journalists are, in fact, more or less aware of what we talk about in this book, as will become clear in each chapter. Yet there is still far greater room for the theoretical/sociological studies of news to be integrated into what is commonly thought of as journalistic practice. Journalists have the job of being watchdog to the powerful, making sure a range of voices are heard in society, giving important information to the public in order that a democratic society can operate. Yet we have little debate about what they do apart from some criticism of the so-called 'gutter press'. This lack of open discussion is a feature both of the public domain and within the profession itself. This book seeks to open that discussion.

Journalists have shown themselves to be open to reflection. For instance, there has been a great deal of reflexivity in evidence in terms of the weblog, editors going online, the autobiography and the emergence of the journalism professor from senior editorial management. This has been in response to the unprecedented news environments that journalists are finding themselves in, their expanding use of technology which raises many questions ethically for them, and the awareness that audiences are ever-more demanding and promiscuous in their media consumption. There is a search for a critical vocabulary that can be shared by scholars and practitioners to enable reflexivity and best practice. We need to start by revisiting some of the most abiding theoretical approaches to news journalism, in order to identify their strengths and applicability. It is also pressing that we in academe acknowledge the gaps and fissures that prevent a clearer understanding of the pressures faced in real-life journalism.

The traditional separation between those who practise news journalism and those who theorise about it is beginning to close. Events in world history and the unprecedented close-up coverage by technologically advanced news media have heralded debate and reflection not only from scholars and critics but also from journalists themselves. One of the obstacles to a clear dialogue and debate has been the ever-present critique of the processes, practices and motivations of news professionals. This chapter will provide a critical account of the history and ownership context of news journalism, while the next chapter will explore theoretical approaches to news, which span many disciplines. The account is by no means exhaustive, but will provide a useful overview. The underlying premise behind critical studies of news production is that journalism is a set of practices, located within a sociocultural and socio-economic context. In this sense, when we attempt to analyse and evaluate that set of practices, we must do so by acknowledging and synthesising cultural, economic, geographical and historical factors that may impact upon them. It will be noted that it has been a tendency within academic approaches to look at just one, or maybe two of these factors. This book will argue that there should be a more broad-ranging approach in order to accommodate some of the limitations of key theories. Most strikingly, it will be apparent that there has so far been a lack of analyses of news journalists themselves, to explore their philosophical and psychological motivations in pursuing stories and also journalism as a profession per se. A few tracking studies of professionals have been undertaken, some of which will be referred to, but more work needs to be done in this area.

Accordingly, this chapter will commence with a brief overview of the development of news journalism in western democracies through the eyes of some leading commentators on the history of journalism. Next, we will examine the current ownership and control of global media, drawing on the critical theories of political economy of journalism.

News as a set of historical practices

The practices that bring headline events into our homes have evolved over thousands of years. Despite the technological sophistication of media formats, the underlying principles and protocols of news delivery are fundamentally unchanged. Accounts of the history of journalism help us to understand that news, far from being something reported objectively from a 'real' world, is in fact inextricably tied up with the development of society, politics, industry and culture. The everyday, routine practices of news editors and reporters arose from particular circumstances and philosophies. Journalism scholars, therefore, assert that we can find explanations for current approaches to news journalism – say, tabloid exposés of celebrities – by looking to their origins over time.

Human beings have always had an innate curiosity about the world around them. The great psychoanalytical theorists, including Freud, Lacan and Klein, agree this curiosity is vital for survival, stemming from the earliest days of infancy when the child realises that they are a separate entity from their mother. Throughout our lives, and throughout civilisations, we are anxious to learn about events and issues that will impact upon our lives. It is the human capacity to investigate their environment and the people around them in order to make our societies and the world better to live in that has given us our selective advantage over other species. Historically, travellers' tales and gossip have evolved into specialised technological means of gathering and disseminating news on a regular basis with increasing speed and regularity. Early forms of transmission were word-of-mouth, though attempts to retell events in writing have been recorded during the rule of Julius Caesar in Rome. A daily report of politics was compiled in Rome and distributed to its colonies. The visual and oral dissemination of news that prevails today has its origins in 'mass' communications, albeit on a much smaller scale than today, to people with poor literacy rates, especially prior to the Industrial Revolution. Paintings and ballads were alternative means of reaching those who could not read or afford written forms of information.

The invention of the printing press, attributed to Gutenberg in 1456, heralded the opportunity for much wider dissemination of written information. Periodicals and newspapers emerged in Europe from the seventeenth century, including the semi-annual *Mercurius Gallobelgicus*. This Latin publication was produced in Cologne, Germany, and is considered by many historians to be the world's first periodical. The *Oxford Gazette*, originating in 1665, was among the first regularly published newspapers and appeared twice each month. It would have been produced in London had the English court not been relocated to avoid the plague. The world's first known daily newspaper, the *Daily Courant*, was launched in 1702 in the United Kingdom, and lasted 30 years.

Journalists and politicians have always had a difficult relationship, and not only in terms of reporters' probing. Press activity was limited from the outset by regulation. For instance, in the US the Press Restriction Act required the printer's name and place of publication be included within the document, and a 1662 law in Massachusetts forbade printing except by licence. It is claimed this led to an early form of press censorship as licences were only permitted to those outlets that did not criticise authority. For instance, during the American Revolution, a Stamp Act was passed which required all newspapers only to use newsprint bearing an official stamp to show tax had been paid. Newspapers could be suppressed by denying the stamp. Similarly, in the UK the Stamp Tax had the effect of raising the price of newspapers to such a degree that few ordinary people could afford them, thus limiting the power of the press to reach wide audiences.

By the middle of the nineteenth century, the newspaper was typically published once or twice a week. They were usually partisan, and much of the content was duplicated, sometimes verbatim, from other newspapers, bar local coverage. Entertainment has been a long-standing feature of news media, with the earliest regular publications containing poetry, fiction and humour.

It has been a recurring pattern that technology has driven the processes and practices of news journalism. In the 1850s, huge presses that could print thousands of copies of newspapers every hour increased the possibility of mass circulation. Whereas access to news media had traditionally been the privilege of wealth through annual subscription, it was now possible to purchase a newspaper from a street seller for just a penny. Newspaper publishers such as James Gordon Bennett, who launched the *New York Herald* in 1835, capitalised on the forces of industrialisation, the exodus of workers from the fields to the factory and the increases in literacy. Newspapers would become independent of government and party control and be subject to the forces of capitalism. The *Herald* achieved a circulation of 40,000 in just over a year. Its editorial structure inspired the modern pattern of staff reporters and specialist and foreign correspondents giving first-hand accounts of events.

During the second half of the nineteenth century, further development of journalism practices to which newsrooms are now very accustomed took place. These developments were effected by technological developments, growing competition between proprietors, and also the unprecedented challenges that covering bigger stories brought. English newspapers, for instance, were among the first to use bold, attention-grabbing headlines to maximise readerships.

The global dominance of Western news agencies has its roots in the nineteenth century. The invention of the telegraph by Samuel Morse in 1837 improved the speed and reliability of news reporting. Wire services began in 1848 in New York when six large newspapers formed a co-operative agreement to provide joint coverage of Europe. This co-operative was later to become Associated Press, now a world-famous international agency. News was transmitted to and from North America and Europe through the new transatlantic cable. The first European agencies – the French Havas, the German Wolff and British Reuters (the semi-official news agency of the British empire) set up a financial data service for bankers before launching a news service. It has been argued that these agencies, which had a remit to provide neutral, impartial reporting, in fact reflected national viewpoints in their editorial stance (Boyd-Barrett 1980). The big agencies made massive amounts of money through supplying financial and other information needed for military and political reasons. Most of their enormous wealth was made in the new mass markets of the colonial powers. The two dominant news agencies in the 1930s, British Reuters and the American Associated Press, signed an exclusive deal during the Second World War which gave them a duopoly over news supply. This basically sealed up control of world news ever since (Tunstall and Machin 1999). This has led to considerable criticism from many Third World countries that they are either excluded from world news or are represented through Western stereotypes.

Just as technology enhanced and influenced the gathering and dissemination of news, it also impacted upon the style and delivery of news language. The American Civil War prompted intense competition to report battles and developments, to get new and exclusive information. This led to the creation of the specialist war correspondent. The war correspondents' despatches to the newsdesk were made by telegraph, which demanded that the writer express their message using the fewest words possible. For the news journalist, this technological tool necessitated an economy of language that is taken for granted and expected of professional journalists in contemporary newsrooms, whatever the story.

Human interest journalism, which means stories that are designed to attract an emotional reaction rather than containing intrinsic news scale, are a vital component of any bulletin, page or screen in the current context. Dismissed by some critics as a frivolous dilution of hard news values brought about by modern-day competition, stories about offbeat events, extra-marital affairs and scandals actually have their origins in the nineteenth century. Charles Anderson Dana, editor of the *New York Sun*, coined the oft-cited description of the newsworthy as 'man bites dog'. While the new-found vibrancy and sensationalism of the news media has been and still is criticised by some critics as pandering to profit-making, other historical accounts make connections between so-called tabloid values and the development of investigative and campaigning journalism. Joseph Pulitzer who, with William Randolph Hearst, was one of the most powerful forces in American journalism in the later part of the nineteenth century, established papers with a reputation for sensationalism, but also integrity. The impulse to deliver shocking stories was directed towards the public good with a commitment to social conscience and exposing corruption and hypocrisy. Using a similar approach, Hearst became one of the first powerful media moguls, building an empire of publications, a newsreel company and other related industries.

It has been a concern of journalism scholars that the growth of the powerful media owner, or mogul, contributed to a reduction in the scope and variety of news. With concentration of ownership and resources, papers belonging to large groups were able to stave off rivals, often causing them to collapse. While the profitability of large newspaper groups might be said to provide a larger newsroom budget to aid reporting, it has been argued that proceeds of mergers have not always been to the benefit of the journalists. In the 1960s, partly in response to the dominance of the news agenda by major groups and networks, different forms of experimental journalism emerged from the underground press which combined traditional reporting skills with creative methods of storytelling. The late Hunter S. Thompson's reporting for *Rolling Stone* has been seen as definitive in its challenge to the notion that mainstream news is objective and neutral.

The introduction of broadcast news at the turn of the twentieth century heralded tighter regulation of output and the eventual growth of competition, not just for stories but also for control of media outlets. Limited airspace meant that stations had to apply for a licence to broadcast. Licences depended upon stations demonstrating that they would broadcast for the public good. What the public good was could clearly be open to subjective, political and cultural interpretation. Nevertheless, television and radio stations in their early incarnations had an advantage over newspapers in that they could broadcast breaking news stories minutes after they had occurred. Newspapers responded by going into increasing depth and context, including pioneering investigative work by the likes of reporters Carl Bernstein and Bob Woodward. Working at the *Washington Post*, they showed the world how powerful print investigative reporting could be when they broke details of the Watergate scandal to the public in 1973. The impact of their story, into corruption in President Nixon's administration, sparked major political events including Nixon's resignation. The potential for the news media to offer a ground-breaking watchdog on democracy was great.

News operations, with the exception of the news wires, historically, had a locale, such as in the case of local, regional and national newspapers. Nowadays, with the Internet, we are accustomed to receiving news from throughout the world in an instant, and may choose to forgo local events and issues. The advent of the snapshot headline 'global' report came with the launch of *USA Today* in the 1980s. This paper harnessed new technological developments in on-screen page make-up to provide low word-count snapshots of international and national stories. It was influential in using a modular layout and white space to attract a particular demographic of reader and to organise the flow of information to the audience. Design came to the forefront of newspaper production, not least as a marketing device to capture different types of audience. This was enabled by the advent of desktop computers and software that allowed journalists themselves, rather than printers, to envision and control how the news would be presented visually. Thus the cheapness and accessibility of the technology beckoned a greater awareness of the visual impact of stories, and the subtleties of typography to engage or distance readers. However, the rapid expansion of digital technology in print and broadcast contexts led some journalism scholars to speculate that the newspaper's demise was inevitable. Rolling 24-hour news operations available through satellite and cable, would, they argued, obliterate any need to read yesterday's news today. However, far from perceiving electronic media as a threat, newspapers embraced the Internet and claimed it as their own by offering multiformat delivery and archives. An interesting development arising out of this is that newspapers can publish news as rapidly as broadcast outlets, though the pressure to be first means that there is an ever-increasing reliance on agency feeds rather than first-hand verification of facts. However, the fact that it is possible for readers and viewers to interact with their chosen mode through email and web-chats offers a new and instant feedback mechanism. Technology may have closed the distance between world events and newsmakers, and in turn it may have brought journalists and their audiences in closer proximity. It is interesting to witness how the advent of the news blog mirrors the oral tradition of news that this section opened with.

Accounts of the historical development of journalism raise important questions for considerations of journalism practices in the contemporary newsroom. They are a significant starting point for entering into a dialogue with journalists themselves about their daily work. These include: whether journalists operate freely in the context of government and industry regulation; whether media moguls and press barons have too much editorial influence over content; whether technological developments and market forces have impacted positively or negatively on news output. We will be discussing these points with journalists a little further into the book. First, we need to look deeper into some of the theoretical work on an important contextual area of journalism that seeks to address these questions.

Political economy approaches to news journalism

Earlier, we described how society has expectations about the ideal role of the journalist – including that they should ensure that a diversity of views are heard. A question arising from this is how can news media be impartial when they are controlled by so few people? News outlets have become concentrated into fewer and fewer hands both at the local and global level, facilitated by successive changes in media regulation. These changes have allowed huge increases in the numbers of media outlets that can be owned by one organisation, and have permitted owners to acquire cross-media interests. For example, in 2005 in the UK the Trinity Mirror group owned around 250 local newspapers including many major city titles such as the *Leicester Mercury.* They were in a position where they had ownership of previously competing local titles such as in South Wales with the *Western Mail* and *South Wales Evening Post.* It also had shares in a number of radio stations and networks and shares in Reuters. In France the Le Monde Group was controlling 43 different daily and weekly titles. In Spain the bulk of newspapers were in the hands of four large groups: Prisa, Correo, Zeta and Pearson. Across Europe and the US most newspaper titles are part of such large media groups (European Journalism Centre Online 2005).

For some theorists studying the political economy of media, this increasing concentration of private ownership is at odds with the media being able to act as watchdogs for a democratic society: news outlets that are part of massive corporations will be unlikely to be critical of views that are favourable to corporate capitalism. Additionally, it is argued that they will be unlikely to represent views that are critical of themselves, in other words, of large corporations. Such news media may be able to cover world poverty, for example, showing audiences heart-rending images of starving Africans, but the reporter is unlikely to connect this developing world crisis to its roots in global capitalism and the activities of global corporations and banking. We might find reports on anti-social behaviour in our cities, but little on the way that the associated poverty is related to economic policies and forms of social organisation that are favourable to large corporations.

Media ownership as a means to control what people read about, to promote particular views of the world, is nothing new. So-called 'press barons' at the turn of the twentieth century, such as Pulitzer and Hearst in the US and Northcliffe and Beaverbrook in the UK, used their newspaper chains to disseminate their political views in order to promote their business interests and to criticise those views that might hamper them. (Curran and Seaton 1991; Tunstall and Palmer 1991). Since the 1970s and the rise of conservative free-market capitalism, those on the right have argued that private ownership of the media facilitates a free press and is good for democracy. This means, it is believed, that a number of private voices will keep the state and government in check. This idea led to successive waves of deregulation in the US, UK and then Europe.

In the 1980s and 1990s there were many big changes in the ownership and structure of news organisations. This was part of a more general bulking up facilitated by changes in broadcasting regulation. The US Telecommunications Act 1996 was the catalyst for speeding up mergers and buyouts. The law encouraged competition, hence dragging down prices of news products. One school of thought to the right believed that the winners would be news consumers: market logic meant that in the end there would be more choice and producers would seek to meet market requirements. From another perspective, it meant that more could be owned and companies could get bigger. One advantage of increasing ownership of outlets for news journalism is that of economy of scale: if content is made centrally it can then be syndicated across the outlets. For example the 1996 Act freed up how many radio stations could be held by one company. US-based Clear Channel soon had control over 1,200 stations (www.clearchannel.com). Similar cross-media groupings soon formed all over Europe, such as SER in Spain and EMAP in Britain, as deregulation spread – all done in the name of improved choice for listeners (Tunstall and Machin 1999), it was claimed, but their use of syndicated material dramatically reduced local content (Grossman 1998).

After deregulation all the major US news networks were bought up by media conglomerates: ABC by Disney, CBS by Viacom and NBC by General Electric. Consider the example of Viacom, the owner of CBS News. This is what it owned in 2005: 40 television stations, cable stations including MTV, Nickelodeon, the Movie Channel, Sundance Channel, 176 radio stations across the US including New York, Dallas, Seattle, Los Angeles, Denver, Philadelphia, a Hollywood film studio Paramount Pictures (makers of movies such as *War of the Worlds*), international film distribution company UIP, the global chain of UCI cinemas, Blockbuster video and international book publisher Simon & Schuster. Audiences watching CBS News are watching a news product that is produced by a billion dollar a year transnational media conglomerate. Furthermore, this corporation has interests around the globe in different media. Mergers by companies such as Viacom and a handful of other conglomerates such as Disney, News Corporation,

Time Warner and Bertelsmann, were part of a strategic aim to become vertically integrated. This enables cost-effective control of multiple stages of the media process – production, distribution and exhibition.

This kind of bulking up also has the advantage of synergy, meaning that corporations can cross-advertise and self-promote. They can also use material across different media, which brings about massive economy of scale; the larger the corporation's output and the more parts of the process it controls, the more that it can get a return on productions through multiple outlets, the cheaper the product. Globally, other countries have followed this US pattern. Depending on the size of the country, one or several media corporations are buying up news outlets. Furthermore, some media corporations are now closely tied to finance and industrial capital. (Curran 1991; Tunstall and Palmer 1991). Commentators argue that such corporations are unlikely to be critical of the corporate world in general.

Also challenging the idea of news organisations as neutral media researchers point out that many of the major shareholders and investors in media corporations are investment banks and other large institutions that have interests across a range of other industries (Wasko 1982; Herman and Chomsky 1988). Some writers (Hollingsworth 1986; Herman and Chomsky 1988; Kellner 1990) see this as a process whereby media corporations will tend to support conservative policies, and will be uncritical of neo-capitalism, seeing it as a natural state of affairs. Herman and Chomsky give a number of examples of international atrocities, such as in Cambodia or East Timor, where the US government were directly involved, that were completely absent from the national press. Movies such as *Black Hawk Down* (2001), made by 20th Century Fox, which tells the story of the US military attempting to help a country in a state of famine, hides the role of the US government in actually causing the famine through its support of ruthless regimes in return for military bases close to the Middle East (Lefebvre 1991; Schraeder1990). If the movies made by these corporations are like this, can we assume that the news will be different?

McChesney (2004) shows that media corporations are among the biggest companies in the world. Using data from *Forbes* magazine, McChesney calculated that over a third of the 50 wealthiest Americans generated the bulk of their fortunes through the media and related industries (2004: 21). He argues: 'Our media, then, far from being on the sidelines of the capitalist system, are amongst its greatest beneficiaries' (2004: 2). These central players are able to lobby Congress and government sometimes with large amounts of cash, and other times in return for favours (Tunstall and Machin 1999). The implications, therefore, of centralising news production in few hands are significant, according to journalism theorists.

As a journalist working for a newspaper in the US or Europe it is very likely that your title will be owned by a large organisation which may control a large slice of the daily circulations in that country and possibly also have large interests in radio and television news. In later chapters we will look more closely at what this means for journalists in a number of contexts and expand in more depth on some of these implications, including a lack of diversity in news content, the susceptibility to advertiser influence and the drive towards attracting mass audiences and readerships through entertainment.

Narrowing news agendas

One of the effects of the deregulation of ownership has been the slimming down of the news production process in order to increase profits. Throughout the 1990s there were waves of redundancies in journalism. In print journalism, these waves were caused by developments in on-screen page make-up technology that made certain roles obsolete. Sub-editors could now do the work of page compositors, for instance, while local reporters began to carry cameras instead of being accompanied by a photographer. Simultaneously, increases in commercial competition have enabled larger chains and conglomerates to use production cost-cutting as a way to maximise profits (Hallin 1996; Bourdieu 1998). The syndication process itself, where output from a central source is then piped out to an unlimited number of outlets, is such a commercial profit-driving force. Such trends mean that the US and Europe, with their deregulated local media networks, are not very local at all (Tunstall and Machin 1999).

Combined with these commercial pressures have been the effects of new media. Bromley (1997) and Parker (1995) described changes in journalism where new recruits to broadcast stations were being trained in digital editing and script writing rather than traditional core investigative techniques that centred on producing well-substantiated news. Some of the daily news, for example, that we hear on our radios from commercial stations in the UK will come from perhaps one electronic newsroom, spliced together from news feeds and archive material. This will then be syndicated free to users, funded by advertising revenue (Niblock and Machin, 2007). In these times of downsizing, journalists must be multi-skilled and technically competent in swift editing practices (Ursell 2001). Garcia Aviles *et al.* (2004: 87) demonstrated that journalists in both Spain and the UK were concerned that the demise of traditional reporting values in the speeded-up digital newsroom was leading them to become 'mouse-monkeys'. Pessimistically, Ekstrom (2000) has written of the television of 'attractions'. His point is that the use of the new technologies themselves can lead to digital theatrics. News viewers now often see maps, tables and computer-generated reconstructions, where in fact he claims little time has been dedicated to actual investigation.

As we have stated, much of the news that we ever come across in the press, online, on TV and radio comes from a handful of Western news agencies. In the 1980s, Bell (1991) wrote that Western newspapers would normally include up to 70 per cent of agency material. But with increased syndication, cuts in newsroom staffing and digital technology some news outlets will now use up to 100 per cent (Niblock and Machin in press). This means that a very small number of organisations have the power to define what is in the news. It is unusual to find a news outlet without access to agency feed including text, pictures, video footage, prepared news items and audio. All these can either be used as received from the agency, or edited to some degree to correspond with the outlet's brand identity. Unless the news outlet is very well staffed, the agency feed will be used more or less as given. It will not be investigated or corroborated.

The big four news agencies, Associated Press, United Press International, Reuters and Agence France Presse, dominate world news collection and dissemination. Only a few news outlets around the world could claim to have any kind of independence from these agencies (Boyd-Barrett 1980). News outlets simply do not have the resources to provide any similar level of international news. Individual outlets would not be financially able to support a global or even national network of reporters. A single international bureau requires several staff, rent, living expenses. Once again, agencies like giant media corporations have the advantage of economy of scale. World television footage is dominated by Reuters and Associated Press Television News (APTN) along with Worldwide Television News (WTN) (Paterson 1998). Reuters television claimed 260 client broadcasters in 85 countries (Paterson 1998: 79). It has been estimated that well over one billion people each week see at least several minute's footage of material from these agencies (Tunstall and Machin 1999: 195). This is why viewers switching between channels, even across international satellite feeds, will see identical footage of carefully selected and edited world events. The services sold to clients are edited-together sets of clips and accompanying scripts; for those broadcasters with no facilities for extra levels of editing or presentations complete broadcasts are provided. Newer stations are often designed to be run directly from agency feeds. Established broadcasters such as Time Warner's CNN will produce much of their own material and also use material from the other agencies (Tunstall and Machin: 79.)

The influence of advertising

One of the arguments in favour of a commercial media is that market demand ensures diversity of output which, in turn, is good for democracy. Given a free rein the media, this argument goes, through the laws of supply and demand, will provide something for whatever market is out there. If audiences do not like something they will simply move on to something that they do. If we take the example of a newspaper, we could assume that if a title does not reflect the views of its readers then circulations will fall and eventually it will close, leaving behind competitors which give the market what it wants. However, political economy theories of media warn that this model of choice and diversity does not operate accordingly in the context of news journalism. This is because audiences and readers alone are not in all cases the primary source of income for news providers. Rather, for the main part media get their income from advertising. Newspapers, for example, would run at a loss if they had to rely on cover price alone. Curran and Seaton (1991) showed that newspapers have long relied heavily on advertising for their survival. In their book *Power Without Responsibility* they show how the need to attract advertisers was crucial historically in the development of the press. Titles that were most attractive to advertisers could afford to spend more on content and appearance, and reduce their cover price to encourage mass appeal. Under market principles this suggests that readers are in a powerful position to demand content. However, we cannot assume advertisers want to reach all kinds of people equally, or that they are indifferent to the content of the newspaper. Curran and Seaton show that if we go back to the mid nineteenth century, when professional journalism was consolidating, advertisers were much less interested in newspapers that were read by the lower classes that had little expendable income. It was only after the Second World War when there were paper shortages that advertisers supported the left-wing workers' press. Once paper shortages ended advertisers boycotted left-wing newspapers in Britain. Curran and Seaton give the example of the *Daily Herald* which had 4.7 million readers in its last year before closing, more than three times the number of the three 'upmarket' titles, *The Guardian, The Times* and *The Financial Times.* The *Herald* was still running at a loss on cover price alone. It had to close. Other well-read left-wing titles, they show, also closed due to lack of advertiser support, such as *News Chronicle* and *Sunday Citizen.* Gradually the only downmarket newspapers that survived were those that were much more centrist in their politics. Therefore through the loss of these newspapers, left-wing politics were denied any means of mass media support.

Many advertising companies will not support media who are openly critical of consumerism and capitalism. Herman and Chomsky (1988) argue that 'Advertisers will want . . . to avoid programs with serious complexities and disturbing controversies that interfere with the "buying mood"' (1988: 17). And we must not forget that the advertising industry, now globally dominated by a handful of mega agencies like Omnicom, exists integrated into news media which rely on them for the finance that allows them to operate. Many commentators have expressed concern because this means that around the planet news must be integrated into media that reflect Western consumer ideologies. Chan (1996) makes this case for Hong Kong; Ray and Jacka (1996) for Asia; Arback (1999) for Egypt where television originally intended to rival Western output soon found it required advertising to operate.

The large advertising groups have also moved into owning public relations (PR), marketing and market research companies on a global scale. As we will see later these PR companies, operating on behalf of politicians and other lobbyists such as corporations, often work as news factories producing ready-made news feed for a news media ever more pressed by funding and staffing problems. These advertising companies are generally now public on the stock market and ownership is widely spread with pressure for increased profits. The control, or at least as Curran and Seaton showed, the support for certain kinds of news content and therefore news outlets by advertisers, has taken on a global nature, at the same time that the media corporations themselves stretch out across the planet.

Wooing readers through entertainment-led news

Since the 1980s news organisations have experienced great changes due to changes in ownership, technology and the need to attract advertisers more effectively. Yet news broadcasts and newspapers have faced a greater challenge, as they have simultaneously been experiencing declining audiences since the 1980s. For example, the US news networks saw their ratings fall by one-fifth through the 1990s. In 2005 the evening broadcasts of the networks were down 44 per cent since 1980 and 59 per cent since their peak in 1969 (Nielsonmedia 2006). There is evidence that younger people do not like the older news formats and are more interested in web sources (Bennett 2005). Bennett cites media critic Jon Katz at *Rolling Stone* who said 'Forty years ago when television was born, television news consisted of middle-aged white men reading 22 minutes of news into a camera. Today, network news consists of middle-aged white men reading 22 minutes of news into camera' (Bennett 2005: 84; see also Miller 1992). Referring to newspapers Underwood (1995) says that younger generations do not want to read them, while older generations are moving into other areas of leisure and may obtain their news from 24-hour news channels.

The financial misfortunes of newspapers and television newsrooms (Garcia Aviles *et al.* 2004) have taken their toll on budgets and staff cuts. Since the 1980s there have been big changes in newsrooms in order to make news more competitive and to target audiences for advertisers. Ex-journalist Doug Underwood in his book *When MBAs Rule the Newsroom* (1995), writes of when a new editor at *The Seattle Times* at the end of the 1980s gave his arrival speech and spoke of his intentions to reorganise newsroom management, to co-ordinate newsroom focus groups in marketing, editorial budgets, circulation and readership. At no point, Underwood notes with concern, did he mention news and stories. This is but one example of how editorial priorities have shifted more towards providing and packaging news that is tuned to marketing the newspaper in harmony with advertisers. Underwood saw this as turn away from 'news-as-news', whereby the news events themselves set the agenda, to a fixation with the reader, to woo them, to target them. It has become known as 'reader-driven' or 'customer-driven' newsgathering. This kind of news contains much brief and packaged information, entertainment and city life news, in visually appealing formats such as upbeat short news items, easily scanned indexes, fact boxes, charts and graphs (Underwood 1995: 18). This has inevitably brought about changes in the types of story that journalists were to cover. Many had to scrap traditional beats such as law courts for new beats based around consumer culture. This has led to an emphasis on simpler news frames. Where there is a tragedy journalists are told to get reactions to it and then a sense of determination to move on rather than carry out original investigation. In a three-year study of US newsrooms Underwood found that many journalists were very concerned about these changes, although on the positive side many sought to find some way to stay in contact with professional standards. This trend towards editors being business managers is reflected in many of the books published in the 1980s, according to Underwood, which showed how to integrate news and marketing in order to increase advertising revenue.

This process has led news outlets to think more in terms of branding. Like other products, radio stations, television bulletins, newspapers and web sites use images, sounds and a coherent visual and textual style in order to create distinctiveness, just as a clothing company might a pair of jeans. News must be dressed up so that it conveys a relevance to particular groups. These groups will be first described by market research. This research allows products to tell stories about the kind of people they are meant for in terms of ideas, values and social status. The research will also allow outlets such as newspapers to think in terms of layout and appearance. It is this kind of approach to news that attracts advertisers who can be certain of the niche audience being reached through the outlet.

Sociologists of the news media such as Habermas (1989) and Postman (1986) have theorised the effects of this commercialisation upon the quality of information that is now offered to the public. Habermas argues that the news media now provide a simplified political world based on entertainment and personalities. Wherever possible issues are dramatised with the effect that they become simplified. All this has the effect of reducing their capacity to inform, to create awareness in the public. Afraid of viewers or listeners switching over, or newspaper readers getting bored, they look for sound bites, simplification and easily understandable themes. There is a reluctance to contextualise, to explain, to show complexity. McManus (1994) concluded that the need to entertain in the contemporary media has lead to a dangerous demise of genuine political analysis and political argument. Franklin (1997) referred to this new kind of journalism as 'Newszak'. Connell (1991) argues that most detailed reporting is now directed towards lifestyle and consumer affairs.

Some of the most abiding theorists from the political economy school of journalism studies have been pessimistic about the possibility of journalists operating freely as watchdogs for democracy within the context of transglobal media conglomerates and attempts to maximise readerships. It is feared that news reporters, sub-editors and editors are severely constrained in their everyday roles to the extent that it is not so much the news events that define the content of newspapers, bulletins and web pages but the drives of proprietors, shareholders and advertisers. Concern has been expressed about the limited array of sources for news information in real terms. The key questions that arise from this overview of historical and contextual developments are twofold. First, what impact does the news journalism that emanates from these organisations have upon its consumers and upon society as a whole? Second, how accurate are these theories when they come not from news journalists themselves, but from academics with their own backgrounds and practices looking in on journalism from the outside? The next chapter will identify and critically account for some of the oft-used seminal theories about journalism and culture. These theories, as with those encountered in this chapter, will then be unpacked and re-evaluated by exploring their efficacy in contemporary newsrooms throughout the rest of this book.

2 Analysing news output

News production, despite what the training manuals might say, does not take place in a cultural and social vacuum. In other words it is a more complex process than objective, independent journalists gathering facts and presenting them value-free to the public. Journalistic practices and processes, it has been shown, have developed over thousands of years, nuanced and inflected by changes in ownership, technology and regulatory frameworks. Accordingly, the products and practices of news journalists – their bulletins, stories, headlines and selection – have been scrutinised for evidence of the impact of cultural forces. This chapter will provide a critical account of some of the most influential studies of news journalism by academics. These studies have been widely incorporated in scholarly analysis over decades, and have for the most part been negative in their findings. The news industry has been robustly criticised for bias, distortion, inaccuracy and lack of context. Its practitioners have been seen at best as elitist and out of touch with predominant concerns in society, and at worst kowtowing to authority and the establishment. While these studies have been invaluable in highlighting valid concerns, and for providing a critical vocabulary for the analysis of journalism, this chapter will add further much-needed questions to this quest. These questions concern the need to fill in some of the gaps left by theoretical accounts that focus on the products rather than the practices of journalism.

In addition to historical and political economy approaches outlined in Chapter 1, the study of journalism has always been closely allied to the study of media and television which, in the UK, had close alliances with the origins of British cultural studies. This is the university subject associated with the study of popular culture and consumer society. Indeed, some important work on news journalism and its power in meaning-making was undertaken by academics at the Centre for Contemporary Cultural Studies (CCCS) at University of Birmingham. Founded in 1963 by Richard Hoggart, this group of researchers drew especially on the theories of Marx and Gramsci, which were politically of the left. Many of the CCCS studies focused on the impact that the political and economic forces of capitalism, later enacted through the policies of Prime Minister Margaret Thatcher, had on society and the cultural sphere. The news media were identified as agents for communicating myths to support political and economic powers to the mass public, to justify the closure of industry, to blame the poor for society's problems, for making monetarism and privatisation seem like necessary processes. In the US, similar concerns were raised by scholars in the context of a prevailing right-wing political agenda. It was believed that the news media, along with film and other entertainment forms, as economic as well as cultural texts, held enormous power to shape public opinion. As a consequence, studies of journalism from media and cultural studies perspectives were underpinned by concerns over the potential for news media to project political bias onto an unsuspecting public.

In this light, decisions journalists make about what should be reported and what should be discarded, or 'spiked', have always been contentious. Analyses of news values have centred upon examining what recurring factors appear in stories selected for coverage in national newspapers. The public are given a sense that they are offered the news stories in accordance with what is important to everyone. But it seemed that certain arbitrary codes had been established that had a greater influence over what was selected than the nature of the events themselves. Yet, in newsrooms, news selection is actually primarily a process of rejection, and criteria alter from shift to shift according to a range of intrinsic and extrinsic factors (Niblock 2005). Similarly, the kinds of people that journalists approach for facts and comments has been evaluated as steering too much towards authority figures and too little towards ordinary and marginalised voices.

Developments in the technology used to gather and disseminate news, outlined in Chapter 1, have drastically sped up the pace at which events are relayed to the public. This has been most notable in the reporting of war, an aspect of journalism that has received probably most scrutiny from scholars. According to critics of war coverage, journalists adopt partisan stances so that their reporting is biased in favour of the strategies of 'home' nations. Furthermore, reporters and editors, it is claimed, are overly susceptible to governmental propaganda and do little to challenge censorship. The fact that wars are now brought to our screens and breakfast tables in real-time raises many more complex issues about the internal and external pressures faced by journalists in times of conflict.

Among these issues is the pressure on reporters to draw out emotional angles, to focus on heart-rending case stories and eyewitness accounts. There has been an apparent shift in the focus points for reporters covering international stories, which is the emphasis on humanising issues that have traditionally been covered more from economic or military angles. Reporting trauma and covering humanitarian crises challenges ethical guidelines on intruding into grief, and journalists have been criticised in some quarters for seeming to boost audiences in this way. A further strand to this has been the criticism of Western news organisations for covering the developing world only when its people are suffering natural or man-made disasters.

Significantly, journalists are using ever more powerful visual means to convey complex situations and stark horrors to readers and audiences. The news industry has always used images as a key part of its mediation process, and has increasingly drawn on developments in hand-held digital technology to capture breaking stories. Academic studies have highlighted the power of the press and TV image to mediate events in biased ways, which has led to some mistrust, sometimes warranted, about editing and retouching. We must also consider sophisticated means by which designers are using typography and images to target reader groups, so that news is very much packaged – visually and textually – for psychographically determined consumer groups.

All these factors have led to oft-repeated concerns amongst the academic community that journalism is dumbing down; that is, resorting to sensationalism and surface gloss in order to grab audiences and readers from their rivals. From another perspective, particularly when talking to reporters and editors, it might be argued that new, simpler approaches to politics, economics and social affairs will appeal to wider audiences who might previously have not felt they were being addressed. Missing from these debates and conversations with academics has been the news journalists themselves. Apart from a small number of important ethnographic studies of newsrooms, which will be recounted in more detail further on, academics have not tended to enter into dialogue with reporters. Some have theorised that newsrooms are self-supporting environments in which new entrants are socialised, so that they unquestioningly internalise journalism values as 'natural'. Many higher education journalism institutions try to keep track of their graduates through questionnaires and other means, which can reveal illuminating data on job progression, gender, ethnicity and other factors. But there is also a clear need to talk to journalists in more depth about how they navigate their way through their training and development. If we are to gain a better understanding of everyday decision-making in contemporary newsrooms, we need to work with journalists, witnessing the pressures they face. The final section of this chapter will explore how that conversation will take place in the rest of the book. It will draw on some recent accounts of the reflective practitioner, that is, the working person who tries to stand back from what they do for a moment and consider their actions in light of wider forces.

Theorising what makes news

When journalists come to select events from the range that are made available by news agencies and official sources to use as news, many editors might say that it is the 'news instinct', the 'nose for a good story' that allows them to choose which should become news. But sociologists of news have shown that there are certain preordained patterns in the kinds of events that do get chosen. These will be events that have certain characteristics, or those that can be placed within established news frames. In other words, these observers suggest a tick list, which should allow us to predict what kinds of events will and will not be selected. Of course this could be seen to go against the idea of news as being simply a reflection of what is going on in the world that is important to everyone.

The pioneering description of news values was made by Scandinavian researchers Johann Galtung and Marie Ruge in 1965. Studying the coverage of international news, they identified 12 recurring criteria that determined whether or not a story was published.

- Frequency: how close a story happens to the moment of publication.
- Threshold: the level the event must reach in terms of scale for it to stand out.
- Unambiguity: the story should be clearly understood.
- Meaningfulness: the story should be relevant to the readers' frame of reference.
- Consonance: the build-up to an expected event.
- Unexpectedness: how unpredictable an event is.
- Continuity: a big story will remain in the news for days or weeks.
- Composition: a story may be selected because it helps balance the other stories.
- Reference to elite nations: some places are covered more than others.
- Reference to elite people: events affecting famous people.
- Reference to persons: news that has a human focus.
- Reference to something negative: bad news usually contains more of the above criteria than good news (Niblock 2005).

The 'news instinct' that journalists prize could be said to be the internalisation of these values (Patterson and Wilkins 1994: 26). Trainee journalists are often said by their seniors to not be able to 'see the story'. What they mean really is that they are not yet familiar with the 'unofficial' criteria that Galtung and Ruge sought to make explicit.

In practice these criteria indicate that a story familiar to readers' existing frame of reference, such as a talking point around drug-related crime, will be more likely to run than one that is not. Similarly, if there is an earthquake overseas affecting people from the same country as the audience, the story has more chance of 'making it to page'. All of these criteria suggest that news selection is not a neutral act of covering the events that affect all people. Rather, they suggest that the news agenda is driven by a set of cultural values, by decision-makers operating according to unseen historically formed codes. Simply journalistic practice over time has established a set of arbitrary values which themselves govern what becomes news.

Galtung and Ruge's formulation proved highly influential. Since they published their criteria, subsequent researchers have added further categories to their list. Gans (1980), for instance, added 'surprise stories' while Bell

(1991) added 'predictability', suggesting that journalists prefer stories that can be prescheduled, such as major sporting events, political conferences and the like. Bell added that journalists appreciate prefabrication, referring to the existence of ready-made texts, such as press releases. Harcup and O'Neill (2001) suggest adding entertainment, picture opportunities and sex.

From another perspective, what makes news may not actually have a great deal to do with the inherent qualities of a specific event or issue at all. Daniel Boorstin (1973), for instance, has argued that a great number of news items are in effect created by journalists and others in order to easily fill space with ready-made coverage. Boorstin describes these stories as 'pseudo-events', that might not have taken place in that way – or even at all – had journalists not been available to mediate them. Examples of these stories include what are known by journalists as 'diary' events, which are expected and prepared for beforehand. An example is where a nation's leader lands in a military aircraft with the press waiting, as did President Bush at the start of the second Gulf War. Or the event may involve coverage of military actions, as in Somalia 1992 when US forces daringly stormed beaches in amphibious craft, to be filmed by thousands of waiting reporters. Most political events, meetings, rallies are just such events, as are preplanned police raids on the homes of suspected criminals. In the latter example, journalists and photographers are invited to bear witnesses to events, acting in their consensual role as watchdogs (see Chapter 1). But from another perspective, their presence is also to show police officers are 'doing their job', thus supporting that agency's ideological function. And it could be seen as one way that politics becomes about spectacle, theatre and telegenic gesture rather than policy.

Boorstin (1973) expressed concern at the manner in which journalists can be accused of 'creating' news themselves through canny interviewing techniques. In this way, a reporter will frame a question in such a way that the response will be something that can be presented as news, such as 'The Minister today denied . . .'. He suggests that the pressure of time and the need to fill news space means that reporters use interviewing techniques in ever more imaginative and forceful ways to produce newsworthy pseudo-events.

These studies raise important questions for contemporary journalism scholarship, notably the extent to which everyday pressures on meeting production deadlines and filling space and airtime has on news selection. They also identify the way in which sources of stories can themselves become the news even more than the original event and issue. This may be ever more likely in contemporary conditions of competition where journalists have to pursue original approaches compared with their rivals. The relationship between journalists and their use of sources has been subject to academic scrutiny, as the next section will outline.

Beats and sources

A journalist's most closely guarded possession used to be their 'contacts book'. This directory contained the names, addresses and telephone numbers of all the personal sources they had encountered over their career. In striving to be first with the news and to break exclusives, journalists cultivate a range of contacts who they hope will give then the first 'sniff' of a story or a fresh angle on an ongoing issue. News organisations themselves also keep databanks of contacts that their journalists can access online. Sources will range from the chairperson of a local residents' association to a government mole, such as Deep Throat who helped Pulitzer prize-winning reporters Carl Bernstein and Bob Woodward uncover the Watergate scandal. Where news comes from can be an important determinant of whether or not it will make the page or get on air, according to academics. It is frequently claimed that journalists are more likely to give credence to the account of a high-ranking official – even if the information they provide only comes from a single source – than from the shared accounts of dozens of ordinary citizens. In this way, the theory goes, people in power are said to shape the news we read and hear far more than is needed to represent what is important to most people in society.

Tuchman (1978) and Ericson *et al.* (1987), in their studies of the relationship between journalists and their official sources, noted that sources are able to organise themselves to provide readily available news for journalists. In other words they can prepare press releases and give press conferences which provide the journalists with the copy they need to give to their editors. This, these authors show, means that the sources are able to have some control over exactly what kind of information becomes news and what angle it is given. Many organisations now employ large numbers of public relations personnel and press officers in order to make certain that a favourable image of them is maintained. Much time and money goes into producing copy and picture opportunities that provide ready-made news that fits news logic and news frames. McChesney (2004) argues that it is the reliance on official sources and need for news hooks that has led to the massive growth in PR. Corporations and official groups supply journalists with masses of ready-made copy. Surveys have shown that PR accounts for between 40 and 70 per cent of what appears as news (Rampton and Stauber 2000; Ewen 1996). They show the incredible role that PR plays in providing copy that looks like news, which includes supplying broadcast-ready scripts. The studies note that there are now more people working in PR than there are journalists in the US. These PR companies, aided by the media deregulation of the 1990s, have now merged with and are part of the handful of large advertising corporations that dominate the globe such as Omnicom and Interpublic, based in New York, and WPP, based in London.

To illustrate, McChesney (2004) discusses the war in Iraq as one case where governments controlled reporting by supplying journalists with ready-made news opportunities. War reporters were embedded within military units to provide captivating scenes – but without context. Additionally, it is claimed much of the footage and photographs shown of the war were pre-existing archive material prepared by the Pentagon (Griffin 2004). There is a long history of pre-packaged material being handed to the news media. Schudson (1978) speaks of the rise of public relations in the 1920s. Journalism schools started to be a source of public relations workers for companies and for government agencies. Politicians started to replace interviews, where the balance of power rested more with the reporter, with media conferences: this meant easy access for journalists but in a structured environment controlled by the organiser. Schudson (1978) shows that press releases became a mainstay of news in the latter part of the twentieth century, flooding newsrooms with ready-made copy carefully written to 'help' journalists fill their pages and airtime. Reporters were encouraged by editors to interrogate claims made in press releases and balance their tone by substantiating their claims through approaches to other sources.

A major development for television and online journalists has been the arrival of the video news release (VNR). A study by Nielsen Media Research showed that all of the newsrooms questioned had used VNRs at some point (Pooley 1999). Pooley stated that a VNR released by pharmaceutical manufacturer Pfizer to promote the anti-impotence drug Viagra was seen by 210 million people. Stauber and Rampton (2000) say that this practice started in the 1980s and has had great success through phases of cost-cutting in newsrooms.

Stauber and Rampton show that there is a busy world of corporate-funded PR-based groups lobbying the news media such as the Global Climate Information Project, the National Centre for Public Policy Research and the Advancement of Sound Science Coalition. All of these groups have funded research which has yielded sceptical conclusions about global warming and it has been widely cited in the news media (Rampton and Stauber 2000: 276). Such PR material and press releases will be highly tempting for journalists who are short of time, especially when they seem reasonable in terms of the kinds of news values that we looked at above.

Bennett (2005) examined strategies that are used by public relations for promoting politicians. These, which he draws from PR manuals, include:

- Composing a simple theme or message for the audience to use in thinking about the matter in hand. Call this message shaping.
- Saturating communications channels with this message so that it will become more conspicuous than competing messages. Call this message salience.

- Constructing a context of credibility for the message by finding a dramatic setting and recognised sources to deliver it. Call this message credibility.
- Delivering the message with the right scripting (particularly sound bites) and post-delivery spin to lead journalists to pick the right category for accentuating the message. For example, when a president signs a law and says 'this is an important victory for taxpayers in America', an obvious frame for the story is 'President scores political victory'. Effective news management helps journalists accentuate the message by putting it inside that frame, which becomes the central meaning communicated by the story. Call this message framing (Bennett 2005: 125).

Again we can see that these guidelines work with the news values we described above. Such releases will, most importantly, be designed to be meaningful for existing frames of reference. This means that it will be less likely that news will deal with things that are in fact completely new or outside of existing frames. We discuss this in Chapters 3 and 4.

This emphasis on official sources means, according to academic studies, that what we will often find printed and broadcast by the news media are different stages of this PR process. When we read a news item on a topic like the invasion of Iraq, we will come across official versions of events that will be designed to fit into an easily understood news frame (Carruthers 2000). We are used to thinking of this process as 'spin', but few realise that due to journalists' reliance on official sources, which are managed by PR, it is very difficult for news outlets to present anything else. Where there is little time or resources for further investigation, there has been the rise of the journalist-as-expert, whereby specialist reporters and editors are themselves called upon as sources by other media and by their own (Bennett 2005). This often happens in the form of the 'two-way' where one broadcast journalist will interview another either on air or in a pre-recorded format. Bennett sees this phenomenon as a further symptom of reduced budgets and the need to fill air-time.

The reliance on a smaller number of sources has been aided by new technology. Niche-marketed journalism – news targeted at carefully defined groups – has been enabled by developments in digital broadcast technology, which allows relatively small agencies, run by a handful of staff, to quickly splice together and transmit bulletins and packages to hundreds of radio stations and direct to mobile telephones. The content of the bulletins and packages is obtained by the agency from a range of providers, including large news agency feeds, archives and sound effects. Bulletins and packages can then be carefully assembled in creative ways for the market-researched target audience of each news outlet. Receiving bulletins and packages from an agency is a cost-effective practice for hundreds of national and regional client stations, who are not able to finance their own in-house production or editing of national and international news. In Chapter 4 we will show that news journalists' reliance on certain official sources may have significant implications for their role as the eyes and ears of democracy.

War reporting and propaganda

According to many studies, the role of journalist as eyes and ears of the public is questionable. Misrepresentation of international conflicts has led scholars such as Herman and Chomsky (1988) and McChesney (2004) to speak of the propaganda role of the news media. In cases where our own countries are in conflict we might hope that the news media would perform much better. However, many academic studies of news reporting have been extremely critical of the level of propaganda that is disseminated as news during wartime (Taylor 1992; MacArthur 1992; Carruthers 2000), both in the case of total war such as the Second World War and limited war such as the Gulf War. Many argue that even with real-time war reporting actually very little is conveyed about the real war (Ignatieff 1998).

Herman and Chomsky (1988) have written about five 'filters' which prevent the news media from being critical of the actions of governments.

1. *Ownership* In the previous chapter we discussed the way that news media are part of large corporations, such as Time Warner Turner. Such organisations may be less likely to be critical of the actions of governments who act in the interest of Western global capitalism, such as in the interests of oil in the Middle East.
2. *Advertising* In the last chapter we looked at the reliance of the media on advertising. Advertisers do not like to be associated with media that is critical of society.
3. *Sourcing* News organisations are more likely to report accounts coming from official administrative sources over any possible contrary accounts from other sources.
4. *Lobby from corporate interests* Corporations regularly come together to lobby and pressurise.
5. *Anti-communism* The news media support the idea that Western capitalism is good and natural.

In fact it may not be so much the case that governments lie to journalists. Propaganda may be more a matter of how events become framed within these established definitions of 'evil others'. Graham *et al.* (2004) studied calls to war from political leaders over a 1000 year period from Pope Urban II (1095) through Hitler to George W. Bush and Iraq. They say that the same themes repeat in all. These are the strategies that are use in each case:

- An appeal to a higher power source that is inherently good
- An appeal to the history of the nation

- The construction of an evil other
- An appeal to unity behind the higher power source.

Parenti (2002) has demonstrated that propaganda does not have to involve falsehoods but framing. He showed this through an analysis of the language used in news to report conflicts. He gives examples of labelling such as 'terrorists' 'militia', 'civil disturbances', 'extremists', 'reform'. All of these are highly value-laden and serve to frame events and the actions of people in the world into ready-made categories. Of course these labels may be created by politicians or their PR teams rather than journalists, but a journalism heavily dependent on politicians as sources will tend to reproduce these uncritically.

In a study of media content after 9/11 Kellner (2004) showed that there was very little analysis of what had happened and why. The mainstream media used a 'clash of civilisations' news frame (Kellner 2004: 44) creating an opposition between terror and civilisation – a threat to the social order. The clear message of this frame was the need for some kind of retaliation to eradicate the threat, to protect civilisation. The people of the US and Western world were familiar with images of terrorists, both in the news media and many Hollywood movies, who were evil and psychopathic. Edwards (2002) says that these kinds of frames mean that events in the world always find the Western powers as benevolent. Poverty and conflict in the world are therefore never shown as being a result of the activities of those organisations that act in the name of Western corporate interests, such as the World Trade Organisation and World Bank, which could lead to pressure on governments to cut welfare and health services. They are never shown as being a result of the involvement of Western corporations and military pushing for control over resources.

The reporting of most contemporary wars has been completely managed by governments. One exception was the American war in Vietnam where journalists played a huge part in ending the war through bringing its horrors and brutality to the US public. The result of the reports was that the military was unable to carry out certain manoeuvres, such as extensive bombing of civilian areas, as these would later be shown on TV (Kimball 1988). Many US politicians blamed journalists for losing them the war, by reporting all its gruesome details and shocking the public. But if journalists were actually showing what was happening were they not just fulfilling their duty in a liberal democracy as they should? Western governments learned from Vietnam and have since dedicated much expertise and finance to managing the news media during wars. Both Reagan and Bush have spoken of the military having to fight with one hand tied behind their back if journalists are not regulated (Taylor 1992).

During the Falklands/Malvinas conflict and in Grenada during the 1980s journalists were hand-picked or excluded from the zone of conflict (Carruthers 2000: 122). There was also censorship of stories in the name of troop morale etc. (2000: 125). In the Gulf wars journalists were selected to be allocated to placements by the military or were put up in hotels for press conferences and debriefings. A list of forbidden subjects was provided by the Pentagon.

In the case of the Gulf there were complaints from British and American journalists, and from news organisations (Carruthers 2000: 136), although this never amounted to a serious challenge by the more powerful media organisations (MacArthur 1992). Although in a war situation governments will expect, to some degree, certain compliance from news organisations Carruthers (2000: 55). Carruthers (2000) and Tumber and Palmer (2004) show how in the case of the American and European news media there was little contextualisation of either of the wars in the Gulf. Little was revealed of the kinds of suffering of civilians and combatants that was shown to the public during Vietnam. Tumber and Palmer show that Pentagon officials were very pleased with the results of embedding as this gets across their messages: 'the embedding process was carefully managed and well prepared. It was planned long in advance of Gulf war II, and evaluations and refinements are already underway for future conflicts' (2004: 59). Kirtley (2001) points out that there is a huge conflict of interests between the military and journalism in times of war. The former needs to win the battle not just on the battlefield but also in the minds of the public. The latter seeks to report what is happening out there in the world. Sometimes, however, the media are more than willing to go along with what could be described as self-censorship.

Reporting humanitarian crises

When grainy mobile telephone video footage of the Asian tsunami disaster of 2004 was broadcast by news media giants, journalism's methods came under acute scrutiny. Audio, video and text generated by ordinary members of the public saturated web sites and bulletins, poignantly bringing home the scale of human devastation wrought by the giant tidal wave. Previously, journalists had included farewell mobile telephone messages from passengers on ill-fated airplanes on 9/11. They had published emails from citizens holed up inside cellars in war zones, in an attempt to project immediacy, accessibility and diversity of opinion as central to its journalistic integrity. Jonathan Dube, publisher of CyberJournalist.net, said that 'hearing about individual experiences directly from the people who survived the tsunami offered readers a different, more personal perspective on the human side of the tragedy than most of the articles published by news organisations'. Jay Rosen, chair of New York University's journalism department, described user-generated content and blogging as, in the words of Internet expert Clay Shirky, a victory of affinity over geography: 'People with aid are finding those in need of aid' (all quotes from *On TV: Day of Destruction*, National Geographical Channel). From another perspective, however, this shocking and heart-rending coverage distracts from the underlying causes and less televisual implications of human disaster.

Benthall (1993) has shown how news journalism directs our attention to certain disasters such as famines, but coverage appears and disappears at times which have little to do with the real beginnings and ends of the famines themselves. He shows how this is more related to what else is available as news at the time, and what other surrounding events make the famine more newsworthy. For example, during a national election a famine in Africa may not appear in national news media in Europe. Later, for example, at the time of the 'Live 8' pop concerts, Africa and famine become newsworthy and so appear as new information. Benthall also expressed concern that an analysis of such news stories reveals little contextualisation of events. There is a tendency to rely on news frames of Third World chaos, photographs of suffering children and African refugees. In the case of famines, the West's involvement in causing the famines in the first place is never considered. Millions of deaths in the 1980s in Somalia and Ethiopia could be attributed to Western support and arm shipments to dictatorships, but this kind of contextualisation is information of a sort that is unlikely to come from official sources. Nor does it fit with established news frames.

As well as the simplification and human interest distraction that emerges from stories of humans in peril, there are the inherent difficulties of verifying the authenticity of the source material. Internet sources are often anonymous, and media organisations have had their fingers burned. Newspapers and broadcasters in India, the UK, Canada and South Africa published or aired images believed to be of the actual Boxing Day tsunami when they were in fact of a tidal surge in China in 2002. Yet the rise of citizen journalism and the proliferation of user-generated content suggests audiences are growing frustrated with the normative role of the journalist to tell the audience 'how it is'. This may not be the fault of those journalists themselves, according to some accounts. For reports say that when they do file stories that go into depth on the causes and solutions to a social or humanitarian issue, they have to modify the manner in which they report it to cohere with the core brand values of their outlet. In many cases, they find editors do not want 'worthy' reporting on 'depressing' matters. (Tanguy 1999). A combination of international editorial indifference and the physical dangers of visiting Rwanda meant there was virtually no international coverage of the 10,000 deaths per day that took place in the early to mid-1990s (Chopra 2005). Similarly, the medical humanitarian organisation Médecins Sans Frontières releases an annual list of under-reported stories, which they claim conflicts with anecdotal evidence that audiences want to know more about these issues.

The relationship between journalists and aid agencies has come under some scrutiny by journalism academics, but more work is needed to interrogate the reliance that journalists have on charities and others in funding overseas trips to disaster zones. A significant number of news features are produced funded and directed by aid agencies, sometimes with celebrity-led images and angles. Researchers note a causal link between media coverage and the quantity and distribution of aid (Chopra 2005) while affected states warn that news media need to deepen coverage to attract meaningful international support, instead of sympathy (Chopra 2005).

The way the attention of news audiences is drawn to particular events at particular times has been referred to as agenda setting. This was first discussed by US academics McCombs and Shaw (1972), who were interested in the influence of news on what people thought. The theory refers to the way that news has the power to draw our attention to certain events, rather than others. The researchers questioned members of the US electorate in the run up to the 1968 Presidential election. From their findings, they concluded that what was defined as important by the public was closely linked to what was being defined as important in the news media. The authors of the study concluded that the news media cannot tell us what to think or directly create our opinions on events and issues, but the media still hold power by being able to direct our attention towards a limited number of key topics – in other words, the topics they feel we should be having opinions about. Therefore it cannot necessarily influence what opinions we will have about the occupation of Iraq or of famines. But we will certainly not have opinions about issues of which we know nothing. Herman and Chomsky (1988) and Pilger (1999) have shown that not all conflicts in which Western powers are involved make it into the news media.

Theories of visual news presentation

There has been relatively little work done specifically on the visual styles of news, the conventions of assembling news sequences, the kinds of patterns of representations used in video footage photojournalism. This does not match the far more extensive academic material on representation in film and television. Nevertheless, several important critical points have been made where further extensive research is required.

Symbolic images

Stuart Hall (1983), drawing on the work of Roland Barthes (1977), used an approach called semiotics, which treats images as being made up of individual signs that combine to create meaning, to look at new photographs. Images or elements in an image can work in two ways. First, they can denote something. In other words they show something as it is. So an image might contain a child and therefore is a description of a child. But an image can also connote: in other words, it can have symbolising power. For instance, a news item on a war situation is accompanied with a photo of a child – the child connotes, or symbolises, innocence. Clearly this has an ideological function, by suggesting how war and warmongers affect the innocent. The children themselves may very well become the enemy, if they have seen their homes burned and family killed by aerial bombardment, for example. But in the West we do not see children in this way.

These kinds of clichés, that are basically extremely ethnocentric views of the world, have been discussed by Lutz and Collins (1993) in their focus on the magazine *National Geographic*. This magazine both defines and reflects more general themes in photographing the world outside of the West, which is reduced to a very limited number of clichés: very wrinkly old men, dirty but smiling children, dignity in poverty, colourful clothes, beautiful women, motherhood, ceremony. They suggest that such photography does not help us to understand the world but to reduce it to a number of Western values that claim to be human universals. Taylor (1992), in a survey of war photography in the twentieth century, shows a complete absence of the pointless deaths and squalor of war but a predominance of plucky survivors, innocent children, soldiers wounded but still smiling, soldiers with children. In both cases of photographs of the world and of war, we are dealing not with images that record or document, but those that symbolise.

Machin (2004) has argued that since the 1990s news photographs have become increasingly symbolic rather than descriptive. This is for two basic reasons. One is that it is now much cheaper to buy photographs from large globally operating image banks such as Getty and Corbis. For very little money an editor can download and buy a photograph of a politician looking guilty or a British soldier holding a child. This cheapness and ease of access is important in the context of the financial and staff cutbacks that we discussed earlier. Second these more symbolic images are designed to look good on the page. This is important in a time when the visual design of newspapers is crucial in branding and marketing.

Photographs as news frames

The way that photographs can work symbolically means that they can have a particularly powerful role in anchoring the kinds of news frames that we spoke of earlier (Hall 1983: 232). We might think about the example of 'terrorists' in the Middle East conflict. Here the visual seems to provide evidence for the spoken. In the same way the photograph of the child in Iraq is evidence, we might say, that a peacekeeping force is required to protect such innocence from evil 'insurgents' and 'enemies of freedom'. Such photographs, Hall believes (1983: 238), come to index, to stand for, the nature of events, making different interpretations more difficult to find their place. In the case of the 'terrorist' or 'innocent child' the nature of the events is mapped out for us by the photographic symbolism and the weight that this can carry.

Photographs carry such weight because they offer themselves as literal representations of the world. Barthes (1977) has written of the way that we tend to see photographs as truthful rather than as interpretations. Taylor (1992) argues that the photograph gives a sense of eyewitness, even though each one is a selected segment of a selected moment in time. Price (2000) argues that because of its claim to truth photography has always played an important role in the legitimation of wars from the Crimean war and the work of Roger Fenton, right through to more recent wars. Most famous war photographs, such as the US troops hauling up the Stars and Stripes on Iwo Jima, are posed and not spontaneous. Yet our faith in them as an accurate and authentic record remains. We seem to credit even more realism to photographs that appear to carry markers that we associate with authenticity, such as if they are slightly grainy and blurred or if they are black and white. Barthes (1977) suggests that just because a photograph is grainy we cannot assume that it is true, but these photographic conventions help to give the sense of realism and truth.

Simplification

Susan Sontag (2004) has suggested that news photographs are problematic for two reasons. First, a news photograph must be somehow seen to summarise events. Therefore photographs cannot represent longer drawn-out processes but tend towards extreme moments. This is one reason why there is a tendency to personalise issues. These are more easily reducible where individuals represent complex issues. Second, Sontag suggests that this quality of photographs has tended to make us think about the world of events in terms of the immediate, big moments, rather than as subtle and complex. So from the war in Iraq we have photographs of a child holding an automatic weapon, or a statue of Saddam being pulled over. These may then become iconic of what the war meant, rather than the whole history of colonial activity that preceded this moment and the actual political complexity of the region.

Conventions of representation

There is a small body of work that has attempted to draw out some of the patterns in the way that techniques of visual representation can influence the way that events will be perceived by the viewer. Hall has looked at the way that photographs are cropped has a huge influence on the way that they will be read. A close-up shot of a face, say of a politician, means, he suggests, that emphasis is given to emotions, to personality, to individual experience. This is one way that attention might be drawn away from the actual broader context of the story itself. We might say the same for the conflict in Iraq being represented by the close-up of a child. One criticism of news is that the tendency towards personalisation moves us away from complexity and detail. So a conflict can become centred around the personalities of political leaders such as Bush and Saddam, rather than the under-lying issues of oil and Western imperialism. Machin (2006) found that photographs of the conflict in Iraq had certain patterns in the way that US soldiers, enemy and civilians were photographed. These techniques were used, he suggests, in order to visually support a news frame of the necessity of the presence of peacekeeping forces.

There is relatively little work done on news film and on the way the visuals of film help to tell the news story. One exception is Hartley (1982). His analysis draws from the same basis as Hall uses for photography. He draws out some observations from analysis of a demonstration. These techniques are used to frame the event as of order versus disorder. *Official sources* (the Prime Minister) are shown in formal settings, invited into the television studio perhaps. The official source speaks for herself. The piece uses a neutral camera angle framed mid-shot. Official sources may look at camera.

Unofficial sources (union member) are shown in street settings, literally out in the cold. Unofficial sources are spoken for by the journalist. They are shown with edited together hand-held shots to give a sense of being in the thick of the action. They do not look at camera: clearly only certain people are allowed to do this and address the viewer directly. Hartley concludes that the challenge to the government is characterised by clashes with the police. Therefore this frames the whole of the demonstration – it is about disruption, disorder and law-breaking. The actual political issue is sidelined.

Sensationalism

As noted in the coverage of human disaster, sensationalism (or making stories seem more exciting, humanised and simple than they really are) is used as a strategy to 'sell' items to editors and audiences in an increasingly competitive news industry context. Bennett talks about 'feeding the beast' (2005: 145); news, especially with its 24-hour nature, demands drama and new developments even if there are none. For if these are not provided by you and your news outlet, they will by your opponents. He wrote: 'Those who market ideas for a living learn quickly that dramatised events, spin, rumour, and reaction are helpful to journalists trying to operate within the low-budget, high hype constraints of the twenty-four-hour news cycle' (2005: 146). While he points out the existence of in-depth varied news coverage in some areas, such as abortion or enduring moral controversies, other areas such as economics, war, foreign policy and areas of elite power will be reported simplistically through official sources and remain obscured (2005: 155).

The idea that news events can be over-dramatised was studied for its social implications by sociologists Stanley Cohen and Jock Young (1981).

They described how inflammatory news coverage of battles between youth subcultures 'the Mods' and 'the Rockers' led to these groups being portrayed as so-called folk devils. Drawing on social anthropology, folk devils describes phenomena that strike fear into communities. Cohen and Young demonstrated how the folk devils of youth subcultures entered into an 'amplification spiral' whereby their threat to society was emphasised and re-emphasised through sensational reporting. This results in, or at least mirrors, a 'moral panic' in society. Subsequent to this panic, due to reporting and dissemination through other public fora, the spiral draws in official agencies resulting in tighter controls on the activities of youths and eventual policy changes and legislation.

This model has been critiqued and developed by academics interested in exploring journalists' influence over this amplification spiral. Writers such as Frank Furedi (1997, 2003) have explored the media's role in heightening and sometimes creating fears about paedophiles and health concerns. Other moral panics arose about the reported dangers of pit bull terrier dogs being kept as pets, which led to the Dangerous Dogs Act as a response to emotive news reporting. More recently there have been moral panics about phenomena including mobile phone thefts, bullying epidemics and happy slapping in the UK press. The concept of news frames has been identified by scholars as a mechanism by which news journalists simplify and dramatise the everyday. These frames determine the ways that news events, once selected for coverage, will be presented. The headings we use here are drawn from Bennett (2005).

Personalisation

Complex issues are simplified in order to personalise them in terms of the individual faults, mistakes, gains and losses that lie on the surface.

Dramatisation

Only the aspects of a news event that can be dramatised are covered. More complex issues and sociological context cannot be so easily conveyed in an entertaining way.

Fragmentation

The need for dramatisation and personification of issues means that events when reported can seem quite independent of one another, when they may be interrelated. Broader sociopolitical contexts remain unmentioned.

The authority–disorder bias

The news likes to frame things in terms of threats, such as to social order, to democracy and to our children.

Several important points emerged from the methods employed by the researchers. First, is it enough to draw conclusions about the intentions of editors by looking at their products alone? How might the processes and practices of news-gathering affect the news agenda? Second, what evidence was there to suggest that editors were consciously setting news agendas for political ends? It seemed somewhat unrealistic to place so much power to direct public attention in the hands of a few editors. Who were the journalists concerned, and what were their own backgrounds and opinions? Moreover, did they bring those opinions to work or leave them at home? Third, what evidence was there to suggest that the news media were the primary influence on public opinion? Could it be that the news media were reflecting public opinion, rather than directing it?

In order to address all or some of these issues, journalism scholars decided to enter newsrooms as part of their research, to witness the news-making process first hand. Ethnographic studies of the newsroom, such as Fishman's *Manufacturing the News* (1980), revealed a very complex set of circumstances at play. Agenda setting, it was claimed, is not necessarily about political bias but is rather a result of a reliance on official sources. In addition, it was confirmed that news frames, as discussed earlier, were of paramount important in crafting angles, to attract and maintain reader/audience interest. This gave some of the earliest indications within academe that the need to tell interesting stories can often be the driving force in what appears as news, as much as any independent qualities of the events themselves. Moreover, those stories were often relayed with limited sources.

To demonstrate the driving impulse behind news selection, Fishman used the following example. In late 1976 there was a major crime wave in New York City. The news media were awash with reports about crimes against elderly citizens by juvenile offenders. There was pubic outcry and politicians voiced their determination to address the problem. The mayor of New York leaped in to promise safety for the people, pressing more police into action. Conversely, at that time, police statistics showed a decrease in these very kinds of crimes compared with the previous year. So why was there this outcry? Fishman claimed that many journalists had doubts that there was any such crime wave, but the story was 'news' and therefore had taken on a momentum of its own, which journalists felt impelled to follow: 'Within the space of a week a crime theme can become so "hot", so entrenched in a community of news organizations, that even journalists sceptical of the crime wave cannot ignore reporting each new incident that comes along. Crime waves have a life of their own' (Fishman 1980: 8). According to Fishman, it was the news organisations that manufactured the crime wave. While reporters did not fabricate the crimes committed, it was they who edited events together, using source material which in turn generated links to further material. There were indeed crimes against the elderly in the city at the time that justified coverage. But in Fishman's view, the news media set the context for the way in which audiences interpreted events.

In a similar vein, simultaneous UK studies indicated the way that news stories had in effect been constructed by news organisations. Hall *et al.* (1978) examined a series of news reports about street robbery, for which journalists coined the term 'mugging'. The researchers identified ways in which the manner of reporting created fears that black people were primarily responsible for this crime. The term mugging became specifically associated with ethnic minorities, As with the crime wave described by Fishman, 'mugging' was placed on the news agenda. As a consequence, politicians became involved and police started to recategorise the crimes that they recorded. Yet again, it emerged that the problem of mugging as reported bore no relationship to actual crime statistics. Drawing from Cohen and Young's amplification spiral, outlined at the beginning of this section, Hall *et al.* (1978) argued that this need to simplify events into news frames of conflict has the opposite effect of informing the public. By continually presenting the world through a limited set of frameworks, 'real' life is reported in predictable narratives. It is argued that the way events in society may be interconnected, such as social exclusion and rampant consumerism with crime, is rarely if ever raised in the news. For journalism academics, the overall view appears to be that sensationalism and human interest reporting necessarily distracts from complex causative factors and implications which, though less immediate and dramatic on the surface, are more important for the public interest.

Socialisation of the journalist

The process of news-making and production is complex, as researchers such as Fishman have sought to illuminate. Many influences that have little to do with what academics think the reported topic 'deserves' can affect content selection and the packaging of news events. While the academic approaches to journalism that have been briefly introduced here vary, they share the underlying agreement that the products that news organisations mediate all bear some sign of the individual journalist. These signs include the byline in print that denotes the author, the reporter's face we see on the screen, the voice of the radio journalist. These glimpses of human agents behind the headlines give the impression that editorial products are made by people with the power and freedom to impart information in any way they choose. It suggests a direct and close connection between the individual journalist and their bylined story that we see in the news. This liberal-pluralist view has been supported by some influential academics, notably Seymour-Ure (1968) and Blumler (1969).

But what we see, hear and read through TV, radio, online and the press is the end product of a complicated process, subject to many influences and constraints normally invisible to the audience. As a player in the mass media, the journalist is but one link in a long chain. The work of the individual journalist is shaped, cut, moulded, nuanced and quite often spiked as it passes along a conveyer belt of editorial decision-making and packaging. Journalism is clearly a much sought-after and prized occupation, shrouded in a myth of prestige, glamour and mystique. Getting onto the first rung of the career ladder is difficult enough; staying there and rising up involves new entrants rapidly absorbing and applying the values of their institution. There has been a limited quantity of work from journalism academics on how journalists navigate their careers, and even less direct research into how these influences might impact on news content by these practitioners.

In order to understand this process better, it is necessary to examine at the context in which most journalism work takes place: the newsroom itself. From as early as the mid-1950s, it was proposed that 'social control' played an important role in the induction of the novice reporter. Breed (1955) showed how senior editorial staff applied institutional authority and also sanctions in order to coach the trainee into approaches and practices agreeable in that setting. These sanctions include ignoring or drastically changing a story, cutting its length or withholding a byline. Internal competition for high-profile space or air-time, with resulting peer esteem, also serve to inculcate young reporters into set norms and approaches, wrote Breed. Opportunities for promotion may suppress 'deviant' behaviour which is too political or too critical, as professional success depends on smooth relations between workers and superiors. This would seem to tally with the later class-based Marxist analyses into media power proposed by Hall (1977) and Murdock and Golding (1977), articulated through less explicitly political vocabulary by Glasgow University Media Group (1976).

When thinking about the decision-making of individual journalists and the myriad factors that may influence that process, we see crystallised the very limitations of approaches to journalism from media studies, cultural studies and sociology. While these approaches can be very helpful in illuminating the sociocultural and sociopolitical structures and forces that impact upon news structures and output, they have so far been unable to conceive of the individual journalist. This inability to conceive of individuals has been well documented by those working in these paradigms with consumers and subjects (McRobbie 1997). The prevailing approach to media and cultural studies approaches has been to 'lump together' certain groups in society, including gendered groups, subcultures and occupational groups, without taking into account the differences between the individuals that make up those groups. This has been highlighted in the work of social psychologists such as Walkerdine *et al.* (2001). McRobbie (1984) and others have criticised ethnographic approaches as being too elite, whereby researchers from outside a social grouping enter it and draw conclusions. More recently, as higher education has moved towards professional and vocational training, there have been developments in work-based learning and reflective practice to enable practitioners-in-training to self-evaluate; however, these models do not necessarily encourage a critique of the practices and processes of the host professions or organisations on the part of the trainee.

In order to develop a better understanding of the processes and practices of news journalism in a contemporary context of conversion, competition and globalisation, a dialogue with working journalists is long overdue. An important dimension of this dialogue must be questions around the composition of the news journalism business. These questions must centre on the diversity of its staff, in terms of gender, ethnicity, faith, disability, socio-economic background and education. For instance, it has been shown that in editorial departments, women and men tend to be associated with different kinds of stories (Gallagher and Von Euler 1995). Other studies have begun to explore the more psychological dimensions of gender practices in a journalism environment, such as whether men and women will seek out more sources of their own gender (Weaver 1997). For journalism to be seen as equally accessible for all, trustworthy and representative, it must reflect on its history, political economy and practices and its stakeholders. Among its stakeholders is the rapidly expanding realm of journalism education, which also carries with it a long-standing set of practices and processes of selection, recruitment and pedagogy, as well as burgeoning commercial imperatives.

Summary: engaging journalists in reflection

This summary of some of the most influential approaches to journalism studies raises some fascinating and urgent questions for journalism research. These questions are fascinating because they have emerged as a consequence of the growing interdisciplinary awareness of news journalism as a rich and significant focus for scholarly activity. Furthermore, work is emerging from journalism academics who also have long-standing experience within professional journalism, such as Richard Keeble (1998, 2001, 2005), Ros Coward (1989, 2004) and Roy Greenslade (2004). What is urgent about this quest is that journalism studies needs a rounded critical vocabulary and methodology to enable it to achieve its dual goals – of shedding new light on existing studies and of articulating the wealth of critical reflection that characterises the practice of news journalism. This book will attempt to develop this methodological vocabulary through a critical dialogue in which journalists and their everyday lives and decision-making are central. Consequently, the questions emerging from this summary of theoretical approaches will be asked from the perspectives of journalists and their audiences, the two least-researched stakeholders in the news research triumvirate of producer-receiver-scholar.

First, to what extent do the theories of news selection confirm and contradict everyday newsroom practices? Through close examination of the news selection process, it is possible to see a more complex array of factors at play in news decision-making. This is especially true on news shifts where no major news events are taking place. How do journalists employ their critical judgement on ordinary news cycles when so much theoretical attention has been placed on exceptional news events such as war and terrorism? Do scholarly approaches to beats and sources sufficiently account for the real difficulty journalists have when facing deadlines and competition? It may have been possible to withhold stories while they were thoroughly verified through multiple sources, such as in the *Washington Post*'s reporting of Watergate. So is it the academic case that journalists rely too much on authority figures, news releases and agency feed really fair? There are many views in the world, and not all stories lend themselves to simple binaries of right and wrong. How many of these views do journalists have to cover in order to be fair?

The next set of questions relate to the way international events in particular are reported. Are journalists consciously presenting biased coverage or are other contributory factors at play? How accurate and consensual are academics' notions of what the news medium is compared with those of journalists? This issue is crystallised in the immediacy and emotiveness of reporting crises. Can these academic approaches account for the seismic shifts that user-generated content has brought to the news producer/audience relationship? How true is the general academic assertion that news coverage is deflecting attention from causes and solutions when audiences are looking to see their own lives and feelings reflected in coverage?

Given that a critically important area of news journalism has been overlooked in academic studies – that of the sub-editor – it is vital we examine that role fully: especially so, now that news has become so visually led. Therefore, does journalism studies need to engage with theories of the visual to gain a better understanding of the thought processes of key decision-makers? Has the role of the sub-editor become more aligned to that of a repackager rather than a factual verifier, and does a bold headline automatically equate to patronising readers if more readers are drawn to that story? It has been shown how the rise of picture-led approaches and featurised news has led to academic concerns that news is over-simplified and sensationalised. In taking this line, is academe falling into the same elitist trap that journalists may be trying to escape from?

In undertaking this study we are mindful of Donald Schon's attempts to bring 'reflection' into the centre of an understanding of what practitioners do. The introduction to his book *The Reflective Practitioner* (1983) states that he is wishing to explore decision-making in a new way, so that knowledge inherent in practice can be illuminated. Schon distinguishes between two concepts: reflection-*in*-action and reflection-*on*-action. In news journalism, the first concept is 'thinking on our feet'. It might involve rapid editorial decision-making that combines experiences with hunches. The reporter will form a decision on unfolding events based on what he or she has experienced before. Schon wrote:

> The practitioner allows himself to experience surprise, puzzlement, or confusion in a situation which he finds uncertain or unique. He reflects on the phenomenon before him, and on the prior understandings which have been implicit in his behaviour. He carries out an experiment which serves to generate both a new understanding of the phenomenon and a change in the situation.
>
> (Schon 1983: 68)

The journalist's 'thinking on their feet' is also connected with reflection-on-action, which is done after the event. Journalists may have a debriefing, a handover at the end of the shift or an informal chat with colleagues, exploring why they acted as they did. This allows the journalist to develop a set of questions and new strategies that might be applied to improve their performance next time. Donald Schon saw this as central to reflective thought:

> When a practitioner makes sense of a situation he perceives to be unique, he sees it as something already present in his repertoire. To see this site as that one is not to subsume the first under a familiar category or rule. It is, rather, to see the unfamiliar, unique situation as both similar to and different from the familiar one, without at first being able to say similar or different with respect to what. The familiar situation functions as a precedent, or a metaphor, or . . . an exemplar for the unfamiliar one.
>
> (Schon 1983: 138)

In this way, this book will do more than simply ask journalists to describe their experiences. They will reflect-in-action and reflect-on-action to reveal new insights and hopefully form a closer engagement, albeit critical, with theory. But is it the case that journalists, as Bennett (2005) has suggested, live too much in their own little world so that they are out of touch with the real issues that affect and interest their audiences? Or, as journalists may assert, is it important for reporters never to be part of the status quo that they are meant to critique? We could equally ask the same questions of the academics that investigate and criticise their work, as the ensuing chapters will reveal.

3 News values for consumer groups

The case of a radio newsroom

In the last chapter we looked at the way that experienced journalists might describe the criteria they use to select events for news as being down to a 'news instinct' or 'nose for a story'. Sociologists of newsgathering have shown that there are certain preordained patterns in the kinds of events that do get chosen. These will be events that have certain characteristics, or those that can be placed within established news frames. We looked at some of the arbitrary criteria that might define what events do get chosen.

This goes against the idea that news should simply be a natural reflection of what is going on in the world that is important for everyone to know. When we open our daily newspaper or switch on a news bulletin we assume that we will be served up the most important and relevant things that have happened over the past hours or days. This is how we can maintain our role as informed citizens in a democratic system. For this system to operate journalists must be able to work as the eyes and ears of the public, as watchdogs over the powerful, in order that we can make informed choices about who we select to govern us. However, news sociologists and writers from media studies have shown that a systematic analysis of what kinds of events do find their ways into news outlets shows that they are governed more by values such as whether they can be placed into news frames that are already familiar to audiences, whether they involve elite nations and people, whether they allow a balanced news flow and whether they are entertaining.

In this chapter we look at the example of news production in the newsroom of Independent Radio News (IRN). This is the news agency that supplies tailor-made news bulletins for the majority of commercial radio stations in the UK. We spent time in the newsroom in September and November 2003, attended meetings and carried out interviews with editor Jon Godel and news editor Simon Cadman.

What we show is that the kinds of news values described in earlier studies by Galtung and Ruge (1965), Harcup and O'Neill (2001) and Boorstin (1973), are still evident in news selection. But we also show that the kinds of changes in news production that have characterised the past decade – concentrated ownership, drive for profits, staff cuts, digital technologies

– have changed the way that these news values are applied by journalists. The choices made by journalists cannot be explained by the kinds of factors described in these earlier studies. We now find that stories are selected and angled in different ways for different markets. The news events that are chosen as news, rather than being those that are naturally important for everyone, become those that are important to members of niche market-defined groups. These have been identified through extensive careful market research which gives information about the values, pastimes and consumer behaviours of lifestyle groups. This renders the idea of the 'nose for a story' as deeply problematic.

Yet this does not mean that the news team did not operate professionally with a commitment to delivering accessible and engaging news to listeners. What we need to emphasise is that they did so with an awareness of the restrictions of the environment in which they worked.

Nevertheless IRN's strategy raises important questions about journalists' consensual role as impartial eyewitnesses and information providers. What we find in this chapter suggests that the gatekeeper role in news is now shared by journalist, advertiser and consumer. The evidence for this is most apparent in the three tasks IRN journalists undertake to ensure their stories are well targeted – selection, simplification and remodelling.

News values: what gets to be news

Imagine an evening news bulletin starting like this:

> This is the evening national and international news. A man in Beirut has planted a tree in his garden. In Burkina Faso there were elections. And in the north a local man is still unemployed after 15 years.

Of course this is not what we would expect from a news bulletin that claimed to give us national and international news. As news audiences we expect to be receiving important events from around the world in our newspapers, our news broadcasts and on our web pages. By important we mean important to *everyone*. Stories about an unknown man in Beirut are not of importance to the rest of the world. A story about an event in a small African country doesn't seem important to everyone. The unemployed man isn't really hard-hitting immediate news and sounds more like a feature item.

In the model of journalists being the eyes and ears of the public we rely on a supply of important and relevant events being made accessible to us so that we can be informed citizens. The man in Beirut and the elections in Burkina Faso are not the kinds of events that we would associate with becoming so informed. Many feel that we have a responsibility as citizens to know what important things are going on in the world. Events around the globe can be interconnected or may involve our own government.

We should know about and understand a particular armed conflict, for example, and be able to develop an opinion on whether or not we think our government should get involved. Should they do so we would then be able to monitor their progress and judge whether or not they are acting in our best interest or in fairness to the people of that country. There are some events, such as natural disasters, climate change, etc., that we might feel we should know about – perhaps the victims can be helped, or perhaps there is someone who should be held responsible. It is simply healthy that we understand what is going on out there in the world, what is affecting other people in the world. In this way news helps to create educated, sophisticated, informed citizens who can have a better political, economic and social understanding of the world.

Of course each day in the world many, many, things happen. Even if most of them were important, a news bulletin is only so long, a newspaper can only carry so many stories. So we rely on the journalist to select those that it is most important for us to know about.

Amongst experienced journalists it is often said that a new reporter must develop a 'nose for a story'. Editors we interviewed spoke of a 'news instinct'. These descriptions are used to describe the way that journalists, through experience, are able to acquire a sophisticated sense of what comprises a newsworthy event, of what kinds of things should be revealed to the public and in what kinds of ways. When a news team have a morning meeting to discuss which of the day's stories should be followed or developed they will generally have a shared sense of what kinds of newsworthiness different stories carry. This will guide them in how they decide what is the lead story and what should follow.

Sociologists of news, however, have shown that newsworthiness is less to do with an instinct and more to do with internalising a set of arbitrary values that have become established over time through institutionalised practices. In Chapter 2 we looked at the news values described by Galtung and Ruge (1965). It was they who first attempted to describe the kinds of values that underpinned the way that certain international events and not others come to be chosen as news. Studying the coverage of international news, they identified 12 recurring criteria that determine whether or not a story was published. These values could be seen to threaten the idea that events have intrinsic importance. Let's look at some of these values in detail so that we can think about what kinds of stories will be selected or ignored.

Meaningfulness

This refers to whether the story can be made easily recognisable to an audience. A story that already fits into an existing frame of reference will seem naturally newsworthy. This will mean that the story will need less contextualisation and therefore be less likely to lose the attention of the audience or readers. The problem with this is that established frames are unchallenging. Journalism theorists like Hall (1977), Hartley (1982) and Bennett (2005) have expressed concern that this creates two problems. One, stories that fall outside of existing frames of reference will be ignored, or two, stories will be given an angle that makes them fit an existing frame. So, for example, a suicide bomber in Israel is simply a terrorist. There is less chance that this will be placed into a socio-political historical context of colonialism, US intervention and Israel's ignoring of Geneva Convention rules on occupation of land and several UN resolutions. A hungry child in Africa is yet another hungry child in Africa irrespective of the political or economic processes that have brought this about.

So the following stories would sound strange to a northern European audience.

> Here is the national and international news. Today there was further violence in Israel as a legacy of European colonialism and map-drawing in the Middle East. Is it time for these countries to take responsibility? In Africa poverty caused by colonialism and international economic pressures gets worse. We see footage of the people who are to blame.

These simply do not fit into established news frames.

Another typical news frame is order versus conflict: events tend to be placed into a context of them being a threat to established society. Crime is one such event. Bennett (2005) suggests that crime in the news does not include corporate crime, nor does it include political crimes, for example where policies are made that favour certain groups in society that might then cause massive unemployment and social upheaval. Crime is simple bad versus decent moral citizens. Sociologists have long shown us that what we call crime is related to the way that we organise our societies – it will increase when we exclude larger numbers of people. So large run-down housing estates with poverty, high unemployment and poor facilities will spawn more of this simple level crime than an affluent area. Yet the news does not routinely deal with crime as an example of a decision to run our societies in a particular way.

Consonance

This describes a build up to an expected event. A five-year survey of news content in the US (PEJ 2002) revealed that there is an increasing reliance on official events, sporting events, political events, council meetings, etc. News organisations like these kinds of events as they can plan resources, use established routines and above all they are cheap and require no investigation or follow-ups (Bell 1991). These might include press releases. Of course, as we saw in Chapter 3 this means that organisations themselves, rather than being monitored by journalists, are simply able to promote themselves or control the agenda. For example, a private water company could provide a press release on water shortages and people wasting water. This could hide years of neglect of the infrastructure and lack of investment by the company which needed to provide upturns in profit for shareholders. Yet the press release seems to explain the shortages and provides a useable news type event. We are given the impression that the news is informing the public.

Composition

News must have a variety of content. After all it is for the most part a product that needs to be sold. What if there were, and there often are, twenty wars happening across the planet? Does a news bulletin just cover them all? Editors normally like a balance of material that includes some lighter human-interest stories, but if this is the case how does the need to have a range of subjects tally with the idea of intrinsic newsworthiness?

There has been much criticism of the 'hook and hold' format of news bulletins. In this format material is ordered to get our immediate attention with an alarming story, perhaps on public safety to begin with, then immediately gives the viewer a promise of something else later on which will usually be a human-interest or celebrity story. The viewer will be reminded of what is to come at different points in the bulletin, encouraging them to stay tuned. So news must be chosen in order to have the right events to fill this template. In the US this has led to audience complaints about repetition of too much crime, infotainment and repetition. The PEJ (2002) study found a massive reliance on press releases, daybook events and feed material. Problems lay in the financing of news-gathering infrastructure (Potter and Gantz 2004). In their study they found that audiences requested more quality programming on consumer issues, health issues, local education and actual events in the community. In short, one respondent said, 'real reporting'. The problem is that this kind of news-gathering requires resources and investment and in the current economic climate of cut backs in the newsroom this may be less and less likely.

Reference to elite places and persons

Events that involved elite countries or famous people are more likely to be covered. Ordinary people are less interesting as are countries outside of the major economic powers. The elections in the small African country may in fact be highly relevant, particularly in its history of European colonial control. But for the one part this kind of control is not a known news frame and for the other this country would not be considered sufficiently elite to interest the public. In 1984 the New World Information and Communication Order (NWICO), which comprised countries who felt that they were excluded from the Western domination of news, complained to

UNESCO about the fact that the Western news paid scant attention to events that fell outside of its immediate interest. This had led to the Western public having a distorted view of the rest of the world, where, in fact, most of the world's population lived (Ochs 1986). For example, 50 socially and politically diverse African nations were generally all lumped together under famines and poverty (Ebo 1992; Fair 1989).

From what we have said so far we can see that what we often get on our news may not be the most important events for everyone chosen by journalists through their news instinct. Rather they are delivering what is felt to be interesting to a target audience. Consider the following bulletin:

> Here is the national and international news. More famine in Africa – we see footage of attempts to get food to starving children often thwarted by rebels. A robbery goes wrong as drug-crazed youths shoot an elderly shopkeeper. Water authorities warn of future water shortages in the south. And we see how Hollywood stars now see Britain as the place to holiday and relax.

This is more recognisable to us as a news bulletin even though it tells us much less about the world and the nature of events than the previous hypothetical bulletins, yet all of these items fall within the news values just described. In this case the idea of news as providing important information to everyone is seriously challenged.

Market-driven news

More recently sociologists of journalism have become concerned about the effects of the commercialisation of news. Practically this means that the same news values act as a guide to which events get chosen to fill bulletins and newspapers, but the pressure to be entertaining and not lose the attention of viewers and readers is an increasingly important factor.

In Chapter 4 we look at the fact that journalists are deeply concerned about the way that news is now a commodity through which companies wish to increase profits. Journalists' memoirs have often lamented the fact that news is a commodity. More recently, academics such as McManus (1994) have observed that news is becoming much more market-driven. Falling audiences and circulations, competition from 24-hour rolling news outlets and the diversification into online media forms has led news providers to look for ways of making their news products more commercially appealing. This change is true of all news formats.

Sociologists of the mass media such as Habermas (1989) and Postman (1986) have theorised the effects of this commercialisation upon the quality of public debate, suggesting that it will become trivialised and uninformed. Pressure to entertain will mean that news frames will emphasise polarities of good and evil, rather than boring complexities of shades of grey. They will tend towards the personal rather than the factual. Similarly, McManus warns that we need to look at what happens when we replace 'the journalist with the consumer as the "gatekeeper"' (McManus. 1994: xii). McManus asked: 'as news becomes more explicitly a commodity, will it lose its informational value?' (McManus 1994: 1). Such concerns about the potential consequences of market-driven news have been expressed by respected journalists such as the US's Walter Cronkite and UK's Jon Snow, who claim that the news media are becoming trivialised in the name of profitability (1997). Cronkite had seen the effects of the drive by owners of the US television networks to increase revenue, which led to cutbacks on journalist numbers and other related staff.

However, while we agree with the concerns raised by the likes of McManus, we feel that his analysis of the effects of marketing on news are in some ways simplistic. His main worry is on the replacement of information with the trivial, fun and the sensational. When we encounter debate about falling standards in news in the news media itself most would identify this as being the major concern about trends in news. The example of IRN that we consider in this chapter shows that journalists' attention to market forces does not necessarily result in dumbing down, nor sensationalism.

In IRN's case, we show that it is market forces that lead to the reshaping and repackaging of news in order to fit with the given marketing research criteria for a particular audience. It is not a matter of news simply becoming entertaining to please audiences in contrast to the ideal model of news as informing a public: rather news production has become a process of tailoring a set of events in the world for a specific audience in terms of criteria, established in terms of market research which tells the journalist what it is that is of interest to this audience and how this should be written for them. Of course this challenges the purposes of news. Rather than informing the public as citizens, news becomes a way of addressing the public as groups of consumers who can be characterised by sets of values, opinions and shopping patterns, which raises important issues for the training of journalists.

News values for consumer groups

Commercial products such as clothing, make-up, sun-glasses and furniture, are produced with a particular niche market target audience in mind. The same is now increasingly the case for news. This is not something that is included in journalist training manuals. The 'use value' of a product such as a kind of soap or a beer is now no longer so much a concern as the way that product can be located as meaningful in terms of a consumer-based lifestyle. Such products are marketed not in terms of how they can be used but by being loaded with particular kinds of values such as independence, friendship, freedom, etc. The precise cluster of values that should be loaded onto products is identified through market research. This allows advertisers to determine how products can be made meaningful to target 'lifestyle' groups. Such processes are now also part of the process of branding news, yet this deeply important part of the work of the contemporary journalist – targeting – is not referred to in one of the most enduring critical studies of news values, produced by Galtung and Ruge in 1965, which we considered in the previous chapter.

Market segmentation research allows consumers to be identified by clusters of attitudes, opinions, beliefs, pastimes and consumer preferences. This is different from an older kind of demographic research which researched consumers in terms of categories such as age and gender. This new research is called 'psychographic research' and allows people to be clustered into 'lifestyle constellations' (Gunter and Furnham 1992: 58).

The term psychographic, used in marketing since the 1970s, describes research in which audience groups are not classified around a more traditional group of categories referred to as demographics, including social categories such as age, gender, and economic background. Instead they are grouped according to lifestyle constellations. This kind of research was pioneered by Arnold Mitchell (1978). It results in describable categories of people who are clustered together on the basis of opinions, attitudes, pastimes and consumer behaviours. For example Hoyer and MacInnes (1997) produce the following descriptions:

- *Actualisers:* have most resources. They enjoy the finer things. Receptive to new products, technologies, distribution. Sceptical of advertising. Frequent readers of a wide variety of publications. Light TV viewers.
- *Experiencers:* are action-oriented. Follow fashion and fads. Spend much disposable income on socialising. Buy on impulse. Attend to advertising. Listen to rock music.
- *Believers:* are principle-oriented. Buy American. Slow to change habits, look for bargains. Watch TV more than average. Read retirement, home and garden, and general interest magazines.
- *Strivers and status oriented:* Image conscious. Limited discretionary incomes, but carry credit balances. Spend on clothing and personal-care products. Prefer TV to reading (Hoyer and MacInnis 1997: 82).

These categories will be used in the production of any kind of consumer product and in the design of a promotional programme to target and reach the appropriate lifestyle constellation. The same kinds of categories are now also used in news selection and production because they allow advertisers to predict the way that a particular market segment might respond to a particular kind of news.

The output of a radio station at a particular time of day should engage not just an audience but a specific market segment or lifestyle group. This strong brand identity can be achieved through the kind of music played, the kinds of people that are interviewed, the personalities of the presenters and in the content and style of the news bulletins.

Radio programmes, along with newspapers and news channels, work hard to create a brand identity that allows such lifestyle groups to associate them with a particular set of core values that will have been identified through psychographic research.

In the same way that newsworthiness could be described systematically by Galtung and Ruge, it is now possible to describe the new contextualisation of these values. For a radio news producer news must be coherent, in terms of the brand identity, with the rest of the schedule. An interview with Gordon MacNamee, previous owner/controller of KISS FM, carried out by one of the authors, revealed that when he was taken over by EMAP, all programmes had to be changed in order to fit more closely with audience segments for advertisers. This covered all kinds of content including news.

This need to reach advertiser-friendly market segments has deeply influenced the identity of the move to Independent Local Radio (from the 1996 Broadcasting Act), which left audiences with radio stations that were not very local and which had very similar playlists (Tunstall and Machin, 1999). Advertisers were interested in the new social categories of people as consumer categories rather than an older model of people as part of geographical communities. As part of the same trend John Birt 'rebranded' Radio 1 in the late 1990s to appeal to younger audiences. This included sacking middle-aged disc jockeys, and also a rethink of the news bulletin style.

Commercial radio news should now be thought of as part of the targeting of the media flow for a particular kind of reception. An interview with Jon Godel, editor of IRN, showed that he had a strong sense of his target audience, who he referred to as 'Craig from Birmingham'. In contrast, an interview with a news editor at BBC Radio Lincolnshire revealed her market segment as 'Dora from Mavis Enderby', who had a completely different psychographic profile.

Independent Radio News

In the rest of this chapter we will be looking at the way the marketing criteria govern the way that Independent Radio News (IRN) choose and shape news. We want to show that while the news values we considered earlier in the chapter still apply we can now see the way that the need to reach target consumer groups influences news selection. Importantly we show that this does not lead to sensationalism and dumbing-down, for the simple reason that this would not be suitable for some lifestyle groups.

IRN is the UK's leading commercial radio news agency, serving more than 260 clients across the UK, Ireland and beyond. The agency has an average weekly reach of more than 27 million listeners. It supplies prestige national stations, such as Classic FM, as well as the biggest radio news groups in the UK, including GWR and EMAP. IRN was established 30 years ago at the start of commercial radio in the UK. The organisation is located within the Independent Television News (ITN) headquarters in central London. IRN was bought by ITN in the 1990s, and operates under the auspices of ITN Radio. This means that ITN Radio is the news provider for IRN. ITN Radio has to submit a competitive tender to supply news to IRN every few years. ITN is owned by a single company, ITV plc, the company formed by the merger of Carlton Communications and Granada plc. These groups have a huge slice of ownership of commercial television in the UK.

IRN is free to client stations. The service is funded through advertising, with what are called 'news links'. These are short advertisements that are attached to prime-time bulletins. They might be played at the end of a bulletin between the final story and a time-check. Typical advertisers are national newspapers, banks, supermarket brands, big electrical retailers and cars.

Over a 24-hour period, during which time the service is constantly staffed, IRN provides four hourly bulletin services – a three-minute mid-market, BBC Radio 2-style service, a 90-second faster-paced, upbeat tabloid-style service and two other bespoke bulletin services for Kiss FM and Magic FM. The other major part of the IRN service is text copy, cues (the text lead-in to audio reports that the newsreader uses to introduce the package) and audio feeds to their client services, and longer packages.

The increase in small news processing agencies

Tailor-made radio news has become a pivotal way of developing media businesses globally, although smaller news agencies have grown up in all areas of news. These agencies have arisen as the news organisations themselves have reduced staffing levels drastically, with waves of redundancies among journalists and editors throughout the last decade. Niche-marketed journalism has been enabled by developments in digital broadcast technology, which allows relatively small agencies, run by a handful of staff, to splice together and transmit bulletins and packages to hundreds of radio stations at speed.

The content of the bulletins and packages is obtained by the agency from a range of providers, including large news agency feeds, archives and sound effects. They may also have a further network of secondary sources for press releases. Again this can be seen as taking up where journalists would previously have carried out routine news collection, but rather than personal contacts the agency will rely largely on pre-packaged material assembled by organisations such as the police.

Bulletins and packages are then carefully assembled in creative ways for the market-researched target audience of each news outlet. Receiving bulletins and packages from an agency is a cost-effective practice for hundreds of national and regional client stations, who are not able to finance their own in-house production or editing of national and international news.

For radio, it is the niche market rather than the mass audience that has the power to attract advertisers (Tunstall and Machin 1999). Bulletin and package content and formats are therefore carefully designed by news agencies on the basis of market research to target these specific markets. This service is cost-effective to the outlet station as the agency can generate its own revenue straight from advertisers. Globally, news agencies such as New York-based Bloomberg distribute syndicated news reports to 840 affiliated clients in four languages. California company ScreamingMedia were providing 'affiliate radio stations with customised real-time news reaching 42 million strong audiences across the US and Canada' (Content-Wire 2002). Such agencies produce none of the content themselves but aggregate and redistribute to outlets. These kinds of news reports, say the Hamburg-based Deutsche-Presse-Agentur news provider, are tailor-made for the target audiences of the different stations, and because these organisations produce news cross-media they are able to offer cross-media packages for advertisers.

The IRN newsroom

Each morning news editor Simon Cadman arrives for work by 5 a.m. He works in the IRN newsroom which is located in the basement of the Norman Foster-designed ITN headquarters in London's Gray's Inn Road, on the eastern side of the city centre. The IRN base is a large glass-fronted space filling half of the basement area. The rest of the floor is occupied by two television studios, a canteen and the building's technical heart, the Master Control Room. IRN is open plan, with journalists and editors editing and reporting using digital computer consoles on their desks. There are also three studios for broadcasts and interviews. Cadman sits at the newsdesk in front of a bank of TV monitors and radio receivers, as well as the computer which enables him to receive domestic and international feeds as well as edit at his desk. Behind him, the wall is covered with pieces of paper featuring vital phone numbers, memos reminding the team about procedures for royal deaths, international maps (such as a huge one of Iraq) and plans of the UK motorway infrastructure. As well as the mass of technology at their fingertips, the team have dozens of newspapers to hand as well as reference texts when fact-checking has to be done in an instant. Communication between Cadman and his team is constant as he manages the flow of the operation, through messaging and through a voice intercom system between the desks. The pace is fast, and it is noisy as reporters report, edit and rehearse. At 20 minutes to each hour, an alarm warning rings across the newsroom to alert the team to their approaching bulletin deadline. Simon likes his team to work fast and efficiently, and for the newsreaders to be in their booths well-prepared before their bulletins start.

Sitting next to Cadman are the newsdesk co-ordinator and the newsdesk assistant, whose roles are to support and facilitate the smooth operation of the newsdesk. During his average eight- or nine-hour shift, Cadman is in charge of a team of eight people, comprising the newsdesk team, two reader/writers who prepare and deliver the bulletins, one or two reporters (there are five reporters on duty across the 24-hour period), and the specialist desks. In addition to the hard news remit, IRN has four specialist desks – sport, showbiz and money and the parliamentary unit (Parly) based close to the Houses of Parliament at Westminster, covering political and governmental stories. He also has access to ITN correspondents in bureaux across the globe. Across the room, the senior management team oversee and lead the efficiency and quality of the editorial operation, liaise with clients and with ITN management.

During every shift, the editorial and legal responsibility for Simon is intense. He balances these requirements with the demands of a network hungry for information and audio on breaking stories. He must also constantly monitor other stations, wire feeds, the Internet, TV and newspapers. In an interview, he said:

> You get up at 4 a.m., you're at work at 5 a.m., so you are seriously out of tilt with the world. It's a unique mindset, like a breakfast journalism club. There's camaraderie and a Dunkirk spirit, so that after that first cup of coffee jokes fly around that have everyone on their knees by 6 a.m. When big stories do break early, that tight-knit family feel also works to your professional advantage. It's definitely the best time of day to be working – there's the most happening, you are setting the agenda and you have the most listeners. You are also under the most intense pressure to deliver what very demanding stations require.

Throughout his shift he is in constant dialogue with his team about identifying the best stories for their service, and creative ways of targeting them to their clients' audiences.

The targeted news process

There are three tasks in the targeting process that we can identify from the way that the IRN news team processes news events:

1 Selection
2 Simplification
3 Remodelling

These tasks allow the journalist to ensure news is appropriate for target audiences. Important in how this takes place are two crucial factors that the news values described by Galtung and Ruge do not allow for: time limits and procedural requirements. These are crucial to understanding the work and output of the journalists working in the IRN newsroom. In the first case the IRN news team is small and has a massive amount of news to edit and repackage. The staff must work quickly without time or resources to perform further investigation or analysis. In the second case, procedurally, there is the important requirement that the longest story will be around 15–30 seconds in length and must be easy to follow with no ambiguity. Journalists we interviewed for this and other chapters all spoke of the increasing pace of news production. This was immediately apparent on the IRN newsdesk, where the duty news editor and newsdesk co-ordinator sit before several large pieces of technology. One of these journalists skilfully splices together wire input while the other works on other archive material, such as sound effects, to intersperse street commentaries with crowd noises or conservation stories with animal sounds. When interviewed, these journalists said that we should not underestimate the way that 'process drives content'.

Selecting news for the target audience

We observed the processes by which stories were selected from agency feeds by the IRN team for different bulletins. A longer initial list of possibilities would be selected and then slimmed-down and ordered by the news editor in consultation with the team and the editor. It was clear that target audiences were in the minds of the news team when they were making these choices. Here is an example of the stories chosen by the team for Friday, 26 September 2003. It was a relatively quiet news day just before the weekend. The most attractive stories to IRN that morning were:

- The aftermath of a major earthquake in Japan, which had happened the previous afternoon;
- Reports suggesting controversial injections into the brain of a victim of the human form of 'Mad Cow Disease' seem to have had an effect;
- Mortar attack on civilians in Iraq;
- Labour minister is warning Prime Minister Tony Blair about consequences of taking Britain into war with Iraq;
- Released Colombian hostage is due back in Britain tonight;
- A new film advertisement to be screened in cinemas warning women about the dangers of drug rape;
- Scottish National Party conference underway;
- British conker championships this weekend – recent good weather means poor-quality conkers;

- Three-quarters of drivers say prayers at the wheel, according to the Automobile Association.

To some extent the choice of these stories can be thought about in terms of the news values we discussed earlier in the chapter. An earthquake is of large scale and the follow-up gives the opportunity for human-interest stories on suffering or those who carried out acts of bravery. There is a predominance of elite nations or the concerns of elite nations. There are also stories chosen to create consonance or balance such as the items on conkers and prayer. The way the IRN news team discussed these showed that they were also thinking much more carefully about specific niche markets.

At the morning editorial conference, attended by Cadman and his team, the drug rape film story was agreed as the lead story for the morning bulletins, a view uncontested by any of the team. Cadman said it that it was a story that affects many women, which made it a good lead for their audience. Editor Jon Godel, in a later interview, reflected on how he imagined that his target audience member, 'Craig from Birmingham', would have a sister who would be going out to clubs that evening. 'Craig's worried and so are his parents.' He said: 'This is entirely on-target for us.' He explained how it was not only the time of day and the day of the week that made this story ideal, but also the time of the year. 'This is the time when students return to university and they are an important market segment for the independent stations.'

We must bear in mind that when referring to Craig from Birmingham as one target group Jon and Simon with have in mind a set of opinions and values that have been identified through psychographic market research. This is very different from the idea of writing for a general public who should be informed as citizens.

In Chapter 1 we considered the relationship between advertising and news content, but sociologists of news have tended to describe the way that advertisers will not support newspapers with a particular political affiliation (Curran and Seaton 1991). In the case of IRN which, as we will see throughout this book, is a phenomenon that characterises news in general, the journalists and news editors think 'instinctively' about choosing news to fit a lifestyle group. It is not so much a matter of exclusion of events, but relevance in terms of marketing factors. This will become more apparent as we look at the way that the wire feeds are then remodelled.

IRN's simplification of agency feed

The journalists working in the IRN newsroom received feed from major national and overseas agencies, including Reuters, Press Association (PA) and Associated Press Television News (APTN). The stories were selected and ordered as described above. They then had to be simplified. On the one hand this was due to procedural matters of the items having to be very short, on the other this would also be done by items being immediately recognisable to listeners by placing them into already familiar news frames. This would ensure that the stories chosen were most accessible and engaging to the target group. These examples from our data gathered on Thursday, 18 September 2003, provide evidence:

Below is the APTN feed as received by IRN:

> One of the few suspects to express remorse over his alleged involvement in last year's bombings on Indonesia's Bali island arrived at court on Thursday to hear his sentence.
>
> Ali Imron is facing a possible death penalty, but prosecutors have asked that he receive 20 years in prison because he has shown regret and cooperated with investigators.
>
> Imran's older brother Amrozi bin Nurhasyim, and another key defendant, Imam Samudra, already have been sentenced to face firing squads for their roles in the attack, which killed 202 people – mostly foreign tourists.

The copy goes on to describe Imron, 33, as a school teacher and the investigation's progress. Below we can see the way that IRN modelled this story:

> A man's been jailed for life for helping to plan and carry out the Bali bombings.
>
> Twenty-six Britons were among more than two hundred people killed in the attack in October last year.
>
> Ali Imron was spared the death sentence handed down to other suspects because he expressed remorse and co-operated with the Indonesian authorities.

The IRN copy uses strong, unambiguous language to signpost memories in target listeners' minds – Bali is a holiday destination . . . 26 Britons . . . spared death sentence. The bomber is de-personalised to make the story simpler and to ensure a simple good vs. bad binary for target listeners. The bomber ceases to be simply a suspect but instead is shown as having a much more certain part in planning and carrying out the bombings.

So in the news feed the protagonist is 'One of the few suspects to express remorse over his alleged involvement in last year's bombings on Indonesia's Bali island.' In the IRN version he is 'A man'. Clearly this involves a great reduction in valuable information. The act of removing the fact that the protagonist is a suspect actually makes a big difference. Other similar information is removed regarding mainly court-type legal language such as 'alleged' and 'sentence'. Such legal terminology must be removed as it would take the story away from the simple news frame which is basically one about evil-doers coming to justice. This simplification also means that other complicated questions need not be raised, for example which court and under whose jurisdiction. Whenever terms such as 'terrorist' are used, there is an ideological impact. For example, in the cases of 'IRA terrorists', or 'Palestinian terrorists', both of which are groups of people living under occupation of another oppressive political power. We often hear of suspected Al-Qaida prisoners awaiting trial, but under whose jurisdiction? Constraints of time and story length mean that journalists must steer away from such issues. And the need to hold attention means that the most recognisable frame should be used. Earlier in the chapter we considered how strange and challenging news stories would look if they were to include the actual political and historical basis of events.

Can we explain this simplification by Galtung and Ruge's sense of making the story 'meaningful' to public audiences? In the IRN case, it involves a complex process of condensing complicated stories using vocabulary that appeals to particular targets. The radio journalists are trying to 'get inside the listeners' heads', to quote Cadman, in order to contemplate how a listener would gain access to a story. As Cadman told us: 'Our target audience will not want to think about political complexity. They won't listen. They want to know what the story means to them and their lives.' This differs greatly from notions of the journalist necessarily telling the listener what is newsworthy, and what angle is the most 'important'.

Remodelling

We have shown how stories are simplified with target audience in mind. Now we want to look at the way the same story can be remodelled differently for different target audiences. IRN adapts the way it writes for the target groups that subscribing stations need to address at different times of the day. It is important that stations can indicate to advertisers that content is attracting specific market groups, such as professional people on their way to work, or mothers of a particular socio-economic group who have just returned from the school run.

This was demonstrated by the development of the coverage of Hurricane Isabel, which struck the east coast of the USA on Thursday, 18 September 2003. The inclusion of this story on the news agenda can be understood in terms of the Galtung and Ruge news values. There was the focus on the White House and the President as elite places and elite people. A hurricane carries a level of unexpectedness, lack of ambiguity and continuity. There is also the opportunity for follow-up with human-interest stories about loss, survival and bravery.

What we saw was that the treatment the story received throughout the day ensured that it was meaningful to different audience segments at different times. Throughout the shift there was no fresh factual information gathered. Rather, it was remodelled and repackaged using different voices at key times in the news cycle. Again we can see a mixture of process and time driving content, along with targeting.

The early morning story built up tension for waking listeners at 6 a.m. Accordingly the story was not given dramatic effect or pace for the more gentle state of early-morning wakers. IRN wrote:

> Tens of thousands of people are on the move in America with Hurricane Isabel just hours away.
>
> Airlines have been forced to cancel flights – and the White House is battening down the hatches.
>
> Reporter Robert Moore's on the north Carolina coast where Isabel's expected to hit first . . . (11 secs of audio from ITN's Robert Moore).

By the 8 a.m. bulletin, the pace of writing and delivery had quickened. Nothing new had actually happened, but the story is dramatised through use of language for maximum impact:

> Hurricane Isabel's racing towards the east coast of America – forcing thousands to leave their homes.
>
> A state of emergency's been declared in Washington and four other states.
>
> The White House has been partly boarded up and schools and businesses have closed.
>
> It's expected to hit North Carolina in the next few hours – CNN reporter Keith Oppenheim is there . . . (15 secs audio from Oppenheim).

Terms have been changed to create a sense of immediacy. Words such as '*racing*', '*forcing thousands*', '*declared*' and '*hit*' give a sense of action, drama and impending threat. The vocabulary is highly charged and active in comparison with the 6 a.m. text, likely to be well-received by Craig on his car stereo as he drives to work.

Descriptions also become much more specific. In the first rewrite we have non-specific actions to describe the effects of the hurricane such as 'people are on the move'. But this has changed to details like: 'forcing thousands to leave their homes'. What is being done by the actors is also much more precise. For example, 'A state of emergency's been declared' replaces the White house is 'battening down the hatches', which is more symbolic than factual. There is also a change in category of those affected. In the first we are only told that flights have been cancelled. In the second case we are told that schools and businesses have closed. This is specific as regards the kinds of disruption and is much more about city life rather than general travellers.

By the 9 a.m. bulletin, the story was more humanised, allowing a different range of domestic – and female – voices to be used. Here the news is directed towards Craig's mother once everyone has left the house:

> A state of emergency's been declared in Washington, as Hurricane Isabel heads towards the east coast of the US.
> A hundred and thirty thousand people in North Carolina have also been told to leave their homes.
> The White House is preparing for the worst – boarding up doors and windows.
> But not everyone is on the move – Audrey Holloway lives in Hampton Village and is staying put . . . (13 secs of woman talking).

In this case the language style is a mixture of the first two remodelled versions, in terms of immediacy and specificity. Emphasis is placed on the experiences of women in this package, and the fact that people were reluctant to leave their homes. Craig's mother can identify emotively with the dilemma faced by Audrey Holloway. The pace of the vocabulary is less high-octane, less stereotypically 'male' with the replacement of 'racing' with 'heads'. The pattern was developed further for the 10 a.m. bulletin. The team gathered an array of different voices from feeds and other television and radio services nationally and internationally via the Internet. They collectively packaged a seemingly objective vox pop, though one which is derived from other journalistic sources. The team were particularly pleased that one of the voices was British. This made the story more empathetic and emotive for their particular target group who may have more of an insular view of the world. IRN wrote:

> Washington DC is preparing for the worst as Hurricane Isabel storms towards the east coast of America.
> Much of the city's shutting down – President Bush has left the area and parts of the White House have been boarded up.
> A state of emergency's also been declared in four other states – including North Carolina where Isabel's expected to hit first.
> These people have decided to tough it out . . . (11 sec vox pop).

Duty reporter Kevin Murphy constructed a package for the lunchtime network news programmes. He sat before his console monitoring a vast array of wire feeds, international TV and radio channels and sought a variety of voices. He scanned the networks in the hope of finding an emergency services worker giving those still in the area a 'dire warning'. Using Reuters feeds, he managed to obtain the number of a bar where many people are planning to shelter from the storm. Murphy said the emphasis in his search was on people 'otherwise it's too dry for our market group'.

He presented Cadman with a paper version of his package, who tells us: 'This is a wonderful example of how you take from a variety of sources and make it your own.' The script for the package was presented as follows:

(Sound effect of wind)
Murphy: Hurtling towards the coast . . . Hurricane Isabel isn't quite the monster it was . . . But it still has winds in excess of a hundred miles an hour . . .
(Voice of CNN reporter)
Murphy: Directly in its path . . . North Carolina and Virginia where people have been told to leave their homes.
(More audio)
The advice is to move to higher ground . . . The tidal surge and flooding are as much a danger as the winds . . . But some people are staying . . .
(Vox)
Even a party at one bar in Virginia Beach . . . bar manager Chris Lane . . .
(Voice)
British Royal Marines Cory Maskell and Cy Lume . . . on exercise in the United States . . . joining the party . . .
(Voices)
Some people are going to the beach to watch the waves . . .
(Voices)
Officials are telling them to write their names, ages, and next of kin on their forearms with a waterproof marker . . . Once Isabel gets inland it's feared it could veer towards the north east, putting Washington in its path . . . President Bush has already beaten a hasty retreat from the White House.

In this version, once again the Galtung and Ruge news values are foregrounded, but the writing has been remodelled so that it meets a variety of modular listenerships regardless of the 'newness' of the information. It is much less about verifying facts and much more about targeting.

Remodelling of IRN news feed by client stations

The client stations of IRN often run the bulletins as they are put together by the IRN news team. Sometimes there might be some additional modelling if the client feels that it requires more personalisation, but there is still no further investigation or new information. It is simply more tailoring for the niche market. Again this foregrounds the target-led approach over notions of public dissemination of newsworthy information.

At 4 p.m. on Monday, 3 November 2003, two of the agency's clients, Classic FM and Jazz FM, used IRN's texts in the construction of their bulletins, but with very different outcomes. We asked IRN's Simon Cadman to comment on these differences as we listened with him.

Classic FM's three-minute bulletin presented IRN's text exactly as it had been composed by the team, following the IRN-set story order. This national station playing classical music targets a mid-market audience. Their advertisers include mid-range saloon cars, fabric conditioner and non-profit organisations suggesting they target an educated, affluent listener. In the news that day one item reported on a breakthrough in a national postal dispute. IRN had led with this story. Cadman said that he would have done some rewriting and expanding for that market, adding additional factual depth. But he commented that the news reader's delivery in a 'slightly reserved, mellow style meant that the feed worked straight' for that market.

At the same hourly bulletin, Jazz FM used the IRN feed but the postal dispute was relegated to a business story. Instead the bulletin led with a story about the sentencing of the 'HIV assassin' as branded by tabloids, who had unprotected sex with women knowing he was likely to be infecting them. The treatment by Jazz FM was much more tabloid in approach than that of Classic FM. This station targets a younger, professional audience than Classic FM. Advertisers are different, including major airlines and soft drinks, indicating a target listener who is fashionable, youthful and interested in the arts and travel. Market research will have identified a range of opinions and values associated with this particular lifestyle group. To cater for this market, Jazz FM chose the most emotive stories, such as the ongoing murder trial of a school caretaker accused of murdering two 10-year-old pupils, and used much more personalised language than the original IRN text. 'They've called it the "Holly and Jessica trial" which IRN avoided,' said Cadman. 'They use more chopped-back language. They've also added their own identity to the reporter to say it's Jazz FM's Tamsin Melville rather than IRN's, to give it more immediacy and brandedness.' Melville was in fact employed by IRN. Again we emphasise that there was no additional reporting done and no verification of the facts. There was only further remodelling by Jazz FM journalists.

According to Cadman, what these bulletins show is that IRN's copy is easily adapted by services to cater for their own branded requirements, although the feed is already designed for a limited target group. Minimal rewriting is needed, and the main alteration appears to be in the hierarchy of stories.

Conclusion

We would hope that what is served up as news is the day's most important events for everyone, but sociologists who studied news output have shown that this is not really the case. Rather selection is governed by an arbitrary set of values, which means that news should be easily recognisable in accepted news frames: it should be about elite places and people and provide an engaging news flow so that it is suitably entertaining.

The problem is that the role of the journalist as impartial eyewitness is challenged by this. This is even more the case when we consider the effects of increased commercialisation of news organisations. Market-led news has become another way of maintaining brand identity. In this way journalists have found themselves in a position where their job is to find events – not that best inform everyone, and not that meet criteria for universal established news values – but which can be manufactured in such a way that they are part of a brand, and speak to people as consumers rather than as citizens. In this case being informed is secondary to being drawn into and held in a space where they can be addressed by advertisers who can have a reasonable idea of their opinions, values and shopping habits.

In Chapter 2 we discussed the idea of gatekeeping in news – who is it that decides what should and should not become news? In this case this role is now being shared by journalist, advertiser and consumer. The evidence for this is most apparent in the three tasks IRN journalists undertake to ensure their stories are well-targeted – selection, simplification and remodelling. The pressure on organisations like IRN and major commercial radio groups to attract and maintain advertising revenue has become ever more acute. The *Media Guardian* reported on 20 May 2005 that the UK radio sector's largest commercial player, GCap Media, reported a 17 per cent fall in advertising revenue in April. GCap is a major shareholder in the IRN company. Indeed, as a postscript to this study, IRN has had to cut nearly a third of its workforce. In an ironic subsequent twist, the ITV News Channel has closed down and it used to be one of the major sources of audio feed to IRN.

There is a lack of reference to strategic market awareness in popular UK journalism training manuals, which are widely used in colleges and universities. Yet in this chapter we have seen that targeting audience groups has become an important driving force in news, both due to the need for advertisers to know the groups that they are reaching and with the increasing importance of brand identity. This means that what editors formerly called 'the news instinct' has to be sensitive to newsworthiness in a much more market-specific way than is accounted for in many contemporary manuals, or in sociological accounts of news values. Now it is produced in the context of psychographically determined market segments.

In this chapter we have also begun to think about the way that we can reduce the divide between theory and practice. In the case of IRN we fostered a positive and constructive dialogue with the journalists involved. The team were highly professional and committed to delivering an accessible and engaging news services to listeners, not just a tailor-made product for the network. Studies that examine only the products of journalism, rather than the processes of production, do not witness the everyday challenges and contexts that shape what can and cannot be achieved.

Nonetheless, this access is not always easy to achieve and many news organisations would be unable or unwilling to accept academics for reasons of space, procedure and protecting their brand's practices from scrutiny by rivals.

Towards the end of this piece of research we discussed the findings with Simon Cadman. He said that this had inspired him 'to go into tomorrow's editorial meeting wanting to be sharper about what we do, how we do it and who we are going for'. He stressed that IRN is not a 'news generator, though we do break a lot of exclusives', rather that the agency is attempting to engage real audiences. It is 'news as conversation', he said. Cadman added that the dialogue with academe had 'crystallised something that's so everyday for us and has brought what we do into sharper relief, and made us ever-more conscious that we're fighting in a commercially-competitive world'. More work is urgently needed to determine which, if any, is the major stakeholder in this relationship if we are to ensure news-gathering is sufficiently and appropriately resourced to provide a public service.

4 News beats and collecting news

The beat reporter, also known as a district reporter, epitomises for many the classic idea of the roving journalist, often depicted romantically in movies, who relentlessly roams around their locality on the hunt for stories. While the daily national news media have the role of informing us about national and global events, the beat reporter is our eyes and ears at the local level. Are our local MPs doing their jobs? Are services being run properly? Are there any hidden dangers that should be brought to our attention so that we can approach those in authority and demand answers? Is our local health service run properly? These are all the kinds of areas that the digging investigative reporter can monitor on our behalf.

In the best possible case, local news-gathering would happen something like this: the local reporters would find out the most important, relevant events to the community served by the news outlet. To do this they would have regular everyday contact with that community. Once they had come across a story they would then identify who it was that could best give further information about those events to allow them to be fully understood from every angle. For example, a reporter might find out from a café owner that a local company has been employing workers in dangerous conditions without proper contracts. The reporter might seek out those who could verify this. They might interview workers, find out why they put up with it – perhaps the company takes advantage of shortages in employment in the area. The reporter may then try to speak with a representative of the company and someone who could give them legal information. They may then contextualise this in a picture of a community living with high unemployment. In the piece all points of view are covered. As a result the readers are informed about issues that deeply affect and shape the community around them.

In reality this has never been exactly the case as regards local reporting, although over the past decade the work of the local reporter has moved even further from this model. For newspapers there has always been the massive practical problem of needing to provide a regular, predictable, economically viable source of news events. Everyday pages need to be filled. For this reason journalists are simply not able to act out this best possible case, although this is not to say that quality investigative reporting has not been done, as we will show later.

Historically journalists developed solutions to the problem of supplying steady predictable supplies of news stories by establishing *beats*. These beats, such as crime, court, or a specific district, would take them into regular contact with sources such as police, councils and other bureaucratic organisations. These organisations process the kinds of events that are newsworthy on a daily basis at a pace that is predictable. So, rather than digging around in the community reporters can access files and reports produced by these organisations.

In journalism studies, however, it has been felt that this solution brings its own problems. It has been claimed that since such news stories have their origins in official organisations we get an official version of what is happening in the world rather than a view from the point of view of members of the public, from what is actually happening on the streets, in our schools and hospitals. But reporters themselves often argue that while beats might be based around official organisations which would provide the regular supply of news copy to fill pages, they would also have time to follow up specific stories that they felt were important. And many beats would include regular visits to cafés and local bars where reporters could learn about local gossip and concerns. The problem is that changes in the industry have made this less and less a component of everyday reporting practice.

Since the mid-1990s in Britain there have been huge changes in the organisation of the regional press. In January 2005 The Newspaper Society stated:

> Over £7.0 billion has been spent on regional press acquisitions and mergers since October 1995. The top 20 publishers now account for 86% of all regional and local newspaper titles in the UK, and 95% of the total weekly audited circulation.

At the time, there were 1,286 regional and local, daily and weekly titles in Britain. Ownership was dominated by three big press groups: Trinity Mirror Plc, Newsquest Media Group and Northcliffe Newspapers Group Ltd. Trinity Mirror, for example, had 274 titles. We have discussed in previous chapters how these large groups have driven huge changes in the way their titles have been organised to raise falling revenue and address waning circulations. This has meant market research to target specific readers, redesigns and format changes and huge cuts in the number of journalists working on titles.

In fact many of these regional titles are in some ways models of excellence for contemporary media. Television news seems to have come up with little in terms of innovation to win back diminishing interest as young people turn to the Internet and see news broadcasts as boring and predictable. In the press it is the regionals, rather than the nationals, that have been able to redefine themselves. Like the nationals there was pressure to deal with falling circulations, but also there was increasing presence from the free press that was taking more and more advertising from paid-for titles. Advertisers seemed to feel that these free titles were more able to reach key markets (McNair 1994: 174). While some felt that the frees would most likely go straight into the bin, some titles claimed to reach 80 per cent of households in a region (McNair 1994: 175). Journalist Brian Walters, who worked for Trinity group newspapers, told us that rather than being competitors to the paid-for regional titles, publishers have swallowed up both and now see them in terms of increased potential for cross promotion, meaning that they could increase overall advertising.

This process of rationalisation and rebranding has had other important implications. It has also meant huge cuts in staffing, particularly in news-gathering and editing (Hallin 1996; Bourdieu 1998). Gitlin and Sylvain (2005) show how regional newspapers in the US have been axing staff in the name of increased profits. Big newspaper chains come under pressure from shareholders to increase revenue and staff cuts and changes in news-gathering procedures is one way that this can be done. It has also meant a greater harmony between news and marketing (Underwood 1995). It is the effects of these changes on reporting procedures that concern us in this chapter.

These staff cuts have had huge implications for the beat system. Basically, to save money titles have employed fewer staff to cover the same geographical areas. This has meant that some beats no longer exist and has reduced the reporter's ability to go out into the community. Where one reporter now covers an area formerly covered by eight, there is no time for nosing around, for verification and especially for developing a story. Instead there has been an increased dependence on secondary sources such as press releases. Story development now involves telephone calls to official organisations, press offices or visits to web sites rather than finding sources who can best verify a story or provide it with different angles. Many of the organisations that provide these releases will employ the very journalists who formerly worked for the newspaper to produce them. A local council may employ ten public relations officers who feed press releases to two local newspapers where they deal with only one lone local reporter. Verification of stories may also increasingly involve calls to the kinds of celebrity lifestyle/culture experts that now dominate the mass media.

Regional titles, particularly in the late 1980s, were able to use new technologies to increase numbers of local editions cheaply across the region that they covered. McNair (1994) describes the *Aberdeen Press and Journal* as having nine editions targeted at specific geographic areas. But with less and less journalists operating across the different localities and local offices closing there could be a danger of losing what has been the strongest weapon in the armoury of the regional title: its *localness*.

Commercial pressures have also led to a tendency towards celebrity and lifestyle/consumer issues, which have had some proven success in terms of turning round falling circulations, and have increased advertising revenue which, as we have already discussed, is the basis of survival for any title.

The result of these changes means that discussions at morning news team meetings will revolve around follow-ups on stories, rather than developing local civic or social issues. This will tend towards getting an extra angle on a comment made by a local celebrity or sports star, or a slightly local slant on a news item in the national press rather than investigation. Decisions will be made in a climate of a fear of anything that will lose the attention of the reader. Politics will be downplayed or trivialised. Reporters will be encouraged to use bullet points and other such textual features, to simplify content and speed uptake by readers.

At worst the locality disappears and is replaced by the buzz of celebrity and the opening of new shopping centres or sports facilities, carefully stage-managed by the local council press office. Local people do appear in the pages of the newspaper, but rather than voicing their concerns about unemployment, poor working conditions or poverty, they give their opinions on whether they agree that a local celebrity has put on weight, or whether they like the design of the new council buildings, and it is unlikely that there will be any criticism of any organisation that is an advertiser in the newspaper.

The Newspaper Society announced on its web site in 2005 that:

> Innovation, brand extension and portfolio publishing are the name of the game for Britain's regional press (and) regional publishers are developing a range of targeted publications and channels to expand their footprint and reach increasingly diverse audiences in their regional markets.

As we will see in the later chapter on the rebranding of the *Liverpool Daily Post*, this means that titles need to be upbeat, to include a positive image of the locality. This is the kind of buzz that appeals to advertisers. Such a title will emphasise local features and be supportive of commerce and local investment. Culture and lifestyle supplements will merge features with advertising for the local night-life scene and urban development. Reaching diverse audiences in fact translates to clear targeting of groups for advertisers.

In this chapter we look at the work of the local beat reporter in order to interrogate critically the effects this ever-changing context has brought to journalism practice. We look at some of the key work done in journalism studies on the development of the beat as a way to ensure the provision of copy. Central to the beat was the establishment of a network of sources. We look at studies that have been critical of the reliance on official sources and of the rise of the influence of public relations and press releases. We then examine a number of examples of stories written by local reporters in the Swansea area of south Wales before and after the commercial changes. In the first case the stories show the strengths of being based in a community and establishing a network of personal contacts. The reporters discuss how these stories were developed and verified in ways that would no longer be possible. We then look at some examples of stories that represent this newer office-bound under-staffed reporting where there is a reliance on press releases, telephone calls to press officers and an emphasis on celebrity and lifestyle. We draw on interview material from four experienced journalists who were working in the south Wales area: Colin Hughes, Brian Walters, Malcolm Rees and Mary Rees.

The development of the beat

The beat is central to providing news events. In a typical news cycle, a local newspaper would require around three stories from each reporter before lunchtime in order to have enough copy to fill the newspaper. Reporter Colin Hughes, who worked for the *Western Mail* and local BBC, told us that before the 1990s, when newspapers carried comparably little advertising and few images, there were more pages to fill and great incentives for reporters to find local exclusives. So the reporter would need to find a way to generate a predictable daily supply of news events. A beat is the routine path and set of locations that a reporter will visit each day, which brings them into contact with organisations that produce such news events.

These locations must be the type that produce a regular supply of easily usable, legitimate, newsworthy events. Places that do just this are official institutions and bureaucratic organisations, such as government offices, law enforcement organisations, health authorities, the military, etc. So we might say that reporters do not find events. What they do is put themselves into situations where they will be exposed to them.

Mark Fishman (1980) carried out an extensive study on the nature of news-gathering at the regional level. He gives the example of crime reporting. In any city there might be a number of areas where crime would not be too difficult to find but reporters cannot wait around on the streets until a crime takes place. Stories might come up, but not with the kind of frequency required to fill pages. Reporters, Fishman said, must expose themselves to a few sources that process potential news events rapidly. In a city there might be several law enforcement agencies, jails, court systems where crimes are recorded, where a reporter can get hold of material that is easily convertible to news copy.

There is a second reason, according to Fishman, that the reporter could not simply wait around in a community to find out about a crime.

News requires official sources. Even though members of a community affected by crime might be able to provide first-hand insights into, say, the experience of social exclusion and how this is connected to law breaking, such voices are not deemed to be official. It would not do to have a news story that had its origins entirely in the words of the owner of, say, the local café. As an example of beat crime reporting Fishman describes how one reporter's beat started off with a visit to the Sheriff's office, where he first went through a box of the previous evening's arrests that he could read in the small press room. He would then go through the coroner's reports from the previous evening to look at sudden deaths. He might also chat to any duty officers whose job it was to provide the press with news. He would then leave for the city police headquarters and follow the same routine including accident reports. Finally he would call the police newsline for information on more arrests. He would then head off to the county court house. He would first check the day's calendar to see what was on. During the day on the beat the individuals who work in these places will come to know this journalist. Some of these, with whom the journalist will become friendly, have the role of providing information to the press.

Most importantly the view of a bureaucratically structured society gives the journalists a list in advance of all of the relevant sources for any topic. Of course this focus on such organisations means that sources of news will not necessarily be those who *experience* events. This could mean that a huge chunk of the communities the newspaper claims to represent will be ignored. But experienced reporters we interviewed felt that prior to the 1990s there were sufficient staff at regional newspapers for some of the stories generated from official sources to be followed up and developed. Colin Hughes, Brian Walters and Malcolm Rees told us that while they had worked the beat system for many years at a range of regional titles they felt that they did have time to expand on important stories and develop angles which they saw as part of the responsibility of the reporter to the public. It was after this period, they say, that commercial pressures such as staff cuts and marketing requirements led to significantly greater reliance on official versions of the world.

The dependency on official sources

All the reporters we interviewed said that an important dimension of the news beat was the relationship of trust with sources. This has been examined in journalism studies by Ericson *et al.* (1989) who described the reporter–source relationship as a symbiotic. So the source, such as a police inspector or a government official, will want their organisation to be represented as favourably as possible. It is in their interest to talk to the reporters and have a good working relationship with them. On the other hand the reporter needs the source in order that they have regular access to the best news events. A source must be able to trust the reporter, meaning that certain events might be treated with discretion, but through doing this the reporter would then earn the right to greater access to ongoing procedures. Reporter Colin Hughes spoke at length about his relationship with police sources. He told us that sources would call him at home when there was any breakthrough in investigations. He gave the example of a murder hunt case. Colin was invited out to witness many parts of the enquiry and felt that he had a collegial relationship with the responsible police officers. Colin said that this meant that he was able to give a much more detailed account of the process involved. Sometimes he had to treat certain things with discretion but this paid off in other areas.

The issue of trust and confidentiality in reporter–source relationships has periodically come to the fore in debate amongst journalists in the US and Britain. At the beginning of the US and British occupation of Iraq there was one instance where this issue of the anonymity of sources became hotly debated by journalists in both of these countries. *Today* reporter Andrew Gilligan broadcast that Prime Minister Tony Blair's office had 'sexed up' the intelligence report that claimed Iraq could launch weapons of mass destruction in 45 minutes. Gilligan did not reveal his source for this report but began to hint at what kind of person it might be. Gilligan gave further hints about the identity of the source at a foreign affairs committee he was forced to attend. The source, government scientist Dr David Kelly, it seemed, panicked and confessed to his employers the Ministry of Defence. In the end he was driven to commit suicide. Glen Frankel, the *Washington Post* London Correspondent, was shocked by the process and that sources could be discussed in this way, pointing out among other things that in the US employers prevent their reporters from attending court in this way (2004).

In 1984 British journalism was thrown into ethical debate about sources when *The Guardian* revealed its source in the form of a clerk who had sent them two classified documents about the deployment of cruise missiles in Britain. The British government demanded the documents back, and received them along with the name of the source. The source was subsequently jailed. Many journalists at the time felt that the editor should have protected his source.

The case of Watergate and 'Deep Throat' could be thought of as an example of what might be lost if sources cease to expect anonymity. Deep Throat was the pseudonym given to one of the important sources of the *Washington Post* that led to exposing the Nixon administration. Deep Throat was a play on the term 'deep background', used in journalism to describe anonymous sources closely embedded or connected to political organisations, for example. It was 30 years before the identity of the source was revealed.

But this reliance on official sources has come under some criticism. Fishman (1980) observed that, while reporting something like crime, for example, a reporter will have no contact with local criminals, youth offenders, deprived neighbourhoods, civil liberties organisations, jails or any other deviant subculture. Nor, he says, will journalists have any contact with the corporate world of price-fixing and other global economic crime (Fishman 1980: 45). Reporters are exposed mainly to bureaucratic types of procedures in institutions. Perhaps if there were institutions for processing corporate crime then reporters would include them on their beat. When covering a crime case they will not ride in police cars, and they will not spend time with the accused. Rather, they will utilise arrest reports, coroner's documents etc., that allow the reporter to produce copy quickly. The net effect, according to Bennett (2005), is that these organisations therefore have a huge influence over the news agenda. Critics warn that this creates the right environment for bias to seep into reporting as official institutions are able to select and control the flow of information.

In the 1930s a team of researchers at Chicago University carried out studies into inner city crime (Park and Burgess 1927). They found that criminals were young men from marginalised social groups who shared the same social and moral values as young middle-class men. Crime was about bettering yourself, organisation, leadership, individualism, pride. In short all the values prized by the wider society. The solution to 'crime', therefore, was to find a way to include these young men into mainstream society, rather than leave them in marginalised communities. A reliance on official sources means that this kind of conclusion is less than likely. A news item gathered at a magistrate's court is more likely to hear that that the perpetrators were a 'menace to society' – rather than about the political policies that created the social situation in the first place.

Bennett (2005) considered the reliance on official sources during the reporting of the Iraq invasion by the US and its allies. Before the invasion happened there were reports that there was no link between Saddam Hussein and Al-Qaida. It had also been reported that it was by no means certain that there were weapons of mass destruction to be found in Iraq. But once the war was underway there was 24-hour coverage from journalists in tanks and images of Saddam's statue being toppled. Few news stories continued to question connections between Saddam and 9/11. This is because, Bennett believes, the attention of journalists was firmly on official sources and political administration. His evidence comes from a study carried out by Cunningham (2003) of 414 stories on Iraq in the build up to the invasion shown on ABC, NBC and CBS, only 34 of which originated from outside the White House. Bennett says that even when some started to question the war, which the press did deal with marginally, the news was still primarily framed by White House sources. Criticisms of the war were framed in terms of old-style liberals attacking the President's patriotism – again official statements.

Bennett (2005: 2) argues that in these cases, such as crime, the health care system and Iraq, it is not that reporters are making up the facts or that they are themselves distorting the truth. The problem is that news organisations are more likely to report accounts coming from official administrative sources over any possible contrary accounts from other sources. As we have seen these official sources may not even tally with those who actually have authority over a particular sector.

This reliance on official sources can be seen through even a casual look at the daily newspaper or nightly television news bulletin. For the most part news is devoted to the official action of government and elected officials. In a study of the *New York Times* and the *Washington Post*, Sigal (1973) found that government officials were the sources of at least three-quarters of all hard news. These may be presented cynically or critically, but they are fundamentally about what politicians say and do. Meanwhile critical investigative reporting is sidelined (Bennett 2005: 116).

This emphasis on official sources gives a huge advantage to those already in power for getting their issues on the political agenda. In the long-term clearly we have a case where the kinds of problems and solutions presented in the news become limited to those defined by official sources. Bennett shows concern for this. He worries that people will come to accept things like poverty, crime, war and political apathy as inevitable parts of the everyday world rather than as the tragic results of the concentration of power and the nature of the way that we now run our societies (2005: 118).

This is part of a process of which Edelman (1977) expressed concern in the 1970s. He felt that the use of the pronouncements of politicians as news were replacing detailed analyses of situations. Thirty years later the British journalist Lloyd (2004), exasperated with the lack of investigative analysis over the British involvement in Iraq, warned that the news media had simply become an appendage of the political administrative process, bound to report in detail all official statements and losing the overall picture in the process. A study over five years by Just, Levine and Regan in 2002 concluded that investigative journalism had disappeared from the airwaves in the US. Most was from official sources and press leaks (Just *et al.* 2002).

There is one further danger in relying on official sources. Reporters have long-established criteria for establishing who is the official source for particular events. Sources will be officials in a particular bureaucratic organisation, but the organisation of our societies is changing. Our health care systems are now run by private organisations. There is an extensive literature on the way that the health system and education system in Britain is now under the control of private companies, or 'government by appointment'. But journalists are still focused on an older system of organisation. Deacon (2004) argues that the actual characteristics and running of public services such as health and education will now be obscured from public view and will not become news because journalists are organised to focus on a system of political control that no longer exists. Public services in Britain, he comments, are now governed by quasi-government and quangos, health trusts, advisory boards and other committees which do not register on traditional journalistic radar. In fact, as Deacon (2004: 339) states: 'even experienced journalists struggle to cope with the complex and evolving structure of quasi-government in the UK'. The people, the privatised groups that make decisions in what were state-organised institutions such as health and education, are invisible to journalists, since they are not credible or accepted official sources.

Ready-made news and PR

Tuchman (1973) and Ericson *et al.* (1987), in their studies of the relationship between journalists and their official sources, note that sources are able to organise themselves to provide readily available news for journalists. They can prepare press releases and host media conferences to provide journalists with the copy they need to give to their editors. This, these authors show, means that the sources are able to have some control over exactly what kind of information becomes news. The local reporters we interviewed all spoke of the domination of press releases in the local press. Mary Rees said that staff cuts had meant that there was no choice but to rely on 'handouts'. This, she said, meant that organisations with the ability to provide large amounts of quality material to pass on to journalists had massive control over the management of what the public would read. For example, she said the local council in Swansea, with a team of at least 10 press officers according to interviews we carried out at the local council, was able to stage-manage an upbeat image of a city on the up. A regular stream of handouts would be sent by email to reporters in a form where they would only require minor cut and paste or where they could be run without alteration. The Swansea council was able to run its own twice-monthly newspaper called the *Swansea Leader* which was filled with PR. This had been the creation of the Labour council, heavily criticised by the local Liberal Democrats as an abuse of resources until they themselves came into power.

McChesney (2004) argues that it is the reliance on official sources and need for news hooks that has led to the massive growth in PR. Corporations and official groups supply journalists with masses of ready-made copy. Surveys have shown that PR accounts from between 40 and 70 per cent of what appears as news (Rampton and Stauber 2000; Ewen 1996). They show the astonishing role that PR plays in providing copy that looks like news. This includes supplying broadcast-ready scripts. They note that there are now more people working in PR than there are journalists in the US. In our own research in the south Wales area we found that in areas where both regional titles had closed offices, and were therefore no longer served by beat reporters, there would be large PR teams producing copy for councils and local businesses.

Beat reporting with time for story development

The reporters we interviewed felt that there had always been a dependency on official sources and bureaucracies due to the simple need to generate quick predictable news copy. But they all said that prior to the 1990s there was time to develop stories that they felt were interesting. This would be done with the support and encouragement of the editor. There was also much more time to develop a range of sources in the local community, not only to provide stories but to verify information and give different angles on a story: all of which changed with huge reductions in staffing at both the news gathering and editorial level.

Colin Hughes worked for many years at the *Western Mail*, based in Cardiff. The paper had recently become part of Trinity Mirror Plc (Newspaper Society 2006). Trinity covered 274 regional titles such as *Birmingham Mail*, *The Journal* in Newcastle, *Liverpool Daily Post*, *Liverpool Echo*, and the *South Wales Evening Post*, which had previously been the rival paper to the *Western Mail*. Colin told us of the massive changes experienced by reporters working for the title. This had included two rebrands, the first when it had been part of the Daily Mail group. These had included huge cutbacks in staffing, the introduction of time and motion so that the number of stories written were counted, and lectures by a marketing company from Canary Wharf. Reporters were told to write stories for niche markets. In this case it was for Dave and Jill with 2.4 children who shopped in Tesco or Sainsbury's. Stories were to appeal to women, and contain human interest, personal interest, family values, law and order. He said:

> In this style you provide a lot of personal information about the people in the story before giving the main bit of the story. I found this difficult as it went against what I had been doing for years which was to get to the point of the story, the core of the story, quickly.

Colin worked from the Swansea office for around 40 years, along with freelance work for the BBC. He said that until the 1990s there were around seven reporters working in the Swansea area. The newspaper covered a number of towns over south Wales, each of which would have its own office and set of reporters. Until the 1990s Colin worked a beat which included police stations and local villages, where he would attend meetings and sit in cafés and local bars. Here he developed a link with communities and a network of contacts. This was a beat in the traditional sense, but also one that brought him into contact with everyday life in the community, allowing Colin to generate real hard news about the area.

It was from 1990 that the *Western Mail* started to cut back on staff and close down local offices outside Swansea. At the time of writing there was only one reporter working in Swansea who worked from home and had responsibility for the whole of Wales to the west of the city due to other office closures. This meant that there was no longer time to work a beat, there was no time to visit police stations and certainly no possibility to spend time in the community.

Colin spoke of the huge changes that took place in news-gathering such as reporters leaving and not being replaced, leaving those left to cover the same areas. This meant that there was an increasing tendency to take press releases: 'We would be accepting stories that we wouldn't have before. And we wouldn't really have the time to check them.'

He said:

> On the front cover of the paper you would get the impression that it contained investigative reporting, but inside it was all press releases, official reports and Internet. Reporters might make a couple of telephone calls, but you wouldn't have the time to do any background research, any checking. In many cases you wouldn't have to even make any calls to show that you have sources as the press releases would come complete even with these. It would just mean cut and paste.

He spoke of the increased tendency to use the Internet to get extra material for stories:

> The internet means that you can get background material quickly. This is important as it is no longer possible to call people, to go and interview people. But this means that we are dependent on the information that organisations put onto sites. But since there have been massive reductions in staffing this is the only way to collect information. And the Internet allows journalists to search other news sites to get information as news is not copyrighted. But again this is not the same as investigation.

As a journalist with 40 years of experience Colin was very concerned by this pattern. He said:

> Before you would be able to develop stories. Some of them you would find out by being out in the community, by talking to regular contacts. Or when a story came to you you could spend some time on it. Your editor would support you in this. You could spend a week on a story.

The following is a story written by Colin in the late 1970s. He chose this as an example of a story that would not be written now. The reporter would not come across the story in first place as it would not come to them as a press release. And they would not be known in the communities so they would not be taken into confidence. Then there would be no time for development of the story, just for a few telephone calls to press officers.

Rugby Club that plays on a 'gold' mine.
Western Mail, 17 October 1978

The turf of Blaenau rugby Club's ground (above) in West Wales is even more hallowed than that of Cardiff Arms Park.

It may not have the same lush, green appearance but for all that it is regarded with reverence by the locals.

The reason? Beneath the grass of the Blaenau club lie rich deposits of best quality anthracite coal.

It is coal the National Coal Board would love to get their hands on – but stand no chance of doing so.

A member of the village welfare committee who own the Blaenau ground told me. 'The NCB tried to move heaven and earth to buy the land.

'They offered us an alternative ground in Llandybie with all the facilities thrown in. But we said no. It would have been a betrayal of the village if we had agreed because the rugby club is the only recreational entertainment left here now.'

The coal board's opencast operation at Glynglas, near Blaenau, was one of the last to go through the public enquiry procedure. It was bitterly opposed by villagers and on environmental grounds by Dyfed county and Dinefwr borough councils.

The board wanted to extract 700,000 tons of anthracite from the 422-acre site. They even wanted to include the rugby ground in their proposals.

But the enquiry result – in July 1976 – although giving the go-ahead to the NCB added certain restrictions. The size of the site was ordered to be cut by 15 acres to exclude the rugby ground and the Inquiry inspector ruled that no excavation work should be permitted within 100 yards of properties in Pennygroes Road, the main road leading through Blaenau.

But the two years that have elapsed have transformed the surrounding countryside into a hive of industrial activity.

Today excavation work has turned once rolling hills into huge craters burrowed out of the ground by giant earth-moving machines.

Dozens of lorries and machines are on the move all day. The noise and dust for the villagers of Blaenau are often intolerable and sometimes plain unbearable.

But that is the way it has to be, I suppose if the 'national interest' is to benefit to the extent of 700,000 tons of anthracite over the next five years. For the once peaceful village of Blaenau, though, it is all like a bad dream.

> Regular meetings of a liaison committee made up of the NCB and local villagers are held to discuss complaints and work out a solution – if it is at all possible.
>
> The secretary of Blaenau and district action committee, Miss Noreen Evans, explained, 'Whenever we complain about something they do try to put things right.
>
> 'We had a lot of noise at one time but it is better now. Then there was a terrible dust nuisance but the weather is on our side now – it is so damp that it stops the dust settling over the village.
>
> 'But we can never be satisfied with the opencast sites. People will never be happy with the situation. We fought against it and lost and now we have to put up with it. It is a five-year operation by the NCB – and that is five years too long as far as we are concerned.
>
> 'There is always noise, and dust and now they have started blasting. Where will it all end?'
>
> Village shopkeeper Mr. Giraldus Thomas complained that the opencast work went on from 7am until 11pm. 'There is continuous noise throughout the day', he said.
>
> Mr. Thomas added 'Once we had open countryside all around. Now you can only see slag heaps – we are encircled by them.
>
> 'The village will never be the same again because many people have moved away. It is the sorriest thing that has happened to Blaenau.'

In this story we can see that the reporter has used their knowledge of the community and contacts. Colin said that he was known around the area by the locals. This meant that they would come to him with local issues. The result is, he said, 'we get a sense of issues that concern the people who live in the area covered by the newspaper'. This is very different to the stories we will look at shortly.

We follow with another example of a story that an experienced reporter, Brian Walters, felt was one that would no longer be written. Brian had worked for many regional newspapers around Britain over his career. He had more recently worked in south Wales for rival title the *South Wales Evening Post.* He spoke of exactly the same processes of cuts in staff, closures in local offices and the move towards celebrity and lamented the move towards office-based reporting. He also expressed concern about the demise of political reporting. He himself had been political editor working in the Welsh National Assembly, but it was felt by the new editor that readers would not be interested in politics.

Brian spoke of the way that the journalism of PR now outweighed that of investigation. He said:

> Reporters handle mostly PR material and then make one or two telephone calls to a press office to get comments, or look on the Internet.

> These office-bound reporters are massively outnumbered by the journalists employed by official organisations to feed them this PR material. Since many of these journalists were former employees they know exactly what is required.

He said that he was concerned about the culture that young journalists now came into:

> When they start they see a different culture now. This is not a culture of investigation. Its one where you throw things together and give them a gloss to make them seem to have real local relevance. They are taught to create stories that are more like features. Basically these aren't reporters. They are *news-gatherers.* They gather together pre-existing material from press releases and check this with other press representatives. They no longer know how to investigate, nor what this really means. They have never known this culture.

The following is a story developed by Brian. The story involves a soon to be Tory MP, Ben Pickering, who turned out to have been making a lot of money from people for films he never in fact made. He claimed to have a film company called 'Film Wales' that was making programming for BBC Wales. Brian had carried out background information checks with film organisations, publishers, the BBC and spoke with actors who Pickering said were in the films. The actors had said that the films had never been made and that they knew nothing of Film Wales. Yet large amounts of money in donations and investments had been taken. Brian then managed to interview Pickering at a conference where he spoke of the films as if they had been made: Brian was able therefore to prove that he was deliberately lying. This example contains a number of features of where a beat reporter has the time to develop a story. This involved archive searches, interviews and travelling. Brian believes that this kind of story would no longer be written due to time and resource constraints. Importantly, without the reporter carrying out background research we might have been in a place where we simply accepted the word of Pickering. His 'film company' had a web site where it made many false claims about productions that had never taken place.

Brian said: 'An office-bound reporter pushed for time may have simply "checked" on the website for verification.'

> **Burning questions that need answering.**
> *South Wales Evening Post*, 14 June 2000
>
> Ben Pickering, a popular figure at last week's Welsh Conservative Party conference in Llandudno, was given the opportunity there to answer some burning questions.

Where, for example, was Film Wales based – the organisation with £500,000 to invest in *Come and Go*?

Ben: 'Film Wales? I think they're not doing it anymore.'

But where was it based?

'I don't think they're doing anything anymore.'

Did they ever exist?

'Yes, they existed. They funded a documentary project which I did last year, you what is this?'

'This is supposed to be an article, according to what you said to me earlier, about the fact that I'm the youngest candidate in Britain. It's not supposed to be an article which is a hatchet job.'

When he appealed for money to produce *Backstreet*, did he return the money to people when the film was aborted?

Ben: 'We're talking about films I made a few years back? *Backstreet*? I can't remember exactly how much *Backstreet* cost.

'It must have been about £8,000 in the end – that's all we could raise.'

'I have to say most of that money was mine. *Tragic Irony* was also privately financed.'

So you are saying there was little or no investment other than from yourself?

'Yeah. I mean the director of *Tragic Irony* spent a lot of his own money on the project, but I also invested in it.'

Were *Backstreet* and *Tragic Irony* ever filmed, ever released?

Ben: 'They were both finished but they weren't released.'

What about the web site's claim that well-known actors and actresses had agreed to appear in *Come and Go* when they insist they hadn't?

Ben: 'The web site was online and I referred to the fact that these people were interested in starring in the project, and were prepared to say so to me to, obviously get the funds together for the project because they liked the idea of the project.'

Brian Walters told us:

He was being hailed as the Tory Party star of the future – the William Hague (or David Cameron?) of tomorrow. I decided to do a search in our archives and up came his film-making exploits of yesteryear. Further research revealed he had never actually produced a film, although he had duped a lot of students out of money they thought would hoist them onto the first rung of a career in films. He went to elaborate lengths to produce a pretty professional synopsis of plans for his 'latest' film, and made the mistake of throwing in some names of actors who had allegedly signed up to it. But this con man's big ambition was politics and he was lining himself up for a parliamentary seat. I knew from leading lights in the local Conservative Association he

> was anxious to get some publicity. At the 2000 Welsh Conservative Spring Conference in Llandudno he made his approach to me and a fellow journalist, Garmon Rees of the Welsh language magazine *Golwg* whose IT skills I needed. We agreed to meet him later in the day with a view to writing articles about the guy's candidature. We were armed with hidden tape recorder and a string of embarrassing questions. Rather than shy away from them, he chose to try to defend himself – and hanged himself in the process! Today, there is rarely a routine check of archives. Certainly we would not have been able to nail Pickering had we not been at the conference. You couldn't corner the guy on the phone. It was a bit of investigative journalism that paid off.

Clearly this reporting could be thought of as being as close as we might get to our ideal model of investigative reporting in the public interest. The reporter has nosed around, found something that seemed out of place and then carried out further investigation, checking and building up a story. In this case the reporter acts as the eyes and ears of the public in their interest.

Another related role for the local reporter that Brian spoke at length about was campaigns – another role that has now disappeared. Here reporters would take on a public interest issue and push it as a campaign. For example, Brian had been part of a *South Wales Evening Post* campaign to get Swansea Bay cleaned up:

> The council wished not to publicise the level of pollution due to costs. There were all sorts of unmentionables floating around in the water and the public couldn't go near it. The huge beach of the bay was unusable and a health hazard.

The newspaper began a campaign. This involved petitions to Brussels, meetings involving the public to pressurise the council. In the end the bay was cleaned up and an £85 million sewage works was built. As a result it is now possible to walk on the beach in the bay.

Brian said that such campaigns were now a thing of the past:

> This kind of long-term project wouldn't happen now. Sometimes you find something that has the appearance of a campaign. This will be a comment on a story in an editorial. Such as say a man is imprisoned for non-payment of council tax. And the editor will make some kind of populist comment of how this is wrong. Such comments are generally of a populist nature rather than a genuine attempt to put pressure on authority for the public good. But there will be no investigation to check out the details of the story. What if the council had good

> reason for acting this way? As a reporter you really should check such things out. Nor will there be any real campaign about this. We simply do not have the staff nor the time.

Brian spoke of another large campaign which had been an attempt to get the Welsh Assembly based in Swansea rather than in Cardiff. Again this involved organising meetings with the public and organising coaches to take people to lobby in Cardiff. The campaign failed but Brian said that the issue gained recognition from MPs that the wealth should be shared out. Brian said that these genuine campaigns are now a thing of the past.

Office-based journalism

We asked two local journalists, Mary and Malcolm Rees, to sort through a pile of recent editions of local newspapers for examples of the kinds of stories resulting from this office-based journalism, instances where the kinds of stories we have looked at above would not be written. Mary and Malcolm had been working freelance at local newspapers and also producing press releases for local businesses. Malcolm, many years a beat reporter, explained that currently this was where the work was for journalists.

Malcolm, like Colin and Brian, spoke of former times where he would have developed stories from a beat which took him out into the local villages. This was before local offices closed and staff cutbacks.

> I used to write a weekly column which was based on interviews with people who lived in the villages. They would talk about their concerns. This could be money or benefits or work. Now you would not find the voices of real people in the newspapers. You might get vox pops where people are asked what they think of a comment by a US celebrity reporter that Catherine Zeta Jones has got a big bottom. As reporters you are now told to go out and get these. But previously there was the chance to bring in stories connected to people's real lives.

Mary spoke of the reliance on press releases. She said:

> Where you would previously have a business editor who would write stories drawn from contacts, about local business people and business issues, they will now base a whole business supplement on handouts which will be put together by a non-specialist.

Malcolm also spoke of the same lack of digging around through dependence on press releases and telephone calls. He mentioned a story he had done which involved digging through receipts from council expenditures and finding that the taxpayer was funding private transport costs for certain council members.

> Now there would not be the reporters available to do this. If you go to a council meeting now there is no one there. They just wait for the handout. You can't blame the reporter, this is how they are forced to work.

Mary gave an example of a gas pipeline that was to pass though her village. She had found out about this as a local man had told her after he had read a notice at the top of a hill outside the village while walking his dog. The work would be highly disruptive and messy but no one had notified the villagers of this. She had then acted as an investigative reporter to find out about what was going to happen by going to council meetings. She said that there were clearly no reporters at the council meeting where the major pipeline was discussed. Therefore there were no eyes and ears of the public. She said:

> It makes you angry. Instead you get made up articles. The lead yesterday was that because of the increase in the use of dishwashers there is now a shortage of tea-towels for children's Nativity plays. So instead of reporting we get things like this that are completely made up so that the paper can have a slightly Christmas theme. There would be no investigation in such a story. The editor would probably come up with it and tell a reporter to do something with it.

These are two of the stories they chose along with their reasons. We must be clear that they were in no way critical of the writers of the stories, only of the kind of news-gathering environment that the stories represent.

> **How does your life sit with the sofa habits revealed about our nation?**
> *Western Mail*, 3 November 2005
>
> *[There is a photograph of a designer sofa and another of Laurence Llewelyn-Bowen.]*
>
> **The comfort zone is more important than ever before**
>
> Welsh people are spending more of their time sitting on sofas than ever before.
>
> Where once people left the house to socialise or do chores such as shopping, modern technology has made it quicker and cheaper for people to spend their out-of-hours time in the comfort of their own sitting room, and according to a new survey, that's exactly what they're choosing to do.
>
> According to a survey out today, commissioned by Intel, the most popular activities for Welsh families at home are watching television, listening to music, surfing the Internet and playing games, all of which can be done from the sofa.

And with so much time spent sitting on them it's no surprise the average household has £23 in loose change down the back of them.

Furniture designer and former *Western Mail* Welsh woman of the year, Angela Gidden, described the trend as 'the migration to the sofa' and said because people now spend more time on them, people have become more concerned about what kind they buy.

She said yesterday, 'There's a lot of people who are watching their pennies and are quite happy to stay at home but it means they're more conscious of what they're living with and so they'll make a more considered choice when it comes to upholstery.

'People want a sofa which suits their needs and aspirations.'

She added, 'There's also more of a trend towards entertaining at home and less emphasis on going out to bars and restaurants and so living space is becoming more important.'

But Wales' relationship with the sofa is not a new one. For the better part of the last century the centre of the UK's upholstery manufacturing industry was based in south Wales.

In the last few years cheap imports and a downturn in spending have taken their toll.

Christie Tyler, Wales' first major sofa manufacturer which was set up after the Second World War and employed around 1,000 people in Wales, went into receivership earlier this year. The decline of the company credited with creating the first widely available three-piece suites resulted in factory closures and job losses.

But despite this many manufacturers still remain.

The Sofa Group in South Wales incorporates six different sofa manufacturers in the region and is the largest manufacturer of sofas in the UK that sells direct to the public.

Marketing director Tom Ridgewell said the group, which has a shop in St Mellons, Cardiff, sells just over 100,000 sofas a year, with an annual turnover of £30 million.

He said, 'The sofa industry in Wales goes back quite a long way to Christie Tyler. They were quite a dominant force in upholstery manufacturers and so when they opened a lot of their suppliers set up in South Wales, such as framers and providers of foam and a cottage industry developed in the valleys.

'People then left the company and set up by themselves, creating more manufacturers.'

Ms Gidden, who has been designing sofas for 20 years, described her company, Attic 2, which supplies sofas to The Conran Shop, as a Welsh brand.

She said, 'I could probably produce my product elsewhere but it's a Welsh brand and I'm a Welsh designer and for as long as we possibly can, we want to continue making our product in Wales.'

The average amount spent on a sofa is £1,200 and most are replaced every five to seven years. The most popular colours are neutral colours and earth shades and almost 50% of the sofas sold by Sofa Sofa are made from leather, although the most popular fabric sofas tend to be made from soft textiles such as chenille and velvet.

However, the traditional three-piece suites have been replaced in popularity by new sectional seating, separate sofa parts which fit together and can fit around corners.

Yvonne Jones, owner of Chameleon Interiors in Cardiff, attributed their rise in popularity to the increase of flat screen televisions.

She said, 'Sectional sofas used to be a very '70s idea, but now it's the thing to have. Its partly due to the new plasma screen TVs. The screens are bigger so people want to sit further back and whereas television used to go in the corner, the new flat screens can be positioned anywhere so people want a sofa that goes around the whole room. That way the whole family can sit and cuddle up together.'

Interior designer Laurence Llewelyn-Bowen said modern trends favour 'faddy' sofas over more traditional ones.

He said 'These days people are spending more and more on sofas in quite faddy colours and finishes due to auction sites like eBay.

'People will spend £1,500 on something because they know if it's not still trendy in five years they can still sell it on.

'It's encouraging to see people creep out of their magnolia safety zone but personally I look for a sofa which is classical and practical and also tailored and discreet, one that doesn't take up too much space.

'A sofa should be somewhere comfortable because we have now developed into a nation of couch potatoes with no ability to stand upright any more. Sofas have become a new microcosm in their own right. It's where we live, where we drop our popcorn and lose our pound coins.'

Laurence Llewelyn-Bowen's guide to sofa buying (This lists some pointers such as size and colour).

This article is not hard news. It does seek to be community-based by mentioning 'Wales' and 'Welsh' wherever possible. These terms have tended to replace actual localities where there are no longer the reporters to cover them. The story is also an attempt to be upbeat about Wales. People may be spending more time on their sofas but Welsh sofa designers and manufacturers have a leading role in the industry – 'presumably', said Malcolm Rees dryly, 'good news for all Welsh people, even those living in areas of unemployment and poverty'.

The origins of this story, used as a page three lead, are a press release, a self-promotion by Intel. There is no sociological relevance in the story.

We rely on lifestyle 'experts' to explain this new 'sofa culture'. As Malcolm Rees said:

> This is a journalism in the style of features rather than hard news, although it lacks the depth you might expect from a feature. Like all this kind of news it is upbeat and tries to be fun.

Malcolm said that there is then a sense that the world in the newspaper must be positive, upbeat. This is because the newspaper 'now has close connections with lifestyle and consumerism'. He said:

> In the 1990s we started to hear editors talking management speak. Before they had always ridiculed it. You would laugh about it with them. But then it changed and you would hear it coming out of their mouths. Regional newspapers have now moved away from hard news, to shopping, commerce celebrity. News-gathering is either lazy telephone calls to press offices of organisations or is PR that comes in on email which can then be quickly searched and cut and pasted.

The second story also comes from a press release and is sourced by telephone calls. The release involves statistics which rather than being analysed are used to give the impression of a local angle. Malcolm and Mary saw this as 'gimmicky' and 'certainly not hard news'.

How many lightbulbs does it take to power a Welshman?
Western Mail, 8 November 2005

. . . 32, and that's a lot more than it takes to power an Englishman

Page 3 lead, 8 November 2005

[Two photographs. One is of a lightbulb against a black background, the other a stock image of a refinery.]

It may sound like a twist on a clichéd joke but the answer is 32.65.

And that's 34% more than it takes to power an Englishman.

Government statistics show that creating enough power to run Wales emits far more carbon dioxide per head of population than any other country in the UK.

The bad news is that carbon dioxide is one of the main contributors to global warming, and the figures mean Wales is playing a disproportionate role in what many experts believe is the biggest threat facing humanity.

The good news, however, is that Wales' poor record is attributable to emissions from industry, and on the domestic scale we are no more wasteful than our English neighbours.

But North Wales AM (Assembly Member) Janet Ryder said yesterday that was no excuse for complacency, and the figures showed that everyone should conserve energy.

The statistics are the first to be compiled by the Department for Environment, Food and Rural Affairs in a way that allocates emissions to where the energy is used. This corrects distortions in previous figures for areas with major power stations supplying surrounding areas.

The new figures show that in 2003 Wales produced 12.3 tonnes of carbon dioxide per resident – equating to 28,605kWh per person per year – compared with 9.1 for England, 10 for Scotland and 7.9 for Northern Ireland. A 100W light bulb left on for a year would consume 876kWh, so our average consumption equates to leaving 32.65 100W light bulbs on.

The extra emissions in Wales arise entirely from industrial and commercial users, who emit 7.4 tonnes per capita in Wales compared with 4 tonnes in England. In the domestic and road transport categories Welsh and English emissions per head are almost identical.

Neil Crumpton, of Friends of the Earth Cymru, said the high emissions from Welsh industry and commerce was down to a few large metal factories in Wales, with Anglesey Aluminium, near Holyhead, consuming about 10% of Wales' energy.

'We don't use all that aluminium in Wales' said Mr Crumpton.

'We're not as dirty as the initial look at the statistics suggests.'

But he said the figures underlined the need for Wales to generate more electricity from renewable sources such as the wind and the tide.

Janet Ryder AM, who sits on the cross-party Energywatch group said, 'I don't think any of us have a choice – we have to think carefully about how much energy we use. The Government has a role to play in enforcing stricter conservation measures.'

She said increased carbon dioxide emissions should be taken into account when officials considered closure of village schools and other local facilities, as such closures forced people to travel further in cars. David Rosser, director of CBI (Confederation of British Industry) Wales said the new figures did not show Wales was energy inefficient.

'Wales has got a greater proportion of its economy in manufacturing, and especially in heavy manufacturing. We have far fewer lawyers and bankers than England and far more steelworkers.'

He said business had already cut its emissions to meet Britain's obligations under the Kyoto protocol, and the Government should focus on domestic and transport emissions rather than taking another stick to industry and commerce.

Mr Rosser said rising energy prices provided enough of an incentive for businesses to consume less energy, without further regulations.

'Shotton Paper, in North Wales, has reduced the energy required per tonne of paper product from 3MWh (megawatt hours) to 1MWh.

Companies like Corus (which makes steel in Port Talbot and other Welsh locations) and Anglesey Aluminium have invested heavily in energy efficiency and continue to do so.

'When you look at the average office block, there's more that could be done. But there's also more that we can all do in our homes.

'We all leave our TVs on standby and leave lights on in rooms that we're not sitting in.'

How does your office measure up?
Rising energy prices may have spurred heavy industries to become more efficient, but offices across Wales could be needlessly adding to global warming.

Do you:

- Leave your computer running overnight, at weekends and even when you're away on holiday?
- Use a desktop computer when a laptop (much more efficient) would suffice?
- Leave the lights on in toilets and other rooms which are unused or infrequently used at night?
- Have extractor fans operating continuously in toilets?
- Open windows while the air conditioning is running in summer?
- Work with your shirtsleeves rolled up in midwinter?
- Use laser rather than inkjet printers and fax machines (laser printers use far more energy)?
- Take the lift instead of the stairs?
- Leave front or side doors open?

If you answered yes to all or most questions, you could be doing more to help the environment.

The story is stimulated by a press release. The statistics come from the Department for Environment, Food and Rural Affairs. In the arguments we viewed above these official sources may be criticised, although in this case they are simply accepted, but these have the ability to define the kinds of things that get talked about. Such a story can easily be padded out with a few telephone calls. Again these sources are accepted uncritically. The CBI, who have a particular agenda, are not cited as such. Malcolm complained that there was no real context for the story. For example, the CBI's central concern at the time was problems in terms of how Britain was going to generate energy in the future and avoid becoming dependent on expensive imports. No mention is made of this. The story also manages to be upbeat. While there are reported high CO_2 emissions, this isn't so bad as it shows that Wales has a high level of manufacturing.

Malcolm also complained that the sources who had been telephoned were used for predictable responses. Therefore we aren't actually getting real different angles on a story, but we get the impression that we are. Malcolm asked again what such a story 'would really mean to ordinary people who struggled to pay rising heating costs'. This kind of sourcing means that we always remain at the official definition of reality.

Mary Rees, herself having worked in PR, said that in fact many press releases are now supplied with quotations from other sources so that the package can go straight out with very little additional work. Of course this means that the organisation that generates the press release has secured complete control over the different viewpoints that find their way into the news.

Finally the item ends with a set of bullet point questions so that you can analyse whether your office is good on energy use. Mary said:

> This is the way that the public are now included in the newspaper. Editors always want these kinds of bullet points. But really the public are included less and less. They might ask readers to text in and give their responses to stories, which might be included in some part of the newspaper. But this remains in a very defined area and does not really give much impression of how people live. Reporters now rarely now come into actual contact with the public.

Conclusion

The role of the local reporter as the eyes and ears of the community is clearly being challenged. Many journalists who have worked under a now disappearing system are concerned about the effects of reduced staffing on the kinds of material that are released as news. The lack of the watchdog presence of reporters was illustrated by Mary Rees who herself took up the old style role in a personal quest to discover the likely outcomes of plans to build a pipeline through her village. Sadly she found no journalists at council meetings. While we might be critical of news that comes from official sources this, as we have seen, can be one starting point for further checking and investigation. Yet now, while council meetings go unattended by reporters, local newspapers are filled with material produced by the same councils: stories that are stage-managed to promote local developments and new facilities.

These experienced journalists expressed concern for new trainees who have never experienced the older system. Instead the impressionable rookie reporter will be taught, by editors who work as managers rather than journalists, a kind of practice that is characterised by minor edits to press releases, telephone calls and Internet searches, rather than one reaching out into the community. In the USA research into local television news (PEJ 2002) suggests that audiences are aware of the results of this new kind of budget journalism, feeling that there is insufficient coverage of local politics and civic affairs. Yet for the meantime, in the local press faltering circulations have been steadied with a move towards celebrity along with new layouts and the buzz of the forward-thinking city. And the same kinds of niche marketing that we examined in the last chapter ensures that advertisers are impressed by what they see.

In contrast to the previous chapter where we saw that the existing theories needed updating and reorienting to be useful for interrogating contemporary practice, in this chapter the work of sociologists of journalism such as Fishman and Ericson *et al.* on news beats and sources still have much currency. This is because sourcing and reporting are the most abiding, fundamental skills of journalism. They are essential to proper practice and ethics and it is the view of most in the industry who have been in the game for a few years that this is the biggest area of erosion. But these facts of the industry must be incorporated into the way that journalist trainers and professionals openly speak of their profession. If not there is a danger it may be taken away from them by the need to push for further profits.

Further, while good sourcing is still the basis of sound reporting, journalists have to find a way to reveal to the public that those who make decisions in our societies are changing. Journalism as a profession emerged along with the development of the party political system. Yet monetarism has created new kind of social organisation. While the levels of private control, quangos and government by appointment might fall outside of familiar news frames, we have to find a way to communicate this to the public. If they do not know who makes the decisions about their health care system and about their schools, how can they hold them accountable? And at the most fundamental level making the powerful accountable is what journalism should be about. This is the model of the roving reporter that is so romanticised in the movies.

5 Conflict reporting and propaganda

The consequences of the reliance on official sources

Conflict reporting is widely believed to be journalism's most stressful and challenging territory, and it is possibly getting worse. In newer kinds of warfare, where the disparity of technology and resources between opposing sides is massive, it is less clear who and where the likely attackers are. Sometimes there are no clear front lines where progress can be reported, no explicit acts of heroism on the battlefield. At the time of writing, *Guardian* editor Alan Rusbridger, at an inaugural professorial lecture at Queen Mary's and Westfield University in London, reflected on whether there was any point in keeping journalists in Baghdad any longer. Is the cost of keeping correspondents in hotel rooms in the Iraqi capital justifiable when it is too dangerous for them to leave the building to report? His reservations have been reflected by many senior editors we have spoken to in the course of writing this book. It seems ironic when faced with 24-hour rolling coverage of high-tech warfare, such as ships launching missiles at targets hundreds of miles away, that major theatres of conflict could have become inaccessible to journalists. Now, with minimal access to battlefields and actual combatants, journalists must in some cases rely on official briefings which, it is widely feared, provide little more than propaganda. And what of the conflicts that do not actually make it to the page, airways or screen, as many do not, even those that involve our own armies? News reporting of war and conflict is felt by many in theoretical circles to be flawed at best, and absent at worst. When conflicts do hit the headlines, how much is meaningful information and analysis, and how much is spin, and how can journalists and their audiences tell the difference?

There is another perspective that is less often heard yet which illuminates the emerging context for war coverage – that of foreign correspondents themselves. The analysis of the processes of conflict reporting crystallises the underlying tenet of this book, which is that journalism theory must take account of the rapidly changing context within which news reporters and editors must work. Our engagement with practitioners revealed some dismay with the perceived lack of thorough understanding of the complexity and delicacy of the work of the foreign correspondent. Additionally, prominent studies of this area have tended to take an Anglo-

American-centric perspective that lacks the very context and breadth for which academics have traditionally criticised journalists. This chapter seeks to bring fresh insights and perspectives to what has become a huge divide between academic and journalistic thought. It is here more than in any other area of journalism scholarly inquiry that new approaches must be found.

In 2004 the British journalist John Lloyd began a relatively short-lived but poignant debate about the nature of journalism in British society. His book *What the Media are Doing to our Politics*, using the case of the British government's decision to follow the US into Iraq, claimed that journalism was no longer able to monitor the actions of politicians and political institutions but has become focused on personalities and political administration. Therefore, he argues, it has ceased to have any critical role. The actual reasons for the war and its legitimacy became sidelined. We saw in the previous chapter, for example, that journalism academics and indeed journalists themselves are concerned that a reliance on official sources has a gatekeeping nature. It means that news has a tendency to be heavily weighted towards certain kinds of events. On the one hand the world as we find it in the news becomes a reflection of bureaucratically produced events. On the other we get an official definition of the world, or at least those events that are defined as relevant by official sources. However, this view may be to the discredit of those within the industry who are actively seeking fresh perpectives.

One area of the practice of reporting that has been emerging during the writing of this book has been the status of foreign reporters. High-profile foreign affairs correspondents are increasingly reliant on local fixers to gain them access to key spokespeople and sources. The presence of the fixer is nothing new, but the dangers of reporting war mean that they have become much more prominent. Additionally, because it has become quite dangerous for foreign journalists working in Iraq, they rely on local journalists and local camera crews to gather footage. Some 112 people working for media organisations have been killed, either by insurgents or by US forces, since March 2003, according to data from the Iraqi Journalists' Association in February 2006. The dangers for local journalists were highlighted by the deaths of a woman TV journalist and two camera crew who were shot in Samara. Colin Bickler, a veteran foreign correspondent and editor who we interview later, argues that stories and statements focusing on the dangers Western journalists may face in Iraq ignore the fact that there are still people out there – local journalists – who are drawing out the issues and breaking these barriers.

> It is very important not to confuse the fact that some situations are difficult to report with journalists not being interested. It is significant that Western news organisations are being forced to recognise that a lot of their news-gathering is being done by local people, at great

> personal peril. There is now pressure on these news organisations to reflect their status through insuring them. Little credit has been given in television to the fact that the footage is being gathered by local camera operators, but events like the Balkans and Iraq are raising the profile. In Iraq many crew have to conceal their jobs even from their own families. In Chechnya local journalists were incredibly brave to keep working when international journalists had been thrown out.

The idea of the press as the fourth estate has been the cornerstone of liberal accounts of the news media. The notion has its origins in the French Revolution, though is often associated with J. S. Mill, who in the nineteenth century wrote of the watchdog role of the press, making the powerful accountable. Thomas Jefferson wrote and spoke of the impossibility of having an accountable government without a press. He talked of the three estates or branches of government: executive, legislative and judicial. The fourth estate was the press. This was crucial if the American people were to govern themselves, and the first amendment of the American Constitution specifically refers to the importance of this free press. Yet John Lloyd was suggesting that some news media have ceased to act in this watchdog role and are therefore no longer acting in the interests of democracy. Using the case of the British government's decision to follow the US into Iraq he demonstrates that the news media had little to say about the actual material evidence for invading Iraq. The reasons why the Blair government had chosen to go to war therefore remained unanalysed in the mainstream news. Instead journalists focused on the political debate and processes that revolved around accusations of falsifying evidence and the mud-slinging, and legal/administrative processes that went along with this. Journalists had become, Lloyd argued, too close to the system. If we accept Lloyd's arguments, this is serious. Without the fourth estate, how can a population govern itself? During the early period of the occupation of Iraq one of the authors was carrying out a research project based around war reporting and dissemination of information. Most of the people questioned by the author were cynical of Tony Blair's motives for supporting George W. Bush, but none were aware of the broader historical context. Some were critical of Saddam Hussein and others spoke of a general need to tackle world terrorism. But there was little sense of concrete context of how the situation in Iraq had arisen.

While there has been much analysis of the role of the news media in the coverage of conflict, the majority of this analysis has centred on the news products – the 24-hour rolling news, the newspaper headlines and the radio sound bites. Rarely have academic researchers asked journalists themselves how they have identified and negotiated the extraordinary challenges faced. As well as receiving biased and unreliable information and living in dangerous conditions, journalists may have a lack of access to resources and face language barriers in offering full and proper representations of the different groups involved in conflict. We have found in our review of critical theories that there is much to be concerned about in the content of coverage, as theorists have identified. By hearing correspondents' reflections, we can identify a set of new questions and areas that need urgent illumination and interrogation. These include:

- That academic studies sometimes confuse the fact that something is difficult to report with non-reporting;
- That the coverage of wars and conflicts goes through cycles, and that not everything can be contextualised at the outset;
- That the practices of war coverage are hugely sensitive to changes on a global political, cultural and technological scale;
- That in more recent wars journalists may have actually helped to clarify situations, rather than obscuring them.

What it means in summary is that applying fixed academic concepts to dynamic and evolving areas of practice is highly problematic. That is not to say that journalists themselves do not recognise that standards of reporting can be of concern, as we discovered when speaking with two prominent and experienced foreign affairs correspondents.

The setting for the invasion of Iraq

Before we set out these arguments and questions in more detail, and listen to the views of correspondents, it is of concern to us that so much academic energy has been devoted to drawing conclusions about ordinary journalism through its reporting of extraordinary times and events. At the time of writing, there were 83 results for a search for 'war reporting' on www.amazon.co.uk, and 60 for conflict journalism, though there were probably overlaps. By contrast, there were three results for peace reporting and one for peace journalism. This is a reflection not only on the news industry and the fact that war has massive news value, but also on the debatable fact that so much of our critical knowledge of journalism focuses upon it. That is not to say the reporting of war does not deserve a robust critique. Indeed, it strikes at the very core of the interface between publics and politics and international relations, not forgetting the locus of power in a globalised world. But while there is a mass of critical literature exploring the manifestations of bias, propaganda and spin, there is little by way of a critical or journalistic intervention into how to change this situation. We illustrate throughout this book how news production routines often drive content. The controversy surrounding the reporting (and non-reporting) of recent major conflicts has often come back to the fact that those production processes and routines may be ill-equipped for reporting modern warfare. The idea of finding two sets of opposing combatants simply may not be the case. There may be many. Enemies may have a legitimate cause even if they are not the army of a recognised nation state. Enemies may even be the civilians themselves. And 24-hour rolling news has to keep rolling even when nothing has been happening and no one is telling reporters anything new.

The underlying and most abiding critical question concerning the reporting of conflict is a question that can be extended to all other types of journalism – what if the actions of journalists have consequences for the conflict itself? Good reporting and news analysis should go beyond merely stating positions and should show the conflict in its historical and social perspective. Before we embark on the analysis we wish to begin by setting out briefly the unreported context for the conflict which was absent from most mainstream coverage. Forgive us for dwelling on Iraq, but this was happening at the time of writing and offers a good example through which we can measure the quality of conflict reporting. It could reasonably be argued that the war in the Balkans, for instance, set in place many challenges to established approaches to reporting for the reason that there were no clear-cut definable enemies. Also the conflict's proximity to the West established questions about the journalism of attachment, centring on difficulties of reporting impartially.

The very boundaries of the countries that make up the Middle East, Iraq, Iran, Kuwait, etc., are the result of colonial map drawing dating from around 100 years ago (Hourani 1991). At the end of the nineteenth century the European colonial powers had become aware of the importance of the Middle East for resources and communication links between Europe and their colonies in Asia. By the first decade of the twentieth century its vast reserves of oil had become of vital importance. The British in particular needed to maintain trade links to India and were reliant on the oil supplies acquired in Iran for their Royal Navy with which it could police its colonies. In the second decade of the century the region, under the Ottomans, was aligned with Germany and Austria-Hungary, and had become a target for the British and French as well as the Germans. Britain had already indicated its aggressive intentions as regards the Ottoman Empire. This is generally not foregrounded in its own version of the events leading to the First World War.

During the First World War Britain captured Baghdad in 1917 and created the nation of Iraq in 1920, splicing together a geographically, ethnically and religiously diverse region. Iraq was created out of the three Ottoman provinces of Basra, Mosul and Baghdad. Part of Basra was broken off to form Kuwait, which Britain also controlled. Before this map drawing the region, ruled broadly by the Ottoman Empire, was not viewed as a political entity and was certainly not comprised of nations. Many commentators have argued that this was one of the most tolerant social and religious societies in human history (Lewis 1998; Halliday 1996), precisely because it was not characterised by the centralised rule of the nation states. Iraq gained independence from Britain in 1932, although Britain still maintained strong control over the country. A treaty had been signed that allowed the British military to remain and gave Britain control over the Iraqi army. It was from the senior officers in this army that great resentment against the British grew. Politicians were seen as puppets of the British. During the Second World War the British were in force in Iraq to protect their oilfields and to deal with the support for the Nazis among the Iraqi army officials who saw an opportunity to get rid of the British. The British managed to support the regime ruled by the monarchy.

When the monarchy was finally overthrown by the Iraqi army in 1958 it seemed that Iraq had finally gained independence from the British. The new government was overthrown in 1963 in a CIA-sponsored coup by the anti-Communist Ba'ath party, which in turn led to the rule of Saddam Hussein. American companies soon began doing business with Baghdad. Recently declassified documents have emerged that show the extent to which the US government embraced Saddam Hussein in the early 1980s. Diplomatic relations resumed, yet during this time Saddam had invaded his neighbour Iran and used chemical weapons on its citizens. Directives signed by President Reagan showed the US had priorities for the region to preserve access to oil. US support and military assistance in Iraq, which involved turning a blind eye to the chemical weapons, has now been dubbed 'Iraq-gate'. According to the US National Security Archive, Donald Rumsfeld made two trips to Iraq to meet Saddam to help prevent an Iranian victory that was seen as against US interests. There were shipments of chemical weapons precursors from several US companies to Iraq during the 1980s, but the US government would deny that it was aware that these exports were intended to be used in the production of chemical weapons.

The Middle East was described by Washington as one of 'the greatest material prizes in world history' (United States Government 1945). This has continued to be the reason for US concerns of 'stability in the region' and is one of its reasons for its support of Israel and also of 'moderate' pro-Western regimes. Billions of dollars in military aid have been and still are ploughed into the region to secure US-friendly governments (Stoff 1980). This policy has included helping Israel to develop a nuclear programme while preventing neighbouring countries from doing the same (Seymour 1983).

When Saddam Hussein, ruling over a country contrived by, and controlled for decades by, the British and then the US, claimed rights over Kuwait and attempted to build an army strong enough to stand up to the Western powers, he was described as evil in the Western news media, mainly through the words and press releases of government officials. According to George W. Bush and Tony Blair Iraq should be invaded and turned into a democracy. The main reasons that were given for this were the presence of weapons of mass destruction and that Iraq was harbouring terrorists.

The Bush administration, in attempting to persuade the public to support the war, presented an overly simplistic case. The problems of the Middle East are enormously complex. The Reagan administration's policies toward the Iran–Iraq war show that international relations are conducted not in black and white but in shades of grey. At the time of writing, no weapons were ever found. The unrest and divided nature of the country were hardly surprising given its history, but the news media reported on the violent acts of militia and insurgents, connecting these to world terror rather than the history of the region.

The main point to be made here is why people were not aware of this context when Iraq dominated the news media for many months? Throughout this book we will see that we must not simply view this kind of absence of context as a matter of bias and covert political pressure on journalists and editors to hide the facts. It is the simple aspects of the organisation of the news media, how news is gathered and which sources are used, that we need to look at.

Theoretical discussions

The golden triangle of news beats in the US is the White House, State Department and Pentagon. Journalists will go here first for information. In other countries it is their own political institutions. The press conferences and press releases produced by these institutions will be at the centre of news and defining the nature of events. On the one hand journalists could argue that since these are elected by the people they write for then they should form the heart of reporting but, as in the case of Iraq, we find that this means that their claims go unquestioned. This emphasis on official sources gives a huge advantage to those already in power for getting their issues on the political agenda. In the long term clearly we have a case where the kinds of problems and solutions presented in the news become limited to those defined by official sources. Bennett shows concern for this. He worries that people will come to accept things like poverty, crime, war and political apathy as inevitable parts of the everyday world rather than as the tragic results of the concentration of power and the nature of the way that we now run our societies (2005: 118).

We find these analyses delimit the realms within which real-life conflict reporting are viewed and analysed. It suggests that the power of the media is predominantly vested in the hands of a few news outlets, which fails to acknowledge a wide range of oppositional editorial strategies in the context of Iraq. There were many voices within the European media and in the UK that were challenging the decision to go to war, and these were in the mainstream. Robert Fisk's reporting for *The Independent* was notably anti-invasion, and the BBC was criticised by the UK government for being seen as overly critical. Furthermore, White House sources in the US were also being fed by the British government. In response to concerns about the seeming patriotism of the some of the US news networks, it must not be overlooked that the BBC was not viewed by the UK government as being 'on side', which may be indicative of more diversity, albeit slightly, than critics have assigned to broadcasters.

We have already seen in previous chapters how journalists' use of sources has come under criticism, and this is felt strongly in relation to war. Edelman (1977) claimed that the use of the pronouncements of politicians as news was replacing detailed analyses of situations. Thirty years later the British journalist Lloyd (2004), exasperated with the lack of investigative analysis over the British involvement in Iraq, warned that the news media had simply become an appendage of the political administrative process, bound to report in detail all official statements and losing the overall picture in the process. A study in 2002 conducted over five years concluded that investigative journalism had disappeared from the airwaves in the US. Most news was from official sources and press leaks (Just *et al.* 2002). Orr (1980) accepts that of course journalists can be aggressive and adversarial, but they will keep this on a personal level, aimed at a particular person or at drawing out a clash between two people, rather than actually criticising the institution itself. In British journalism throughout the 1990s it became more common to see journalists treating politicians assertively, but these challenges were personal and about policy, not institutions, and certainly not about careful examination of the outcomes of policies. This aggressive approach gives a false sense that there really is a process of interrogation going on, digging and bravely seeking out the facts.

One aspect of real-life news reporting that this model overlooks is the fact that once a war is underway, journalists by necessity will shift from reporting context and build-up negotiation to covering the action itself. The priorities of journalist once sorties or military action has commenced is to provide blow by blow descriptive accounts of what is happening on the ground. This may not be wholly ideal, as journalists we spoke with acknowledged, but it is an expectation of journalism that coverage will follow this pattern. What is more of an issue for journalists is that they are prevented from seeing those events close up through embedding. According to Colin Bickler, a highly experienced foreign correspondent who we interview in more detail later, it is not that journalists are not trying to seek out and carefully examine the facts. He describes the criticism levelled at journalists who refused to leave Baghdad when the bombing began, because they spoke to official Iraqi sources. 'If we look at the reporting of Iraq historically, we can see that veteran correspondents who reported on the first Gulf War were in fact having to report from the other side in the current conflict.' According to this model owners, or at least their chief appointed editors, work as *gatekeepers*. This is a term that is used to describe the fact that there are decisions made at some level that prevent certain things, and allow others, into the news. One example of this might be where there is relative silence in the news media about thousands of civilian casualties in an act of war by our own governments, such as in the case of Iraq. On the other hand there may be extensive details given about a handful of deaths of soldiers from the UK and US at the hands of local 'terrorists' or 'militia'. We might say that this withholding of information is an act of gatekeeping, but it seems over-simplistic to ascribe so much influence to the media – to accuse the media of actively promoting misinformation. This goes strongly against our conversations with many journalists who have reported or edited war coverage. It implies that it was the media actively creating the connection between Saddam and WMDs or terrorism, rather than the fact that the news media may have fallen into a trap. When we hear the word propaganda we think of a process which involves the composition and delivery of a lie or political viewpoint, with all those involved in the process being complicit. In the case of the news about war, academic research has shown that it is both more complex and more subtle than this. We can characterise three levels:

1 Large privatised media corporations interconnected to the power bloc of society;
2 governments concerned to win a war and maintain public support;
3 journalists who see 'their boys' making sacrifices in combat.

Media corporations are interrelated with other large corporations, banking, finance and industrial capital (Bennett 2005; Curran 1991; McChesney 2004; Tunstall and Palmer 1981). Therefore, we might not expect such corporations to be critical of the corporate world in general. Such organisations may be less likely to be critical of the actions of governments who act in the interest of Western global capitalism, for example for oil in the Middle East. Famines on the horn of Africa, such as Somalia where millions died, were directly connected to US and Soviet need for military bases and control over oil, yet this part of the story was whitewashed by the media in the UK and US.

The corporate nature of news media may mean that higher-level decisions will co-operate with the needs of government. Many advertising companies will not support media who are openly critical of consumerism and capitalism. Herman and Chomsky (1988) argue that their research supports the view that 'Advertisers will want . . . to avoid programs with serious complexities and disturbing controversies that interfere with the "buying mood"' (1988: 17).

Herman and Chomsky wrote about these issues during the Cold War. For them, communism was the demonised other of Western society. In more contemporary times we have global enemies of freedom that come in the form of terrorists, as we saw in the example of the Palestinian terrorists mentioned earlier. The motivations of these 'terrorists' is rarely discussed.

Graham *et al.* (2004), in a paper on the way that people have been rallied to hate enemies over the past thousand years, quote from Goering:

> Naturally the common people don't want war: Neither in Russia, nor in England, nor for that matter in Germany. That is understood. But, after all, it is the leaders of the country who determine the policy and it is always a simple matter to drag the people along, whether it is a democracy, or a fascist dictatorship, or a parliament, or a communist dictatorship. . . . Voice or no voice, the people can always be brought to the bidding of the leaders. That is easy. All you have to do is tell them they are being attacked, and denounce the peacemakers for lack of patriotism and exposing the country to danger. It works the same in any country.
>
> General Herman Goering

At the time of writing this book Saddam Hussein was on trial in Iraq. The account of this process and the reasons for going to war with Iraq were framed exactly in the model described by Graham *et al.* (2004). Saddam was an evil beast who needed to be taught a lesson in the name of the greater good of democracy and freedom. The same was the case as regards Osama bin Laden. After 9/11 he was used not as an example of the challenge to global capitalism and economic policies, but the challenge to 'civilisation'.

Kirtley (2001) points out that there is a huge conflict of interests between the military and journalism in times of war. The former needs to win the battle not just on the battlefield but also in the minds of the public: the latter seeks to report what is happening out there in the world. Sometimes, however, the media are more than willing to go along with what could be described as self-censorship, as can be seen in the following:

> We live in a dirty and dangerous world. There are some things the general public does not need to know about and shouldn't. I believe democracy flourishes when the government can take legitimate steps to keep its secrets and when the press can decide whether to print what it knows.
>
> Katharine Graham, Washington Post owner
> Cited at www.globalissues.org

It is important to state that journalists themselves may not necessarily agree with the stance their own organisations take.

Additionally journalists may find that they lose a sense of neutrality when faced with their own country in a conflict situation. British reporter Max Hastings wrote during the British war with Argentina over the Malvinas/Falkland Islands, that no reporter could be neutral when their own soldiers were involved in fighting (Carruthers 2000: 6). Hallin and Gitlin (1994) wrote of the role of the journalist as cheerleader maintaining links between our boys and the population. Carruthers remarks (2000: 9) 'Once patriotism is mobilised . . . critical voices are rapidly silenced.'

To exemplify, BBC Radio 4's flagship *Today* programme on Thursday 16 February 2006 carried two stories related to the Iraq conflict high up on its news agenda. It reported that a second set of still and moving images appearing to depict abuse by US soldiers against Iraqis held captive at Baghdad's Abu Ghraib prison had been shown on Australian TV. The images were more disturbing even than a similar set released earlier that led to the conviction of at least two US soldiers, yet the story ran that Pentagon officials were criticising the media for showing the pictures. Instead of instantly condemning the treatment of prisoners, the US military attacked the media for showing the images, saying they would only serve to inflame greater hatred towards America by the Muslim world. Pentagon officials said that the images were not recent, and that the matter had been addressed when the first set of images were broadcast. Therefore these pictures did no more than place US and allied forces still stationed in Iraq in imminent danger. Most significantly, in light of theories about propaganda, the Pentagon argument appears to be stirring fears of potential threats to ordinary citizens.

The issues around journalism and conflict seem to be getting no nearer resolution. When the *Daily Mirror* published a set of images that appeared to show soldiers of the First Battallion Queen's Lancashire Regiment humiliating Iraqi prisoners, they were proven to be fakes. Editor Piers Morgan was fired but insisted that they were essentially true. In their editorial for a special edition of the journal *Mediactive*, Anita Biressi and Heather Nunn articulate the impasse:

> During the debate about the veracity of the *Mirror*'s photographs, influential international journalists such as Robert Fisk and John Pilger cautioned that the argument had become a means to side-step wider debates about the role of the journalist, to weaken the power of the journalist's dissenting voice and put a brake on the necessary media dissection of the broader hegemonic discourses of war, security, retribution and 'rights'.
>
> (*Mediactive* 3: 5)

Going back to the actual context of the conflict in Iraq, even if soldiers are seen to be abusing prisoners this is in fact only one small symptom of nearly a century of the West abusing the people of this region. To focus any kind of blame on a small group of soldiers who find themselves at the heart of this mess is by all accounts quite absurd. It must be emphasised that the fact that British mainstream media covered these moving and still image revelations in such detail is evidence of a media that challenges propaganda, rather than capitulating to it. Given the absence of real material to cover it is no surprise that journalists get their teeth into the arrival of some scandalous photographs. There are no longer any enemy lines to watch. There is no longer any clear progress to monitor. And read any good war novel by an ex-front line soldier such as *The Naked and the Dead* or *Cross of Iron* – these will tell you that war and its daily routine of damaged bodies, fear and devastation, brutalises its participants, just as does a century of colonial meddling. Soldiers get nasty. But public knowledge of what goes on in wars seems to have become as remote as our knowledge of why they are happening at all.

War reporting in summary seems to be the case where the social and cultural context of journalism is powerfully evident. Carruthers (2000) concludes of war reporting:

> to look at which wars media cover, for how long, and in what ways, is less to see a recognisable reflection of the 'world as it is' – as the journalists are wont to claim – than a map of the broad preoccupations, interests and values of their particular society (or at least of its dominant groups).
>
> (Carruthers 2000: 17)

Case study – NBC

We have already mentioned that the main terrestrial television news networks in the USA – CBS, ABC and NBC – have been criticised for excessive patriotism during their coverage of the war in Iraq and its immediate aftermath. NBC is part of NBC universal, one of the world's leading media and entertainment companies in the development, production and marketing of entertainment, news and information to a global audience. It has vast corporate interests spanning news and film-making as well as theme parks for English-speaking and also Hispanic markets. NBC News has been in operation for 75 years, first on radio, then television and now via cable and the Internet as well as terrestrial. According to their web site, it is watched by 'more Americans than any other news organisation'. It provides more than 25 hours of weekly programming in the United States, including the flagship *Nightly News*, *Today* and *Meet the Press*. *Dateline NBC* is the signature broadcast for NBC News in prime-time at least two nights per week. Also under the NBC News umbrella is MSNBC, the 24-hour cable news channel and Internet service launched in 1996.

During the Iraq war and its aftermath in 2003, MSNBC was criticised for running promotional advertisements featuring a photo-montage of soldiers in Iraq as a piano version of the *Star Spangled Banner* tinkled in the background. Its news rating rose threefold during wartime coverage (*St Petersburg Times*, 25 April 2003). It is hard to read this type of promotion as anything more than an emotive ploy, and far from independent or objective. However, MSNBC president Erik Sorenson took a different view:

> MSNBC covered US troops, US casualties and Iraqi civilian casualties during the course of this war . . . Given the Iraqi regime's track record

> towards their own civilians, drawing conclusions about civilian casualties was certainly a tricky business journalistically. Finally, I see nothing wrong with an American TV news network focusing on American troops and their efforts, many of which were in fact brave and heroic.
> (email to *St Petersburg Times*, published 25 April 2003)

Significantly, NBC fired the Pulitzer Prize-winning journalist Peter Arnett in the same month for giving an interview for Iraqi state television in which he was critical of US progress. He was promptly hired by the *Daily Mirror* in London, the editor of which, Piers Morgan, was sacked soon after for publishing fabricated images alleging abuse by US soldiers towards Iraqi prisoners of war. It is worth mention that New Zealand-born Arnett was also criticised for his reporting from Vietnam – because he was not American.

We spoke with one of NBC's most experienced news correspondents to gain insights into his experiences. Jim Maceda has reflected on the challenges facing journalists covering conflict, and has spoken alongside peace journalism advocate Jake Lynch and others on how reporters must negotiate their social responsibility for delivering the truth to the public against a backdrop of conflicting interests and restraints. His account reveals the pressure TV conflict correspondents are under to deliver news round the clock with minimal new information from fresh sources. His account also reveals a strong brand awareness at NBC that is reflected in the content and packaging of his material. The process of news-gathering and dissemination, especially in terms of the editing of his scripts, is illuminating in displaying how the words from the autonomous news correspondent are actually carefully pre-vetted in newsrooms hundreds or thousands of miles away.

Jim Maceda, NBC News Correspondent

In a career spanning more than 30 years, NBC's Jim Maceda has reported on more than 100 countries, many of which were in the midst of conflict. Most recently, he has reported on the wars in the former Yugoslavia, including the air-strikes in Serbia and Kosovo, and the conflicts in Afghanistan and Iraq. He has won two Emmy's for his journalism. The first was for his coverage of the Intifada Palestinian Uprising in 1987–8. In 1989 he won the second for his coverage of the Tiananmen Square massacre in Beijing. He has held a range of prominent international positions including deputy bureau chief, on-air reporter and producer. Now based at the London bureau, he travels the globe as a news correspondent.

Jim graduated from Stanford University, California, in 1970 then pursued postgraduate studies at the Sorbonne in Paris.

> I started in the business through the back door (as many do). I was hired by CBS Paris as a copy boy, gofer and courier. That was in 1973 and my first assignment was to follow Kissinger and Le Duc as they

> sped around Paris and St Nom la Breteche, dotting the i's on the Vietnam peace accords. I worked my way up the food chain, slowly, eventually landing a senior producer's job at French TV (FR3) in the late 70s. As a 'French reporter' I had access to datelines (Afghanistan, Cambodia, etc.) that American reporters couldn't easily get to. That opened some doors overseas, and in 1980 I was hired by NBC News in Paris as a producer. I returned to on-air reporting in 1987 (during the first Intifadah). I never studied journalism in school. I was an English literature major with a music minor. But some (including me) would say that was a good foundation. My father was a journalist and, as a youth, I wanted to have nothing to do with the fourth estate, which I saw as a haven for failed – often alcoholic – writers. I guess blood is thicker than vodka.

NBC London is a hub that covers Europe and the Middle East and beyond although, as with areas we have already covered, there are closures of offices and reductions in staffing.

> Twenty years ago we still had over a dozen 'real' foreign bureaux (with full teams), but that has shrunk to only four: London, Moscow, Tel Aviv and Hong Kong. We have around 50 staff employees here, in addition to a large number of freelancers.

Jim explained that he now spends more time on assignments than he ever used to:

> Correspondents and producers average at least 50–60 per cent in the field. Since 9/11 that has jumped up to 80 per cent for me. My professional life seems to triangulate around Iraq, Afghanistan/Pakistan and the Middle East. There is the occasional 'perk' (Pope coverage in Rome, for instance). The hours are pretty predictable: in the field, on assignment, it is 24/7. In London we do around 10-hour shifts. The only 'guaranteed' time off is during holidays and I've had a number of those cancelled by important breaking news. There is no template for a working day. We call a day in Baghdad 'the wheel of death' not because of the ieds (improvised explosive devices) but because of the preponderance of MSNBC live hits, sometimes around the clock, in addition to *Early Today*, *Today* and *Nightly News* stories. A day in London can be filled with doing expenses or reading research and doing little if any broadcasting.

He described how technology and economies of scale have in some circumstances required him to multitask:

> I don't work alone but I have worked with only a 'one-man-band' crewman. In that case I'll report, produce and run sound, the

> cameraman will shoot and edit and feed. So this two-man band will do the job of five. But usually we are a four-man team, correspondent/producer/cameraman/soundman. For a number of years we tend to feed our material to London by satellite where it is edited on high-tech digital Avid edit consoles.

Wherever Jim is reporting, he must be conscious of the production cycle and New York time:

> On an average day I spend a couple of hours in the morning reading the wires and papers online from home. If I see a story we should be doing I'll call the London desk and get some balls rolling, then, at 8 a.m. NY time, will call our senior foreign producer in NY to see what they think. Or, often, it's the reverse and NY sees a story (sometimes a foreign story related to a domestic spot someone is working on stateside) and will call the London desk in our morning. Once we discuss the story and agree on the elements and approach, there is complete autonomy. In 32 years I have only had one story killed by an executive producer due to what I would describe as 'political pressure' coming from above. It's a lot freer at corporate-owned NBC (or CBS or ABC) than most would believe.
>
> We do work very closely with our senior editors/producers in NY, and we have a process called 'script approval' which is totally alien to my British colleagues, whereby the seniors must sign off on the script before we can track and feed the story. Again, this is less fascistic than it sounds. The 'approved' script is 9 times out of 10 an enhanced script. And the revisions often result from the news flow of the whole show – what comes before and after my piece – and how I need to adjust to that flow. But 'script approval' does amuse many of my Brit peers.
>
> I often work for the flagship show, our *Nightly News* programme, which means I live on New York time. An average day begins with the 8 a.m. (NY time) conference call, which gives NY a first look at the day's news. That's followed by a 9:30 a.m. *Nightly News* conference call, at which the NY producers decide which stories *Nightly News* will cover that day. We are usually off and running after a story by that time. I'll return to base, with tapes, in the early evening, screen, script and track by around 4 p.m. (NY time), and we'll feed the cut story before 6:30 p.m. (NY time), which is when the show airs on the east coast. If it's a breaking story we will do updates across the country's three time zones.

There is an overall identity to NBC News output. Jim has a certain type of viewer in mind when scripting and producing his stories. This may affect his choice of angle, vocabulary and use of images.

> Our main identity derives from being a terrestrial – non-cable or satellite – network. Anyone with a TV can get NBC. We are a major mainstream news outlet, and as such we tell the news 'straight', unlike Fox, which is a niche network. That said, given our broadcast times, and our medium, we've found that a majority of our viewers are 45–64. That's why you see so many Exlax and Viagra commercials in between segments. But that has influenced the news fare we offer. We focus much more on issues that concern the older and retired: health, 401(k)s – investment for retirement – social security, insurance scams, etc. Demographics do affect our choice of stories. Our vocabulary plays to mainstream middle America. My greatest challenge is taking a complex story, like the recent people power movement in Lebanon or even the Papal conclave and making it understandable to the average American with a high school education, or less. – And who may have grandchildren fighting in Iraq . . . –

In this case we can see that even where the reporter may have awareness of more complex issues these may get lost in the kinds of news frames that are perceived to be necessary to engage with target audiences. Jim spoke further of other kinds of restrictions.

> We are often restricted by the gruesome nature of our pictures – we are a breakfast or dinner-time family show, after all. But there are no editorial restrictions on what we air. There is an ongoing debate about how much we want to broadcast 'terrorist' web sites or insurgent footage showing, for instance, the blowing up of US military vehicles by roadside bombs, etc. The question is whether we are helping the insurgents by airing their wares. I think we've tried to find a compromise, which gets the story across without over-using the material.

Jim's experience of reporting from war zones is inevitably tough and very stressful. It is apparent from his account that his coverage must by necessity cohere with established routines at NBC in terms of values and production deadlines.

> My last two trips to Iraq were October/November of 2004, and January/February of 2005. Each trip, for a correspondent, is a month, which in reality becomes five weeks. Because of the constant stress there, one tends to hit a wall after three weeks, and you get over that wall by seeing the light at the end of the tunnel. I have a 'handover' session, once inside, with the correspondent who I am replacing, a brief on the stories he had done, is working on, etc. and we get a security briefing from our 'pilgrim' security consultants (body guards). October/November was Ramadan so we know we will be covering

> a spike in insurgent violence. January/February was the election, and our stories and embeds (I was in Ramadi, the heart of the triangle during the election, where the ink-stained voting finger was a kiss of death rather than a badge of honour) evolved around that historic event. On all of our [scripts] (TV stories are 'scripts' not stories) we try to put a face on the players and/or victims caught up in the event. And we try to avoid doing abstract, 'survey' pieces (which is what you'll usually see on CNN). The days in Iraq are structured by NY's needs. You get up, you have breakfast, you read in, and you do your morning hits. You then try to get out and shoot, do interviews, work contacts and work up a story for *Nightly*, all the while trying to come back to base alive, and do more afternoon hits. Then, if you're lucky, you have dinner with your team, then it's back to the newsroom for the long back stretch – the *Nightly News shift*. You get to bed around 3 a.m. You are up at 8 a.m. unless you are heading off for an embed which means you get no sleep. Why do we do it? If we don't, who will? It's a cliché. But it resonates with many colleagues in Iraq.

He also provides insights into his relationship with the military.

> I think my relationship with the military is one of mutual respect. They know I am not out to burn them. They also know I am not Ollie North or Geraldo Rivera and will not sing their glory. I have a long and pretty good record with the US military, and not just in Iraq. That helps in getting on embeds and in getting more autonomy than many when doing my stories. On embeds we live with the military – either the army infantry or the marines or the airborne divisions, like the 101st. Every embed is as different as the units we cover and live with. I think, overall, the US military has gotten a fair deal from NBC News. We don't pander. We call it as we see it. But we don't 'recon by fire' either. I think many soldiers and sailors think we journalists are nuts doing what we do. And I suppose the feeling is mutual.

Reflecting on journalists' experiences

Countries like Iraq are currently undergoing significant social, economic and political changes. In places like Palestine and Lebanon there are complex political processes taking place that are deeply interwoven with their relationship to the West. Reporting therefore requires a sensitivity to history and to actual economic and political interests outside of the official statements of politicians and visible political administration. If not there is a danger that our societies will lack the maturity required to act in our own best interest in the long term.

In journalism research itself what has been lacking is a critical reflection on the actual experiences of the producers of news, the correspondents themselves and how they themselves deal with constraints. There has been a wide range of autobiographies by journalists in which they recount their experiences. For instance, in the second book by veteran BBC foreign affairs editor John Simpson, *A Mad World, My Masters*, he provides detailed insights about his experiences overseas, some harrowing and many amusing. He also refers to attempts to curtail his activities by the powers of the various states he was working in. At no stage is there any evidence that he could be anything but autonomous and independent in a war zone. Though he is candid about the changing nature of the personnel and resources he has worked with:

> Now of course, everything has changed: the world, society, television, we ourselves. There are few sound recordists left in news, and therefore no period of apprenticeship. Cameramen, as a result, are in their thirties rather than their fifties, and working on their own has made them more self-sufficient. Lighting men and despatch riders have vanished utterly from television news. The jobs they once did are either done by the cameramen or are not done at all.
>
> (Simpson 2000: 328)

It may or may not be a coincidence that titles are starting to emerge from media sociology that do in fact interview correspondents, and a less satisfying picture emerges. Howard Tumber and Frank Webster (2006) interviewed 50 front line correspondents for their book *Journalists Under Fire*. Similar, though less theoretically driven, is *The Media at War in Iraq*, a collection of essays by journalists edited by Bill Katovsky and Timothy Carlson (2003). In addition to these personal and ethnographic accounts of the process of reporting conflict, other voices and methodologies are emerging that seek to offer fresh perspectives on this domain. Two that are particularly notable are studies into peace journalism and also trauma. Both of these approaches respond to the growing concern about the routine approach to conflict reporting that seems ill-prepared to handle international affairs. Proponents of peace journalism argue that in the context of conflict and the changes that ensue, journalists should not simply report the facts (though that is hard enough itself) but should also work to critically and creatively explore avenues for conflict resolution. In this way, it is argued, journalism becomes reliable, respects human rights and represents diverse views. Drawing on the work of Swedish sociologist Johann Galtung, Jake Lynch and Annabel McGoldrick, who are themselves experienced international broadcast journalists, advocate a critical self-reflexivity in their book *Peace Journalism* (2005). They summarise key findings in the misreporting of conflict:

- **Violence is never wholly its own cause**: Conflict is made up of structure, culture and process – the context, without which no account of a violent event is complete or, indeed, correct.
- **Non-violent responses are always possible**: There is always more than one way of responding to conflict. Many people, in many places, are devising, advocating and applying non-violent responses.
- **More than two sides**: There are always more than two parties to any conflict – some, whose involvement or interest is hidden, need to be out on the map. Others, presented as having a solid aggregate view, may contain important internal divisions, and need disaggregation.
- **Every party has a stake**: Parties to conflict should be seen as stakeholders, pursuing their own goals, needs and interests – some openly acknowledged, but almost invariably some hidden as well (Lynch and McGoldrick 2005: xviii).

This model aspires to a shift in the balance of power in reporting, from a top-down dissemination targeted at maximising ratings to a closer engagement with and empowerment of the public to play a role in the democratic processes. They deny that their model wishes to conceal the real horrors of war, rather that they want it told in full but carefully and accurately contextualised. This contextualisation, they argue, does not have to take up much space or airtime (2005: Appendix A). For these authors, war is often more than something arising out of simple issues. Often more complex causes underpin what is ostensibly the cause of that conflict.

A further significant body of work is emerging on the toll war coverage takes on the journalists involved which, again, is something that has rarely been cited in autobiographies. Major news producers are now enlisting support from trained counsellors, many of who are former journalists themselves, to help staff deal with the images they have encountered. Al Tompkins of the Poynter Institute for Media Studies wrote the following for Poynter.org in September 2001:

> Reporters, photojournalists, engineers, sound men and field producers often work elbow to elbow with emergency workers. Journalists' symptoms of traumatic stress are remarkably similar to those of police officers and firefighters who work in the immediate aftermath of tragedy, yet journalists typically receive little support after they file their stories. While public-safety workers are offered debriefings and counseling after a trauma, journalists are merely assigned another story.

The Dart Centre for Journalism and Trauma is a global network of journalists, journalism educators and health professionals dedicated to improving media coverage of trauma, conflict and tragedy. The Centre also addresses the consequences of such coverage for those working in journalism. CNN and the BBC have used the Centre to support not only foreign correspondents but also desk editors who have been exposed to unedited footage of traumatic events. The Centre is developing a range of practical and scholarly resources, synthesising journalism with psychology and psychoanalysis in order to do three things. First, it advocates sensitive treatment by journalists towards sources who have experienced trauma, not only in the immediate aftermath but also when asked to recall events years later. Second, it educates journalists about how trauma works so they can recognise it and be sensitive to it with sources, colleagues and also themselves. Third, it considers audiences and the social consequences of mediation of trauma. At a conference at London's Tavistock Centre in 2005, Dart Centre specialists expressed concerns about the depiction of traumatic events through user-generated content, both for the untrained citizen journalist and for the audience. Journalism studies has so far not embraced theories of the self such as psychoanalysis into its vocabulary, but given that practitioners and academics are striving for solutions to flaws in current practices, it is clear that a much broader set of methodologies may need to be addressed.

Responding to the theoretical approaches

Case study: Colin Bickler

Colin Bickler is a veteran foreign affairs correspondent who has worked for news agencies, print outlets and also in broadcast journalism. He worked for the news agency Reuters for 26 years as bureau chief in several countries. Working as a journalist brought him into contact with some powerful world leaders. During the early 1970s he joined the press entourage which followed Henry Kissinger's shuttle diplomacy in the Middle East.

More recently, he was a consultant to UNDP on the reorganisation of the Bulgarian national news agency and was a keynote speaker on press freedom at the Trinidad and Tobago Annual Media Awards. He was also a UNESCO panellist on press freedom in the Caribbean, has done seminars for Article 19 and IPI, and is a member of the Foreign Office Freedom of Expression advisory panel. He is a member of the Communication Information Committee of the UK National Commission of UNESCO and the Human Rights Consultative Committee of the UK Foreign Office. Now he lectures in what he emphasises is 'conflict not war' reporting. He also promotes risk-awareness for all journalists, not just foreign correspondents, having helped found the International News Safety Institute. We asked him about his experiences of covering conflicts and violence, specifically encouraging him to reflect on access to sources and information and his dealings with governments and the military. He described how he gained skills in detecting when authorities attempted to 'plant' stories to promote their own agenda. What is most interesting about his discussion is how diverse the work of foreign reporting is, and how theoretical approaches may not have a wide enough lens to articulate the complexities and breadth of practice in this field.

Having grown up in New Zealand, Colin spent the first six years of his journalism career in the late 1950s and early 1960s covering two domestic beats – police and industry – which he said was excellent preparation for his work abroad covering wars:

> These beats taught me how to keep contacts sweet to get the best stories. They showed me how to get under the skin of a story, and how to cover the story in depth through a variety of sources whilst maintaining my journalistic integrity. As a foreign correspondent you often deal with sources who may dislike what you are doing. But once they know that you have integrity and are determined to follow the story, they recognise that it is better to work with you than not. It was also good training in the use of sources. It taught me when and how to use anonymous sources and, above all, to double-check everything. This is always very hard work. But it taught me always to be sceptical about anyone who wanted to tell me something. As a foreign correspondent, you must always ask yourself that question, especially if it is a governmental or diplomatic representative who wishes to talk with you. Remember, the good guys don't always tell you the truth. It may be unintentional because they themselves think they have the correct information. But the bad guys will often tell you the truth because they want to set the record straight.

Colin describes the changing nature of the way foreign journalists have been perceived by authorities:

> As an agency reporter you were often seen as akin to a senior diplomat and were given a lot of access. Because of that access and openness, we tended to be very careful – sometimes we would not print everything that we were told. In the early days, ministers in certain countries would speak to the foreign correspondent first because they respected them more, and to their national press much later. As governments grew more confident and reporting grew sharper, tensions grew between governments and journalists. My successors have had to fight far harder for access. Nonetheless it is still the case that 'good' reporters, those who are recognised as having influence and integrity, would still get access when others wouldn't. But you have to spend a lot of time building up that profile. Now, as then, there is a great deal of competition for access, particularly with TV cultivating relationships with the military and governments. But that can also work against you.

He reflects on the Hutton Inquiry into the BBC's reporting of controversy over the evidence for going to war on Iraq. The Inquiry centred on a two-way between Andrew Gilligan and a *Today* programme anchor in May 2003, in which he stated that a security source claimed the UK government knowingly 'sexed up' the suggestion that Iraq had weapons of mass destruction in order to justify military action. Later Gilligan's source, leading biological weapons expert Dr David Kelly, was identified and he took his own life. The Inquiry studied the evidence for the claim and produced a report condemning Gilligan's reporting methods, notably his reliance on a single source. Colin stated:

> Some stories have to be based on a single source, and if you don't use it someone else might. But what you need to do before you use it as the basis for your story is to establish the reliability of that source and to have confidence not to use it if unsure. It depends on the weight of that source and ideally you should be able to indicate the source even if you cannot name them directly. There is nothing new in this, and it is nonsense to believe that a single source might not be the best and indeed the only source provided it is treated with proper care.
>
> When Syria was in talks over disengagement, I got hold of the disengagement map. I wrote a story with diplomatic sourcing on both sides. Kissinger, on the record, denied it. We carried that denial but we repeated what we had said. If I had been 10 years younger my editor might have reprimanded me and spiked the story, but we went with it and sure enough it turned out to be true. The problem is that even when you have documentary evidence, it is not always watertight. Governments will float documents which may not turn out to be the final versions.

He warned that sometimes it is governments rather than journalists who will present dubious information as fact, and that journalists have to be wary about the veracity and intention of such disclosures. He was referring specifically to lessons learned in the wake of the Judith Miller affair in the US, in which the star *New York Times* reporter lost her job amid allegations that she had fallen prey to US government defence propagandists seeking to embellish rumours of Saddam's military capability. She was also accused of being ensnared in a campaign to smear an outspoken opponent of the war, former ambassador Joseph Wilson. It has been alleged that she allowed herself to be wooed by senior officials intent on planting stories on her. Colin said:

> I have had documents planted on me, and I have had to be very careful in judging the authenticity of the content. For instance, in the build up to the war in Iraq, I read an account in a respected broadsheet that looked totally planted – it was a piece of propaganda that they could not authenticate, yet they printed it. It was as if the journalist had been carried away by their own ego. Journalists must always

> ask – why is this piece of information being volunteered to me? It doesn't mean it isn't reportable, but you have to check it very, very carefully.

The identity, integrity and conduct of individual journalists working overseas can be crucial in maintaining their access to information. Journalists often have to tread very carefully to ensure they can remain in the war zone, rather than be evicted or have their bureau closed down.

> Every bureau has its own status in the country in which it operates. Its reputation is very much dependent on individuals within that bureau. One of the advantages that agency bureaux have is that they are very international. Since the 1960s when Reuters wanted to be seen as truly international, it increased its employment of international staff, and made a point of keeping the UK foreign office at arm's length. During the Falklands war, there was an unsuccessful attempt by the British government to use a D notice on an editor in chief who was not felt to be sufficiently patriotic. He said he didn't understand the term 'our boys' because he was German. Individual ego is always a problem for a war correspondent. As soon as you start to believe in your ability and authority it becomes a dangerous mindset. Sometimes agencies face special problems when working in countries with a tight regime. In order to keep the bureau open, sometimes you have the balance whether not to rock the boat. You have to balance the weight of information you have to put out against cutting yourself off. And you have to keep your local journalists at work and help them.

At the time of writing, there are fears of widespread civil conflict in Iraq. Baghdad is the most dangerous place on earth where it is alleged journalists cannot leave their hotel rooms to report. The UK's journalism trade paper *Press Gazette* reported in February 2005 that the BBC was spending a major part of its foreign reporting budget on keeping the Baghdad bureau open. Bickler says this is money well spent:

> Whatever the situation there will be serious journalists looking for a chance who will try to get out of the hotel and report independently. You have to keep your bureau open if you want to have any integrity as a news organisation.

He adds that concerns that journalists become the helpless subject of government and military control when they are fed information through briefings is often to underestimate the skills and intentions of individual reporters. He said:

> It is very important for journalists to go to press conferences even if they know nothing much will come out of them. That is the way you

> get your face known. One former colleague used to start off the questioning by being very rude to the spokesperson. At the end of the press conference he would approach the speaker, apologise then get an exclusive interview on matters that hadn't been divulged to the assembled mass of journalists. So much of your work has to be done on the telephone that you should grab every opportunity to ensure the person on the other end of the phone has met you and knows you.

Colin has clear views on some of the emerging theoretical approaches such as peace reporting and the study of trauma. He reported during the 1973 Yom Kippur war, the 1974 Cyprus war and other conflicts. Covering inter-communal violence in Malaysia, he came up against the dilemma of whether to reveal the ethnicity of killers and their victims. Doing so could fuel further killings and violence. Balance between public order and accuracy was necessary. Colin helped found the International News Safety Institute and actively promotes risk awareness for journalists. He was lead editor in 2004 of the *Journalism Handbook* for the Institute of War and Peace Reporting and a former committee member of the London branch of Reporters Sans Frontières.

> I cannot agree with the feasibility of peace reporting, although I have great respect for what the writers are trying to do. Where I break with Lynch and McGoldrick is that journalists have a role to report, not to act as a mediator. The minute a journalist becomes a mediator two things happen; they are going beyond what they are trained to do, and they start to become part of the story. I would more likely go along with the journalism of attachment. If something is evil from your perspective then you should be able to say it. But peace reporting relies on you knowing the whole story and that is simply impossible. If several journalists see a plane go down, each will provide a different eyewitness account. Nevertheless, I strongly agree with the authors that you should go beyond the simple presentation of facts. You should report contextually – all the sides in an argument will have something going for them and should be presented. Any reporter can do 'bang bang' but contextual reporting demands a great deal of work by correspondents. Given the diminishing budgets it is getting harder and harder to achieve.
>
> People often ask me who my favoured journalists are. I may disagree with the perspectives that one or other correspondent brings to the forum but I would rather have a full spectrum of foreign reporting than have it reduced to a formula. Formula reporting means bad reporting.

Colin ultimately prefers the term conflict to war reporting, a view mirrored by several journalists we encountered. He explained:

> It shouldn't matter whether it is a domestic situation or events overseas. I would see a demonstration against high taxes that might escalate

as the basis for conflict. If you look at most conflicts, it is less about different views, religions or ethnicities, it is often down to some fundamental economic inequality. In this sense, conflict is a much broader term and allows us to stand back and look at events more contextually. For instance, we can look at the current tensions in the Middle East in relation to conflict over territory. But actually, if you look at the region as a whole the biggest emerging issue relates to natural resources, access and control over the water supply. In this way, I have never considered myself to be a war correspondent. I was a foreign correspondent. I would even say that there is no such thing as foreign reporting. You are reporting for a domestic audience from abroad. It is always about reporting back to the metropolis.

Conclusion

Powerful theories about the nature and content of war reporting are highly relevant and illuminating. Importantly they point to the necessity of viewing the practices and products of journalism against the context of media ownership, as well as in light of the prevailing backdrop of political and military pressure. What they cannot show are the insights and endeavours of individual journalists. These journalists, as we have shown in these case studies, are driven as much by the process of reporting and the need to produce copy, as they are by the story itself. What is evident is that they are highly conscious of their context and seek to negotiate it in order to ensure the story is delivered. Sometimes this involves compromise; the conditions under which foreign correspondents work and the need to keep the channels of communication mean this is inevitable. This is not so easily sanctioned by some of the more abiding theories that take the individual out of the equation.

One of the most telling changes that has affected foreign reporting in recent years has been the sheer scale of delivering round-the-clock coverage. Correspondents reminisce about bygone days when the only communication between them and the newsroom was the telegraph. Now journalists have to work to time clocks set hundreds if not thousands of miles away, and are constantly pursued and pushed via mobile communications by their desk-based editors and producers. It is hardly feasible for a reporter to blend into their new environment, to have the time to forge new working alliances and make contacts with a range of sources if deadlines loom day and night. It is clear from these accounts that the work of a foreign correspondent is also severely limited by access to sources and information, not least in terms of the resources that are required to permit some freedom on the part of the journalist. A further critical issue, and one that we have not had the space to explore sufficiently, is the fact that as the world changes, so must journalists try to adapt to a shifting context. Covering war is a highly fluid activity, and the huge changes that coverage requires now, compared with when theoretical models were drafted, sharpen our belief that this is an area where most disagreement between journalism and academe lies. A case in point is the emergence of blogs and emailing, a key source of first-hand information from citizens caught behind enemy lines in the Balkans and elsewhere. Journalists are actually working with a vast range of new sources and accounts that are ever harder to verify. This is not described in theoretical accounts. Nor is the role of the myriad fixers and local journalists who work directly and indirectly for the Western media.

We began this chapter by making four assertions that crystallise for us the key disagreements between theory and practice in conflict reporting. The picture that emerges from this study is one of predominantly well-intentioned and skilled journalists being caught at the nexus of a range of limitations – procedural, resource-related and not least political. Colin Bickler told us after reading our study that it is very easy for journalists to be alienated by reading critical approaches that are fixed and sweeping. They do not reflect the dynamics of this sphere and expertise of the journalists that try to navigate its complexities, and we would agree with that.

6 Humanitarian reporting

When conflicts erupt overseas or when natural disasters such as hurricanes and earthquakes wreak havoc, the news media erupt into a frenzy of action to report the scenes of devastation. This is rapidly followed by outpourings of sympathy, the relief efforts and the heart-rending accounts of survivors and eyewitnesses. It seems on the surface to be a natural response to what is the most newsworthy of situations – unexpected events involving thousands, maybe millions, of lives. Television packages contain grainy, hand-held mobile telephone images of giant waves crashing against what was once a paradise beach for holidaymakers. Newspapers carry harrowing picture-led feature stories about vast communities facing starvation or disease brought on by famines or wars. Readers, viewers and listeners are invited to identify with the plight of the helpless and the hopeless, to imagine their suffering and their vulnerability. Not surprisingly, this type of reporting has grown in magnitude in response to the growing emphasis on human-interest reporting, that is, reporting that centres on the emotional, human implications of events and issues. Cases in point have been the recurring famines in Africa, the flight of refugees from ethnic cleansing in the former Yugoslavia and earthquake devastation wrought upon the already embattled communities in Asia and the Middle East.

Yet, for the journalism researcher, there is nothing simple and straightforward about the way such stories are selected and reported. The fact that technology can bring events to the screen in real time has implications for the way that events are perceived, and for the way they are potentially reinterpreted by powerful policy-makers. The rise in the status of the humanitarian aid agency and the powerful role it can play in framing stories and orchestrating the work of journalists has become a significant question. Additionally, the personal subjectivities of editors and commissioning editors can determine whether or not a cause may be reported, and if so how. Furthermore, there are major fears that once again, simplification of world events leads to misunderstandings about the role of the West in the underlying causes of disasters and conflicts. There appears to be an impasse in the relationship between different stakeholders in the humanitarian effort. Yet each of these stakeholders – aid agencies, journalists, the afflicted and governments – has a mutually dependent role.

This chapter will examine some critical accounts of the work of the humanitarian correspondent, who travels to some of the most challenging terrains in the world to bring home the plight of the most needy. It will be demonstrated that most of this work has tended to focus on moral and ethical matters in relation to reporting. This is extremely important, thorough and illuminating work, but there remains further territory that needs interrogating if we are to better grasp the complexity of the reporting process. This territory is the experience of the journalist who is trying to get his or her story covered, the hurdles they face and the parameters within which their access and writing is constrained. Therefore, after reviewing the available literature, there will be an analysis of the working life of award-winning *Sunday Times* journalist Ann McFerran. Here, it becomes evident that the coverage we receive has come about after a lengthy process of negotiation and reflection on the part of journalists, editors and sources. New questions emerge about the power of metropolitan-based editors to shape coverage, about the power of aid agencies and about the journalist's drive to create a picture of hope and possibility when conditions are far from optimistic.

Critical enquiry into compassionate reporting

Throughout the industrialised world, the public envisions developing nations as crisis-ridden, diseased and disabled by corruption according to critical approaches to the media's reporting. The fault does not lie totally with journalists; their efforts to alert readers and viewers promptly as disaster unfolds can motivate fundraising and governmental response. But it is a recurring concern of academics that Western audiences often lack sufficient knowledge – or any knowledge – of developing countries because reports of extreme events such as famines and wars tend to create false impressions of everyday life in those zones. The concerns of scholarly research into journalism's reporting of humanitarian crises have been twofold: first the emphasis on news values that prioritise drama and human interest rather than sustained reporting, and second the lack of background information to contextualise events, so that audiences can visualise but may not understand what they are seeing. In recent years, a series of approaches to humanitarian reporting has emerged, including 'compassion fatigue' and the 'CNN effect'.

In terms of the first concern, Susan Moeller (1999) writes that after the massive global response to Michael Buerk's BBC report of starving children in Ethiopia, which culminated in Live Aid, famine relief was no longer in vogue as a news story. 'Six years later, news of African famine evoked a "been there, done that" attitude. . . . It's the media that are at fault. How they typically cover crises helps us to feel over stimulated and bored all at once' (Moeller 1999: 8–9). The media industry is part of the entertainment industry, she continues, that must forever look for new ways to inspire audience attention (1999: 10). Accordingly, it has been observed that humanitarian crises are unlikely to get in the news unless something has happened or is happening that meets the criteria of newsworthiness covered in Chapter 2. The three key news buttons that must be pressed, it has been shown, are: unexpectedness, human interest and the extrinsic factor of production whereby there must be good pictures and/or audio.

The findings are highlighted in the largest scale survey of humanitarian reporting so far carried out, by Steven Ross of Columbia University, under the auspices of the Reuters Foundation and the Fritz Institute, published in 2004. The relative infrequency of humanitarian issues means that they tend to be covered by general reporters rather than specialists. As a consequence, it is the everyday news values that are used to measure their worthiness. According to Ross, the question becomes:

> 'Why should my news organisation invest in such stories TODAY when they will be here tomorrow and there are so many stories that MUST be covered today?' Factors such as the number of deaths and other potentially 'sensational' aspects of a tragedy weigh heavily in decisions to cover.
>
> (2004: 6)

The study identifies three prominent newsworthiness criteria for covering humanitarian stories:

- Number of deaths
- Suffering of children
- Compelling visuals

This confirms the findings of Niblock (2005) that production values ring high on newsworthiness as much as the inherent content of the story. Likewise, Bailey and Peterson (1989) see the power of the distribution of video footage as having a huge influence over what stories will be covered in world television. Without video footage a story has much less chance of being run. Some stories are used simply because there is footage (Cohen *et al.* 1996). And of course the kind of footage that is available also predetermines the kind of angle that can be given to a story.

The challenge for journalists accused of ignoring stories once they become habitual is how to continue to engage audiences when nothing new is happening. In his editorial for *Asian Age* on 8 January 2005, days after the Asian tsunami struck, editor M. J. Akbar warned the aftermath means a return to habitual indifference. 'Tomorrow – tomorrow, not the day after, for I am in the news business and know how ephemeral is the nature of news – the tsunami will ebb from the headlines.' He added: 'The poor will remain with us. The privileged will return to their indifference. . . . The privileged, in the meanwhile, are wallowing in conscience-management. Every so often the rich need a tsunami after another glut of

Christmas shopping.' In this sense, the timing of the tsunami coverage can be read as being framed by comparisons with normality in Western culture, but keeping the aid pouring in after the first shockwave is difficult if journalists scale down their reporting.

Most scholarly attention to humanitarian reporting has focused on television. The power of the visual media to encourage and maintain powerful and influential assistance has been dubbed the 'CNN effect'. This term is synonymous with the implied impact of 24-hour rolling broadcast news on foreign policy. In 1992, President Bush Snr placed troops in Somalia after viewing media coverage of starving refugees. This decision was questioned sharply on the basis of whether American interests were really at stake. Was CNN deciding where the military goes next? Less than a year later, shortly after the broadcast pictures of a dead American serviceman being dragged through the streets of Mogadishu, President Clinton's decision to withdraw US troops seemed to confirm the power of CNN. Reviewing numerous accounts of the CNN effect by academics and critics, Piers Robinson in his 2002 book *The CNN Effect*, explains its prominence in accounts of reporting of humanitarian crises: 'To a significant extent the CNN effect has persisted throughout the 1990s. For example, members of the policy-making establishment have reasserted their belief in the power of the news media to drive western responses to humanitarian crises' (Robinson 2002: 11). In support, he cites Tony Blair in his 1999 speech during the air raids on Serbia, in which he claimed that politicians were still fending off the 'danger of letting wherever CNN roves be the cattle prod to take a global conflict seriously' (2002: 11).

Ironically, in this age of real-time coverage, camera crews and reporters find it increasingly difficult to get into trouble spots, and are assisted in no small part by aid agencies. It is a concern amongst critics and journalists alike that they must rely so heavily on NGOs as sources and eyewitnesses. It may be no coincidence that aid agency media activity has grown in tandem with the decline in newsroom budgets allocated to overseas work, especially since concentration and globalisation of media ownership since the mid 1980s (see Chapter 1). Until the harrowing TV footage of starving children in Ethiopia which led to the Live Aid records and concerts, few people would have heard of Médecins Sans Frontières or Save the Children, whereas today these are household names thanks to concerted efforts to ensure a high media profile. Their efforts to break through into dangerous territory when traditional survival networks break down, either through conflict or natural disaster, has captured the public's imagination. Their teams of staff and volunteers are depicted undertaking dangerous, challenging and selfless acts that are wholly admirable. Given the emotive nature of their undertakings, and their growing visibility thanks to 24-hour rolling news broadcasts and sophisticated media relations, it is no surprise that aid agencies have proliferated. Today, it is estimated that there are literally thousands of aid agencies in existence throughout the world.

According to the prominent British international editor Lindsey Hilsum, writing in *The Observer*, emergency aid relief business grew from 'a small element in the larger package of development into a giant, global, unregulated industry worth 2,500 million pounds sterling a year. Most of that money is provided by governments, the European Union, and the United Nations' (31 December 1995). A key critic of the rise to prominence of the aid agency is Michael Maren. In his 1997 book *The Road to Hell*, he describes how while the media's admiration for NGO workers is entirely justified, they downplay the power that agencies have in actually shaping the ways these stories are covered. Similarly David Rieff (1997), of the World Policy Institute, wrote that this is because of restricted newsroom budgets:

> Whether it was in Mogadishu, Sarajevo, or Goma, more often than not print and television journalists turned to a member of the humanitarian non-governmental organisation (NGO) for the story on the ground – not to mention transportation, lodging, and companionship.
> (www.netnomad.com/rieff.html)

This might be partly explained by Ross's observation that after newsworthiness, the second factor determining whether or not a humanitarian issue will be reported is cost: 'Responses to numerous questions in our survey reveal that news organisations do not feel they can invest more money to send reporters to areas where aid is being administered' (2004: 6).

During the war in the former Yugoslavia, journalists were prevented from entering large parts of Bosnian Serb territory. BBC reports, for example, were reliant upon the unconfirmed testimonies of refugees fleeing across borders into refuges run by international aid agencies such as the International Red Cross and UNHCR. Consequently, it has been documented how these agencies offered the only eyewitness accounts of atrocities which led to action at international political level. For example Young (2001), in her study of the profile-raising role of NGOs, described how UNHCR reports of appalling conditions in Bosnian Croat-run detention camps received heavy coverage in the international media in 1993. This led to Western political pressure on the Croatian authorities in Zagreb, the main sponsors of the Bosnian Croats. She wrote: 'This in turn resulted in the Bosnian Croats agreeing to grant the ICRC full access to the camps (which had until then been denied for almost six months), and to allow UNHCR to resettle the detainees to third countries' (2001: 785). Young wrote that this war was easy for aid agencies to market to journalists because of resonant newsworthy themes of dramatic rescues, bloodshed and easily identifiable perpetrators.

> The situation was of particular interest to the European and North American public, as to many it recalled memories of the Second World

> War with victims who looked and lived like them, and served as an unsettling reminder that conflict and suffering were not as far away as they had imagined. It was therefore inevitable that the humanitarian operations of UNHCR and ICRC would be very much in the public eye.
>
> (Young 2001: 802)

In addition to feeding the press with information, UNHCR enabled reporters and crews to get into inaccessible areas and to 'where UNHCR wanted the suffering of the civilian population to be exposed' (2001: 803). Staff were encouraged to speak openly to the press and broadcast media, a practice that was criticised by the International Red Cross, seeing UNHCR's programme as a 'humanitarian circus'. While the use of the media helped gain access to victims, in some cases UNHCR was forced to devote a disproportionate amount of resources to a small number of individuals who had captured the media's attention. An injured baby named Irma in the Sarajevo hospital, for example, received massive media exposure in the British press which led to inordinate pressure on UNHCR to evacuate her to safety. Might those resources have been more democratically utilised elsewhere?

The CNN effect has, however, been disputed in research by the Copenhagen-based Centre for Development Research. Gorm Rye Olsen, Nils Carstensen and Kristian Høyen (2003) acknowledge that in some emergencies, humanitarian agencies and the media interact so closely with, and depend so much on, specific governments, that humanitarian assistance becomes a tool of foreign policy and international crisis management. But they counter that other factors, notably national security threats, were paramount in decision-making by foreign governments. The authors state:

> It is also unlikely that the large amount of aid for Kosovo resulted only from the massive media coverage of the area in 1999. . . . The resulting coverage of the humanitarian crisis – propelled by well-crafted NATO media spin – turned contributing to the emergency assistance to the Kosovars into a civil duty. As the military became deeply involved in supporting the humanitarian operation, humanitarian assistance to Kosovo became mixed up with the objectives of the military campaign. So much so that humanitarian assistance to Kosovo became a crisis management tool for the NATO governments trying to deal with yet another foreign policy and security concern in the Balkans.
>
> (Olsen *et al.* 2003: 109)

They conclude that ultimately journalists have very different priorities from aid agencies:

> Sometimes the media may help them in highlighting a particular situation. More often humanitarian agencies will be on their own.

> The media fundamentally have their own very different agendas. It is a bit like a holiday romance: one second he is there but when you really, really need him, he is long gone.

In line with this argument, some senior aid agency representatives have been openly critical of media coverage, employing theoretical discourses to support their assertions. For example, in 1996 Gilbert Holleufer, a Red Cross communications advisor, wrote:

> For what moral justification can be found for broadcasting, night after night, all too summary newsflashes showing throngs of starving people, piles of corpses and seemingly endless scenes of horror? And what justification can be found for showing certain scenes rather than others? Finally, is any serious attempt made to explain what is shown? It would seem that the legitimate moral questions which pictures of human tragedy raise for television viewers or readers too often receive unsatisfactory answers. The media increasingly confine themselves to covering – the word, with its sense of covering up, is appropriate – humanitarian crises and situations of armed conflict in all too superficial a way: by concentrating on visual shock effects, they only scratch the surface of the problems raised.

Holleufer expresses concern about the growing voyeurism of a mass media that is ever hungry to fill airtime. He warns that the speed of journalism allows insufficient time for careful ethical reflection. Images and footage, he argues, enable audiences to visualise events but not to necessarily understand them. Instead of portraying those subjected to immense suffering purely as victims, he says, they should be allowed to speak for themselves of their plight and of their courage.

Nevertheless, aid agencies remain closely in tune with news agendas in order to create opportunities for coverage, such as the use of celebrities to draw attention to overseas initiatives. This is in part in response to seeing their own concerns eclipsed in news agendas by 'sexier' material. Joelle Tanguy, a worker at the New York office of Médecins Sans Frontières, writes how the OJ Simpson trial distracted attention from the Rwandan genocide and how, in 1994, the Monica Lewinsky saga overtook famine devastation in Africa where mortality rates had rocketed:

> In July, a nurse who had just returned from working in a feeding centre in Sudan was sitting in a national television news studio and being fitted with a microphone for an interview when a new twist in the Starr investigation caused the producer to abruptly cancel the segment.
>
> (Tanguy 1999)

In terms of the second theoretical concern about lack of context, if most of the developed world's information about the developing world comes from news media and relief organisations, they may unintentionally contribute to distorted images. Furthermore, critics argue that Western viewers and readers receive and read this information without any context or background information to inform their judgement. It is argued thus that news audiences' perceptions of crises in the developing world are formed largely by accounts of the exceptions rather than the norms of everyday life.

African countries have been critical of the way that the Western news agencies only take an interest in Africa in times of famine or war and that these reports are presented without historical or political context (Benthall 1993). For example, in famines, such as in Somalia and Ethiopia in the 1990s, the Western news agencies mentioned nothing of the lengthy US involvement, arms trading and supporting of a violent dictator, in return for military bases, which caused massive population displacement. The news agencies have been widely criticised for producing news that has a Western interest. They tend to leave unreported the power relations that exist between countries and cultures and do not deal with the fact that the Western powers and corporations have complex economic control over Third World countries.

Such has been the monopoly of control over global news that there has been much complaint by Third World organisations. UNESCO challenged Associated Press and Reuters in the early 1980s claiming that their global dominance was against the free flow of information. Britain and the US, under Thatcher and Reagan at the time, left UNESCO. UNESCO members had been critical of the imbalance of news production and distribution between the First and Third World countries (MacBride 1980). But the head start had by the Western powers, using the resources they plundered during the colonial period, means that it is impossible for the less wealthy parts of the world to develop their own resources. To set up such an organisation requires considerable amounts of finance. One reason that the agencies remain uncritical of global capitalism is that the biggest part of Reuter's $5 billion or so annual revenue comes from financial services. Reuters produces most of this from trading in shares and currencies. Reuters is according to Boyd-Barrett and Rantanen (1998) the linchpin of day-to-day financial markets transactions worldwide. Yet this organisation also has massive power in terms of what information about the world gets disseminated. Some writers, such as Herman and McChesney (1997) and Herman and Chomsky (1988), see this connection as one reason that people around the world who challenge capitalism are reported as being guerrillas, terrorists, communist militia, etc., or even the reason why certain events never appear in the news media. But Ross argues that not all blame should be laid at the door of news organisations. He warns that NGOs have a long way to go before they can be seen as an efficient and reliable source:

> Press relations specialists at NGOs we surveyed noted repeatedly that field offices tend to be staffed by local nationals and that such personnel are inexperienced in press relations and unfamiliar with what might be at stake when working with a reporter from outside the region.
>
> (Ross 2004: 6)

Given this impasse, by what means can we successfully unpack and interrogate the actual work of real-life reporters in this most emotive and challenging of contexts? How are we to develop practices and policies that ensure the highest professional and ethical standards, which perform the consensual function of the journalist as a watchdog and the eyes and ears of the world? It certainly appears to be the case, when talking to journalists, that this type of work is not undertaken lightly or without consideration for its potential effects and implications. A close examination of the professional function and identity of the humanitarian reporter may reveal a more complex and reflexive process than normative and theoretical accounts of content and context. This is because there is little work undertaken on the journalists themselves, and this is possibly because there is a lack of a methodology in journalism studies to explore the motivations and feelings of the practitioner. To this end, we need to look beyond the confines of political economy, history and text, and further to the intersection of philosophy and moral responsibility.

The work of Zygmunt Bauman (2001) may be helpful in identifying, from a socio-psychological and philosophical perspective, the underlying causes and solutions to the apparent impasse between some areas of theory and practice in humanitarian reporting. Bauman (2001: 3) observes how we look longingly at the notion of community – 'it is the kind of world which is not, regrettably, available to us – but which we would dearly love to inhabit and which we hope to repossess'. In a world where market ideologies have become dominant, we have increasingly lost a sense of working together to make change. A critic of liberal capitalism, Bauman identifies our insecurity in the context of competition, so that problems are not viewed collectively as a societal issue. Rather we are offered solutions that are individual and personal. Hence overarching problems are seen as personal, with the effect of dividing communities into 'them' and 'us'. In Bauman's account, individual action is unlikely to bring the results we are after, 'since it leaves the roots of insecurity intact; moreover it is precisely this falling back on our individual wits and resources that inject the world with the insecurity we wish to escape' (Bauman 2001: 144).

Drawing on the work of the philosopher Emmanuel Levinas, Bauman asserts that there should be greater efforts made to identify with the Other. In *Totality and Infinity* (1961), Levinas argues for the need to transcend ethical neutrality, beckoning greater intersubjectivity so that we better understand the suffering of others who may not be familiar to us. Levinas argues that we need to be aware that modern thought is predicated on the primacy of selfhood, the idea that our needs come before those of others. Bauman accepts this and identifies how the poor are miscast always as the Other. As an illustration, he comments on Deputy Prime Minister Gordon Brown's suggestion that the unemployed be given mobile telephones to help them find employment, thus curtailing their freedom to provide them with freedom.

This model seems to find parallels in criticisms of reporting of Africa, such as the media frenzy surrounding the baby who was born in a treetop while torrents of flood water raged beneath her and her terrified mother. There are flaws in this argument when we consider the professional and ethical duty of reporters to be impartial, to be mediators as opposed to commentators. Bauman's approach inscribes the reporter as someone who must present a subjective view of the afflicted. But what informs that subjective view, and does it skew power relations between reporter and reported if one imposes their view onto the other? The unanswered questions that emerge from this review of the limited number of studies into this area include the need to thoroughly explore the nature and extent of coverage. In the following interview with the award-winning *Sunday Times* journalist Ann McFerran we will see the extent to which Bauman's ethical considerations, as well as the other factors discussed, inform her negotiation of myriad contextual and procedural constraints.

Case study: Ann McFerran

Ann McFerran has worked as a journalist for 30 years. More recently, she has written about human rights issues, post-conflict situations, and Aids in Africa and Asia for the British press. Having been theatre editor for *Time Out* (from 1975 to 1983) she now works as a freelance feature writer, mostly for *The Sunday Times*. Ann also reports on international issues, most recently about female Rwandan genocide survivors who are HIV positive; Aids in Zambia; child-headed households in Malawi and child trafficking. She has worked closely with aid agencies but has not been uncritical. In 2004, she won Amnesty International's magazine journalist of the year award for her report on how aid failed to reach the untouchables after the Gujarat earthquake. Her post-conflict coverage includes genocide orphans in Rwanda, rehabilitation of child soldiers in Uganda and much more. Ann has interviewed many celebrities, and has accompanied some, including Susan Sarandon, Robbie Williams, Jessica Lange, Mia Farrow and Roger Moore, as ambassadors for UNICEF, on their travels to meet the world's poorest and most neglected people. Ann became a roving reporter by default in the last 10 years.

> When my eldest son was working as volunteer in Tanzania, the editor I was working for at the *Sunday Times* said 'we must get you out

there'. I loved Africa and I fell over stories that I felt needed to be told everywhere I went. I also met a young photographer to work with, and having covered several stories people grew to trust me. One of the first stories in particular that I came across was all about a Kenyan version of the long-running BBC Radio Four series *The Archers*. This programme was listened to by farmers as it disseminated agricultural information. But it was also used to promote Aids awareness. It was 1997 when the world was beginning to realise the devastating impact Aids was having throughout Africa. When I pitched this very African story but with a very British parallel, lots of editors read about this, they all wanted me to cover it – until they realised the cost of sending me out there to do the story.

Ann has to prepare detailed costings for editors as part of her pitch. It costs 100 dollars to hire a 4 × 4 in Africa, while NGOs often have facilities in place.

One of the first big lessons about doing foreign stories is that it is very expensive. I spoke to loads of editors who simply said 'We just don't have that kind of budget.' I really wanted to tell this story so I got a cheap ticket to Kenya (it was February) and met up with my photographer, the late Nick Robinson, who was living there full-time. I managed to sell the finished piece to the *Times Educational Supplement* as an education story, and to the *Telegraph* as a news story. Just before I went I bumped into an editor at *Red* magazine, who wanted it as a travel piece. I more than covered my costs, in fact I made money on it. But that's unusual – an important lesson I've learnt is that if you are going to be a careerist, money-making journalist you should put the foreign stuff to one side. You have to do it because you want to do it.

Ann's motivations seem to be driven by a love of reporting but also by her passion for her subject matter. This has led to numerous associations with aid agencies.

As a result of that story, Plan International called me up and I began a long period of working with them. When I met with their press people, we brainstormed potential story ideas for some time, including reformed prostitute support groups and other stories to grab editors' attention. My experience and news sense as a journalist was very important to them. They then told me the extraordinary figure of the number of child-headed households predicted in Africa over the next couple of years. This was early 1998 and I certainly hadn't seen any feature on it. Plan said they would cover my travel costs if I could get a commission. Since then that has often been the way I've been able

> to write about Aids and human rights issues in Africa and Asia – and it hasn't compromised my independence.

Ann described a series of protracted negotiations with a national commissioning editor who wanted something different from her, such as a focus on child-headed households in Britain as well as Africa to make the story more newsworthy in terms of relevance. But Ann was unwilling to dilute the story and approached *The Times*, who commissioned it. Ann's reliance on NGOs in Kenya was apparent, not only for practical support on the ground but also for finding sources. Ann is very positive about this:

> The aid agency workers operating in these environments are like social workers and are worth their weight in gold. A journalist can explain to them, without being too adamant, what they are looking for, and they can help identify potential interviewees. We found a 12-year-old girl whose father was alive and very ill with the disease. Her mother was dead, and she was looking after five siblings.

Though Ann stresses that UK editors can often be too prescriptive about the types of case study they want – in this case the paper was not pleased that the girl's father was still alive so that she was not a full orphan.

> Phone calls go backwards and forwards negotiating with them. They also often want to know before you go on the trip who you will be interviewing and something of their story. Often, this just isn't possible, but this demand is becoming more prevalent. I can only put this down to anxiety and concern about budgets on the part of editors, rather than faith in the journalists who will find the story.

At 12, and with one parent still alive,

> Mary wasn't exactly what *The Times* were looking for, but we were adamant her story should be told. We asked if we could come back to see her, scrapped the rest of our itinerary and spent the next day with her. We didn't go with money, we took foodstuff, flour, sugar, something really useful. It was heartbreaking and fantastic at the same time. We went back one year later and saw her again.

This quest for newsworthiness through the suffering of children confirms the findings of Ross. However, Ann's sensitive approach to this, and her determination to negotiate with editors rather than to concede to all wishes, suggests a reflexive, self-conscious involvement with her subject matter, in accordance with Bauman.

Ann also visited Uganda with Plan International to report on the emerging Aids situation, and it caused her to question her role as a journalist working in a tragic context. This was at a time when the reporting of Aids by journalists was quite limited, though Ann says that now, with experience, she would not be particularly shocked by what she encountered. She said:

> They took us to this little remote town, where a line of people were sitting on a bench queuing up to be tested for Aids. The photographer, a very sensitive guy, said that he felt he was looking at death row. I didn't want to listen to someone being told that they had Aids, and wasn't sure I should be there as it felt intrusive, and I wasn't sure I could handle it emotionally. But the Plan representative turned round and said: 'This is your job'. Now I think she was absolutely right. In this situation, my feelings don't matter. It's my job to tell the truth of a situation. She helped me by simulating an encounter between doctor and Aids patient and we role-played it. It was so powerful we both had tears in our eyes.

Here the NGO appears to have played a very direct role in pushing for the story to be covered.

Ann's encounters with families ripped apart by Aids led her to reflect further on her role as mediator.

> We met one family in a remote part of Uganda, where there was a wife with really small children. She was breastfeeding one, another was very ill and her husband was skeletal and days from death. I went in to see him very apologetically, but he said the story must be told. It is very difficult when you see the reality of what Aids means, and when you're a mother yourself. It did confirm to me that I wanted to go back and tell people what was happening – it became a vocation. On the plane back I found it even very difficult eating food and doing things we take for granted, thinking of how little these people had to survive on. It'll hit you at very strange times, like when you are in the bath or in the middle of the afternoon. At first, you will just feel like crying uncontrollably.

It has been mentioned that NGOs have responded to media fascination with celebrity to employ high profile people as ambassadors. Ann has travelled extensively with top stars, though rather than simply write an awe-struck piece that praises the celebrity's interaction with the needy, she has openly addressed the theatrical nature of such endorsement, and has sought to illuminate what has really propelled the stars in question to take part.

> It was very odd literally three days later to go to Sri Lanka with Robbie Williams and Ian Dury on a completely different kind of trip with UNICEF, who were promoting polio vaccinations. The nature of

> working with celebrities is very different to the previous type of first-hand reporting that I have done. Yes it is a way of selling difficult issues, such as polio, but I think for a journalist you are always doing it through the presence of the celebrity which has obvious limitations.

In *The Times* magazine on 17 October 1998, in a feature entitled 'The kids aren't all right', Ann wrote:

> Dury is by turns charming and cantankerous, one moment extolling UNICEF's mission with the panache of a committed zealot, the next fuming about 'the cult of personality. This isn't bloody *Hello!* magazine. I'm here for UNICEF'. Dury's ambiguous take reflects most people's views on celebrities and charity. UNICEF has had its star ambassadors since the Fifties, but it was Bob Geldof's headline-hitting mission to 'feed the world' in the mid-eighties, and the potent mix of film footage of starving children with a popular song that was surely the forerunner to this trip. UNICEF won't put a figure on the kind of money that Williams and Dury help to generate, but a spokesperson says: 'Without the help of celebrities it would be very difficult to make the public aware of the work we're doing. You cannot put a cost on their involvement.'

This shows that Ann is all too aware of the machine within which she operates and is transparently reflexive within it. Nevertheless, Ann knows her target newspapers very well, and has so far found her stories to be barely edited or altered from the original. She also says that she would have most likely written the same story – whether for the *Telegraph*, *The Times* or the *Guardian*. 'I wouldn't say there was very much difference in the way I have written for different titles,' she said.

But conflicts can occur when the reporter close to a story has a different idea of the priorities than a UK-based editor. Ann was heading to central America with Plan International to report on the aftermath of a serious earthquake, focusing on support systems for women. One UK editor wanted her to focus on the impact of the quake on doctors and lawyers, who were a target audience for them. But the women who suffered most were poverty-stricken and socially excluded women who lived in the worst-affected areas. A further editor wanted her to focus on prostitution in the area.

> My editor desperately wanted to lead with the prostitute story, but I was very clear in my head on my focus – I was very committed to ordinary peasant women and I led with an incredibly powerful story about a young woman describing seeing a mountain literally collapse in on itself. Eventually, after much discussion, we achieved a compromise whereby I reported the prostitutes second but did not lead on them. You have to be prepared not to make yourself very popular!

Having witnessed appalling human tragedy, Ann says she is glad the medium of print allows her some control over the way she expresses and retells those stories.

> One of the great things about print is that you can suggest without it being too upsetting or traumatising. With film you only get one go at it, whereas when I come home I can still do lots of things with it. I am anti-censorship, but I do sometimes control my stories if I think words can't express it well enough, and reality can make you feel so desperate and it leaves no sense of hope. You have to offer hope. You want people to be aware of the fact there's this huge and extraordinary continent with amazing people who we have much to learn from, who have been beset by these terrible things. It is our human duty to go in and help. But I also want people to qualify that awareness by sending off some money. That makes you evolve, and become a joined-up member of the human race. You have to be really careful – it's become its own cliché and we have a duty to find other ways of telling and retelling.

She adds that she was very aware of the need to listen carefully and allow those she encountered time to recount very difficult experiences. She said that in some cases, such as in the wake of Rwandan rape atrocities, she would hear stories from women survivors who wanted her to bear witness. She said:

> But you have to listen properly and ask very tough questions. One reporter said to me that she didn't 'go in for the kill', but I believe it is often right to go deeper to allow people to express what they have endured.

Nonetheless she is pragmatic about the limitations:

> Once you've told a story – of the child soldier, child-headed household, life in the day of a mother dying of Aids, it does honestly become difficult to find a new angle. The truth is it's an ongoing tragedy and it is getting worse. There is all the more reason for reporting it. They are the same problems, but when you talk to editors they say, 'well we've done that'. Like Rwanda, the Darfur story is complicated, there isn't a simple case of goodies and baddies, there are lots of grey areas. Certain kinds of newspapers and magazines want a specific type of human interest story. Others, like the *Sunday Times*, want heavy investigative reports and scandals. I don't think placing these Aids, post-conflict and human rights issues stories is getting any easier.

Conclusion

Ann's case study both confirms and contradicts a number of issues raised by theoretical and critical accounts of reporting humanitarian affairs. First, her experiences confirm research on how ongoing issues have to be presented according to prominent newsworthiness criteria, such as drama, children and celebrity to attract editors. The fact that much of her reporting is accompanied by startling images also demonstrates the compelling power of the visual in this area of coverage. However, Ann always negotiates the angles and expectations that commissioning editors put to her. She does not always agree and will strive to follow the agenda that she feels is most important. This has been a successful strategy for Ann, as a confident and expert journalist, though it might be harder to stand up to a commissioning editor as a newer freelance. This demonstrates that news angles can in some cases be negotiated between the reporter, aid agency and editor, rather than it being a top-down approach from senior managers. This still begs the question, what say does the other stakeholder – the afflicted and suffering – have in this relationship? Second, Ann is in many cases reliant on NGOs for financial assistance and practical news-gathering support, confirming critical accounts. Once again, however, that relationship and power is negotiated as Ann's primary commitment is to her story. Her coverage of celebrities enlisted by aid agencies to profile-raise is but one example of her querying of strategies. She herself would like nothing more than to always be fully funded by a foreign desk, though it is clear that she still supports the aim of charities to raise as much money as possible for their causes. This is again demonstrated through her editorial approach, which is to create hope. In terms of the CNN effect, Ann's work appears to be more driven by untold stories and individual accounts rather than through attempts to rally policy initiatives, though her work on Aids in Africa may have some implications for US foreign policy. More work needs to be done with commissioning editors to discover to what effect their rivals' coverage of humanitarian issues might inflect on their own editorial decision-making. Of course compassion fatigue, as discussed by Moeller, could be read as one possible reason why stories such as Ann's are getting harder to place.

Ann's experiences raise a series of new questions for journalism studies, that require a deeper study of the actual practices of humanitarian reporting. The key issue is how can journalism studies help journalists themselves navigate the obstacles and dilemmas they face? Ann's freelance career, like that of so many humanitarian reporters, relies on being able to attract commissions and sell stories to editors which are expensive to produce. Given the economies of scale in newsrooms, compromises have to be made, which includes working to aid agency agendas. Much research has focused on TV coverage rather than the type of work Ann undertakes, where she has a longer time frame and is more interested in personal stories than dramatic footage. But there are still important issues around safety and access for which she relies on the NGO. More in-depth studies of similar work could be evaluated to illuminate to what extent NGO involvement compromises the story's impartiality by framing. Moreover, what journalists bring to the experience of reporting these traumatic stories needs to be interrogated. To what extent might recurring coverage affect a journalist's interpretation of events, which may have been shaped by previous experiences? Is that a good thing or might it be problematic?

Questions around policy also need to be raised and discussed. Suggestions have already emerged from some researchers, including Ross, who argues for establishing a single organisation to support journalists rather than individual NGOs (Ross 2004: 4). Journalists need to cover humanitarian crises more comprehensively and extensively, and tell untold stories, according to aid agencies such as Médecins Sans Frontières, which conducts an annual survey of unreported humanitarian crises. Cate (1994) calls for better training of international journalists so they are well-versed in the backgrounds to stories in order to educate their audiences.

7 Visual journalism

Reading the redesigns

News journalism is primarily thought of in terms of words. Those words may be spoken, in TV and radio bulletins, or written, in online or print journalism. Understandably, job advertisements and journalism training courses focus heavily on writing skills, such as style and concision, as proficiency in communication is essential for accuracy and ease of reading. But there is another key aspect of journalism communication which is becoming ever more prominent and a much-needed skill for reporters and editors alike. This is visual journalism, the ability to project a news story to readers and audiences through image and design as well as through text. From the inception of a story idea through to its editing, all the journalists involved must be thinking about creating a strong visual impact to help grab and maintain attention. Traditionally, the relationship between reporters and layout subs was one of some mistrust, fearing that stories might be over-zealously edited to fit the allocated space. Nowadays, with the arrival of design editors and multimedia newsrooms, there is more of a symbiotic relationship between the news-gathering and news output parts of the operation.

Journalism studies has yet to acquire a critical vocabulary with which to investigate the development of visual journalism. While there have been studies of news photography and meaning, which are predominantly from semiotic approaches to visual texts, there has been little if any prominent investigation on the impact of typography, layout and picture editing. A survey of existing critical literature pinpoints academic concerns about the ideological meanings of images, the encoding of ideology in, say, war photography. Yet this work lacks a close examination of the contexts and practices of news visual design which may affect decision-making.

Looking outside journalism and media studies, in graphic design and areas of cognitive psychology, work has been undertaken to explore the way that aspects of visual design, such as colour and typography, work for audiences. While these studies can bring a fresh approach and vocabulary to journalism studies, they need to be directly relevant to the rapid pace and considerations of the news environment. As a response to these methodological issues, this chapter sets out to describe and analyse the theories, practices and processes of visual journalism critically. In doing so, it will illuminate a highly influential and fundamental news practice. Central to the investigation will be the work of a real-life design editor who played a leading role in the rebranding of a UK regional morning newspaper.

The underlying theme of this chapter is the growing reflexivity and multi-skills of the contemporary journalist. Text-based studies of news pages and bulletins born out of semiology do not account for the actual practices of real journalists on any given production cycle. However, from the perspective of the design-oriented journalist, there is little material available for them to better understand the nuances of font choice, the connotations of colour and the effects of image selection. It will be argued that in visual journalism, practice and theory directly intersect as the task of engaging readers and 'selling' stories requires immense skill and acute intuition. Design editors, and the reporters that work alongside them, have to be creative and innovative at the same time as meeting a demanding production turnaround. To illustrate these points, this chapter will closely examine the process of rebranding the *Liverpool Daily Post*. In doing so, it will expose some of the limitations and challenges of text-based analyses, and opens up a space to think of journalism studies as an intersection of numerous themes. In this context, the themes will be drawn not just from media, but also from theories of the visual and theories of the city. This shows that we cannot think of journalism inside neatly determined parameters.

Redesigning newspapers

Careful formatting of the appearance of newspapers and other news media in order to reach target groups is a phenomenon sweeping the world, driven by systematic market research and increased competition for advertising (see Chapters 1 and 3). Over the past couple of decades, there has been a massive increase in market influence on the news media (McManus 1994; Garcia Aviles *et al.* 2004). This, accompanied by technological advances, has led to changes in the emphases in news production, along with the introduction of newer job titles, such as design editor, and the prerequisite of multi-skilling for new entrants to the journalism career. With the rise of on-screen full-page make-up and the demise of hot metal and traditional photographic darkrooms, newsrooms and news production look very different to those described in the classic ethnographies (Fishman 1980; Tuchman 1973). Nowadays news output, whether textual, visual or broadcast, must consistently, in all of its dimensions or modes, be tailored for the particular slice of the market that is being offered to advertisers. As well as thinking about choice and angle of story (as described in Chapter 3), newspapers, first in the US and now across the globe, are thinking more carefully about visual elements on the page. These visual elements, such as fonts, colours, white space, graphs and images, set the mood for the newspaper. Put another way, they are the tone of voice for how the paper tells the news. Now page designers and sub-editors must choose communicative resources carefully in order to speak to specific lifestyle target groups.

Over the past two decades print journalism was thought to be in steep decline, but attention to print formats through the expansion of news design departments seems to have bucked the predicted trend. In the 1990s, when it became apparent that newspaper sales were steadily falling, editors and publishers were pursued by visionaries bearing electronic tablets and other technological trickery to stem the tide of news consumption to broadcast and the Internet. Yet, as newspaper design gurus such as Mario Garcia (2005) have identified, there has been a hitherto unpredicted turn to tabloid formats, once pilloried as being akin to a lack of quality.

The advent of the tabloid newspaper occurred in the 1830s, motivated by two of the same factors that drive journalism ownership today. First there was, and still is, the desire to cater for readers who are in a hurry, specifically in urban or metropolitan environments where commuters use public transport. The second was the drive towards human-interest journalism, offering bite-sized chunks of crime, sport and emotive reporting. Charles A. Dana, editor of the *New York Sun*, announced to readers in 1868:

> The *Sun* will specialise in presenting the news in a concise manner, with greater clarity, and will attempt to present a photographic report of significant events taking place in the world, but always doing it in a friendly, entertaining manner.

The myth that tabloid equates with lower quality journalism has been partly debunked due to the recent success of broadsheet newspapers that have turned compact, such as the *The Times* and the *Independent*, (which both made the switch in 2003) and the *Guardian* (in 2005). In the US, sixteen newspapers that similarly changed format in 2004 saw an average 4.6 per cent increase in circulation within weeks (INMA 2005).

The critical issue driving these changes is an awareness that redesign can alter the way readers navigate through news. Design factors, and not just text content, allow the newspaper to connect with readers. The stories may be excellent but if they are poorly packaged or cluttered, readership suffers. Commenting on the broadsheets who have moved to compact format, Hugo Drayton, former managing director of the *Telegraph*, described why weekday features now need to be concise in comparison with 10 years ago, stressing the change in reader lifestyle: 'less is more for the over-supplied, multi-tasking iPod generation' (*Guardian* 2005a). It is not just the length of the story; fonts that were around in the 1970s and 1980s can appear dated rather than classic to modern readers. On the day the *Guardian* re-launched with its new Berliner format, editor Alan Rusbridger wrote of the decision to change its 1980s David Hillman fonts to a new one which is 'intelligent', and that a new colour press would 'give greater emphasis and power to our photography and, we hope, make the whole paper a touch less forbidding than it sometimes may have seemed in the past' (*Guardian* 2005b).

It is not just reader demands that propel redesigns. Competition from web sites and other formats has forced newspapers to become very much more visually aware and design-led. Instead of telling the news, newspapers today seek to reflect the *personality* of their readership and locale. It is noteworthy that newspaper personnel in the UK have been looking to Europe and the US for a visual vocabulary to help them to achieve these goals. In Britain, it is mainly photographers and photojournalists who have explored the notion of visual journalism, rather than subs and designers. For instance, there is a visual journalism group as an off-shoot of the UK's Royal Photographic Society. They explain:

> Why Visual Journalism and not Photo-Journalism? The answer is simple. Visual Journalism embraces television news and film documentaries in addition to newspapers, magazines and books, and now, of course, the Internet. Thus the central focus of Visual Journalism is that the images involved are either published (or produced with publication in mind) in order to tell, illustrate, or support a factual story.
>
> http://www.rps.org/groups/vj.html

Outside the UK, a burgeoning print and online sector of consultants and networks has developed, such as the German-based Society for News Design, and the North American organisation of the same name, to support sub-editors and page designers. For example, page design consultant Ron Reason (www.ronreason.com) urges editors to think very much in mood terms: 'Clarify the goals of your paper, and ask whether words like "elegant", "retro", "modern", "sensational" or "edgy" should apply to the design . . . Consider how your paper's community, mission, competition, or staffing might have changed significantly in recent years.' The lack of discourse on visual journalism in the UK may have something to do with the traditional suspicion that layout might detract from the content of the story. The sub-editing 'bibles' for UK journalists are celebrated former *Sunday Times*' editor Harold Evans' series of books on editing and design (1972, 1973, 1974a, 1974b, 1986), and F.W. Hodgson's *Modern Newspaper Editing and Production* (1987). These texts present newspaper sub-editing and layout as a trade or craft, closely adhering to the newspaper printing's history as a unionised industry. Their style is hands-on and pragmatic, downplaying notions of artistic creativity of reflexivity. Yet the advent of on-screen page make-up, and the transformations this wrought on newspaper production personnel and organisation from the mid-1980s onwards, has necessitated and enabled multi-skilling of production staff. Traditionally, becoming a sub-editor was seen as a promotion after a young reporter had indentured.

Sub-editors played a pivotal role in the training of young reporters on local newspapers in the finer points of style and flow. Nowadays, since the explosion of pre-entry training and higher education programmes in journalism, it is possible to enter the news industry straight into sub-editing, sometimes even at national level. Visual journalism is not taught widely in the UK, but should be if new recruits are to have the ability to anticipate and respond to rapid developments in presentation.

Fonts are one of the key changes that occur when papers seek to redefine through rebranding. A study published in November 2004 found that newspapers are opting to use fewer and fewer typefaces despite the myriad on offer. Furthermore, many typefaces used in redesigns were designed specifically for the title, such as the new *Guardian* Egyptian font used on the UK Berliner (made by the Ascender Corporation.) The study of nearly 100 newspapers found that 10 fonts recur most frequently, including Poynter, Helvetica, Franklin Gothic and Times. The report's authors say this may have something to do with their transferability to an on-screen format. But there may be other more creative factors at play in the choice of fonts, colours and mood-creating visual devices that journalism training and journalism studies has not yet pinpointed or accounted for. For instance, there are other factors of change in relation to technology that will determine new design briefs, such as increased pagination and upgraded printing presses. There have also been huge changes in reader expectations thanks to ubiquitous graphic design in other media, such as popular music promos, animation, interactive media and the Internet, that place enormous pressure on newspapers to be seen as in touch. We must not forget that new entrants to journalism have also been exposed to more challenging and diverse visual communication than their predecessors, which will impact upon their own professional decision-making. These developments have not yet been taken into account in the academic studies of visual journalism.

Theories of visual news journalism

News visuals are driven by appealing to target audiences. In Chapter 3, we described how news organisations are using marketing theory and psychographics to closely identify audience segments and target their coverage accordingly. In the IRN case study, we exemplified how audience targeting is a news value criterion, and demonstrated how consideration for the implied listener affects the way a story is angled and packaged. A similar approach applies in print journalism too, as newspapers and magazines compete for readers and advertiser revenue, especially given the downward trend in circulation. We described how in marketing theory and practice there has been a move away from traditional social indicators of how a person might act and think, such as class, gender, age, etc., to a system of lifestyle market segmentation, or psychographics, which classifies consumers through consumption patterns and attitudes. The results of psychographic research are found in the research by the marketing company for the rebranding of the *Liverpool Daily Post*: 'Mr and Mrs target reader are a couple over the age of 35. They work in the professions, own their own small business or work in middle management . . .'

This is basic demographic information. But it soon shifts . . .

> They like to eat out regularly, hold dinner parties for friends, and during the week often eat quality supermarket meals.
>
> They are sophisticated, or certainly aspire to be so, and like to go to the theatre or cinema or shows.
>
> Personal finance is a major issue in their lives, whether it is funding a house purchase, or major home improvements, putting a child through private school, college or university, or saving for retirement.
>
> Their ideal role for themselves is probably the *Cold Feet* TV series couples; they see themselves as cool, modern, sophisticated, moderately affluent, fashionable, well informed, humorous and attractive.

Therefore the newspaper must reflect these values in every way. Market research, for example by the Poynter Institute in the US, aims to find out what kinds of design features best signify the lifestyle values associated with this group. So it is not only story content and style that can signify a particular lifestyle and its associated attitudes and values, but also colour, layout, typography and use of images.

Other psychographics describe different consumer groups. Here is an example from Mehotra and Wells (1979: 54–5)

> 'Fred the frustrated factory worker'
>
> Fred is young. He married young and had a family. It is unlikely that he had any plans to get a college degree, if he did he had to shelve them to find work to support his family. He is now a blue collar worker having trouble to make ends meet. He is disconnected and tends to feel that 'they' – big business, government, society – are somehow responsible for his state. He finds escape in movies and fantasies of foreign lands and cabins by quiet lakes. He likes to appear attractive to women, he has an active libido, and likes to think that he is a bit of a swinger.

Products and news must be suitably tailored to fit with this psychographic information. Therefore, these expressive meanings, these 'new rhetorics of desire and personal involvement' (Chaney 1996: 152), are now deliberately produced by designers and advertisers, and have become the key mediators of lifestyle (Hanke 1989).

When a newspaper or any other product goes through a redesign, it is often referred to as a rebrand. What is important for a brand of any product is that it must be immediately recognisable as meaning a particular set of values. A car might be branded to signify sophistication, a beer with designer fashion or friendship. If a brand is not immediately recognisable then it has failed. We would like to think about a brand as a set of representations and values that that are very much like 'discourses' as described in the work of Foucault (1972) and in Kress and Van Leeuwen (1996, 2001). Their book *Reading Images* looks for rules in visual design. By looking at the formal elements and structures of design – colour, perspective, framing and composition, Kress and Van Leeuwen examine the ways in which images communicate meaning. Drawing on an enormous range of examples – children's drawings, textbook illustrations, photojournalism, advertising images and fine art, as well as three-dimensional forms such as sculpture and architecture, the authors demonstrate that there are identifiable rules that govern visual design. These are rules that we can more or less rely on to create certain kinds of meanings. In other words, we can rely on colour, typography and layout to create specific meanings. In turn these meanings will contribute to creating certain discourses. For example, certain kinds of blue are associated with truth, science and coolness. Therefore blue is a popular colour for corporate logos and for news broadcasts.

Kress and Van Leeuwen (1996) draw on traditional theories in semiotics, such as Barthes (1977). Barthes was interested in the ways that images or elements in images worked as signs to convey meanings, a bit like words in language. For example, an image of a lion might be used to signify bravery, strength or even danger. Barthes thought that images did not have fixed meanings and therefore relied upon words to anchor them: in the case of a newspaper, web site or TV broadcast, this may be in the form of a caption or explanatory text at the bottom of the screen while events unfold.

Journalism studies analysts who have been influenced by Barthes have been concerned about the way that the visual can provide massive cues that anchor our understandings. These are then elaborated on by the text. Hartley's *Understanding News* (1982) identifies four modes of visual presentation in news reporting in his case study of the BBC's *Nine O' Clock News*. These visual conventions anchor and organise the news content. These modes are:

1 The 'talking head' – newsreaders and correspondents
2 Graphics
3 Nominations – captions or verbal introductions that name participants
4 Actuality – the footage (Hartley 1982: 108–9).

These visual conventions influence the prestige and credibility that audiences are likely to credit to speakers. Journalists are represented as an elite along with key spokespeople, while public participants in vox pops are rarely if ever nominated. He expresses concern that news audiences may be duped into receiving certain interpretations of events by semiotic techniques such as these:

> it is by no means clear that news is 'read' as information by many people. . . . It is quite possible that the 'preferred readings' so carefully structured into news accounts of events are simply not noticed – the 'readers' have their minds on other levels within the discourse.
>
> (Hartley 1982: 143)

Therefore we can say that the visual itself, in terms of both signs such as colour and typography and layout and formats, can offer a powerful form of communication.

Machin and Thornborrow (2003) describe the way that consumer-oriented lifestyles of women in the magazine *Cosmopolitan* are realised in texts, language style, layout image style, poses, clothing and make-up. These different modes of communication can be used to signify discourses of women being in control, fun and independent. These are some of the discourses established by feminism – that women should not be subordinate to men or domesticity – but the message of the magazine is not direct action related to women's equality. Readers of the magazine are encouraged to align themselves with the discourses and the values and purposes that they contain, not by direct action in the world, but through using the products sold in the magazine, striking the same poses, wearing the same clothes.

One of the key features of the regime of lifestyle is that people signify who they are through visual display. Products come with elaborate symbolic systems to provide resources for this display. Kress and Van Leeuwen (2001) argue that Barthes, and those who have followed his theory of image–text relationships, are missing an important point. They argue that the visual component of a text is independent of language. Whilst it may be connected to verbal text, it may not automatically be dependent upon it. And they argue that the visual modes, for example, used to communicate the consumer/feminist values of *Cosmopolitan*, can be systematically analysed and described.

What became clear during our ethnographic study which led to this chapter, is the great difference in approach between these semioticians and the approaches taken by practitioners. While the former strive to observe and describe systematic patterns in communication, the latter often describe design choices in terms of aesthetics, or simple practicalities of time, space and convention. Semioticians often fail to carry out a semiotic analysis in consultation with the text's producers in order to understand the economic motivations behind observed changes and to understand the motivations for choices of communicative tools. As a result, from the viewpoint of the practitioner, their analyses can seem absurd. For example, the massive symbolism they might see in the choice of an image might be more accurately explained as due to budget, copyright, or a contract with an image archive.

We attempt to find a more flexible and versatile critical methodology that enables a better understanding of what appears to be a more sophisticated process of editorial decision-making than theorists would have it. Kress and Van Leeuwen (1996) argue that we can develop a better understanding of contemporary popular cultural texts, such as newspapers and other visual media, if we adopt a multimodal approach. This simply means that we must study the linguistic mode of communication along with the visual mode of communication. From advertising, film and television to web sites, game environments and mobile technology, the texts that surround us today are increasingly multimodal. This is not peculiar to any one culture, but is accelerated through processes of globalisation.

Kress and Van Leeuwen explain:

> In the past, and in many contexts still today, multimodal texts (such as films or newspapers) were organised as hierarchies of specialist modes integrated by an editing process. Moreover, they were produced this way, with different, hierarchically organised specialists in charge of the different modes, and an editing process bringing their work together. Today, however, in the age of digitisation, the different modes have technically become the same at some level of representation, and they can be operated by one multi-skilled person, using one interface, one mode of physical manipulation.
>
> (2001: 2)

The emergence of the role of the design editor in the rebranding of a newspaper is a clear example of multimodality in practice, as is the reframing of reporters' perspectives so that their writing complements the visual style of the newspaper. Visual coherence is the order of the day, so that text complements image, image complements typography, and it all complements the marketplace's notion of the implied readership.

Newspaper design as a mediator of lifestyle: a multimodal analysis of the rebranding of the *Daily Post*

In common with the trend affecting many regional daily and evening titles, the *Post* was steadily losing readers. Circulation of UK paid-for regional newspapers fell by a third between 1982 and 2002 (Advertising Statistics Yearbook 2003, cited by the Competition Commission 2003). Senior executives at the paper's parent company, *Liverpool Daily Post and Echo*, owned by Trinity Mirror plc, commissioned in-house and contract research to help identify potential new readers. Editor Jane Wolstenholme and other senior editorial staff responded to the research and the evident shift in the social and cultural identity of Liverpool, Merseyside and the wider north west and north Wales area with a significant rebrand. In 2004 it unveiled a brand new look for the twenty-first century, with a wholesale redesign, a raft of new supplements and a bold new masthead – incorporating the word Liverpool for the first time in 25 years. The changes followed the *Post*'s split from its Welsh counterpart in autumn 2002. Previously, Welsh editions had been largely written and edited in Liverpool, which was felt by many to be out of touch with Wales's strong sense of its own identity. Following the split, the *Liverpool Daily Post* launched its dynamic, marketing-led manoeuvre to reflect the lives and aspirations of the region's increasingly consumer-oriented, cosmopolitan population. Ms Wolstenholme told HoldtheFrontPage.com in February 2004: 'It meant looking hard at our marketing proposition, and editorially it meant being prepared to present our readers with an entirely different package from the one they are used to' (Hold the Front Page 2004). Accordingly design editor Gary Bainbridge, the subject of this case study, set to work as if he was designing a completely new product.

Becoming design editor

Gary's first job in journalism was as one of the launch team of a small independent weekly title. He said: 'They advertised for "newspaper people", rather than specific job titles of reporter or sub. This meant I was involved in devising the newspaper's identity and drawing up the dummy. I really enjoyed it.' This provided Gary with a fundamental and formative sense of the newspaper as a product, with a clear brand identity. As a multi-skilled journalist, Gary combined subbing with reporting roles on other weeklies, before finally immersing himself in full-time production journalism. He joined the *Liverpool Echo* as a sub/designer, for three and a half years. The role of sub/designer combines the traditional role of the top-table sub and down-table sub. The top-table sub is the staffer who draws up the page layouts. The advertising department supplies 'shapes' to the subs department, which have any space sold for adverts clearly indicated. The top-table sub would draw a layout that would accommodate the advert and the stories that have been allocated to that particular page. This would then be passed to the down-table sub. The down-table sub edits copy for readability, consistency, punctuation, grammar and house style. They may be required to make cuts in order for the story to fit the allotted space. They write a headline and any other required page furniture, including picture captions, to the size and style determined by the top-table sub and the paper's visual protocols. As sub/designer, Gary combined the roles to work as a page editor, whereby he would draw up the page and edit the copy. This development in multi-skilling largely came about as a result of developments in on-screen page make-up software, making subbing in the twenty-first century a largely paper-free enterprise.

After promotion to assistant design editor on the *Echo*, Gary became design editor on the *Daily Post*. The design editor role reverted to splitting off the function of layout from copy subbing, allowing Gary to focus entirely on redrafting the visual style of the paper to meet market shifts. He said:

> Design has always been important in newspapers, but has only recently been described as such. Arthur Christiansen (longest serving editor of the *Daily Express*) was a leader in packaging stories. Successful design should reflect the kind of paper it is meant to be.

The process of rebranding/redesigning the Daily Post

In 2002, the *Daily Post* had a middle-market feel, with ABC1 ambitions, and Gary felt it lacked a clear identity.

> Part of that look was necessity. The subs producing the Liverpool paper were also producing the Welsh *Daily Post*. The Welsh edition was a much more populist paper. The paper felt like the *Mirror* with *Mail* typefaces, lots of cut-outs, headlines on top of pictures and great wodges of text. In consultation with the editor, herself an experienced sub, I drew up the beginnings of a design strategy. We immediately made the front-page headlines bigger and we standardised the leading in headlines. We had to establish ourselves as a mid-market newspaper before anything else.

The *Welsh Daily Post* then split from the Liverpool paper and shifted its editorial operation to Llandudno under a separate editor. Gary said:

> We couldn't carry on like this. Slowly, we were trying to move upmarket, which we did subtly with more white space and paler type. Next came the redesign of the English masthead. 'We dummied it up and focus groups liked it. Then the *Independent* went compact. We wanted ABC1 broadsheet in tabloid format. As soon as the *Independent* made that leap, followed by *The Times*, the whole environment changed. We could say 'this is what a broadsheet in tabloid format could look like'.

Gary and senior staff ensure they are fully up-to-date with the latest insights from leading think tanks and researchers such as the Poynter Institute.

> We look to the continent and to the States, where newspaper redesign is looked at along scientific lines. The best newspaper design is both

> an art and a science. There is science in the choice of the width of a column and the width of a headline. The art is in how appealing and aesthetic this is to our target audience.

Their target readers fitted the demographic of Adam and Rachel from the hit TV series *Cold Feet* – affluent, professional, educated, intelligent, middle-class tastes and fashionable. 'They listen to Travis, Katie Melua, Dido. That is the target *Liverpool Daily Post* reader, which is not to say we don't attract other readers as well, but that's who reporters are told to write for.'

This audience would be instilled in the minds of reporters and sub-editors alike to ensure a consistent and powerful voice through the paper.

Working life of the design editor

Gary's working day starts at 10 a.m. He sits at the head of the design desk in front of a large monitor upon which he can see full-size pages on screen. His first job of the shift is to scrutinise the work of the overnight page editors who work on the inside feature pages.

'I check the types conform to visual style, that the headlines are well-written and look right, and that the pictures are cropped appropriately.' Gary and his team of two design subs will begin work on around two of the news pages in the run-up to the main editorial conference. Gary attends the 30-minute conference daily.

'I listen carefully to the news editors and other section editors, to get a sense of what stories are being covered. I will be thinking about the stories discussed visually in that meeting.'

Gary does not make decisions about the placing of the articles – that is done by the command desk of news editors, assistant editor and the chief copy sub.

In the editorial conference, a story emerges about proposals to erect a statue of Neptune in the sea just off the Wirral coastline. The meeting decides that this will make the page three lead.

> The idea of a picture-led page three is very much influenced by the *Daily Mail*. Pictures come first on this page – they must be powerful and arresting as they are the first thing our readers will look at. The second most important page feature is the headline.

Gary draws a page plan and passes it to the chief sub who edits the copy for punctuation, grammar, house style and general readability. The subs will query any factual ambiguities with the reporter if necessary. As it is a lighter story, the headline has a lighter font, whereas the hard news stories on the right-hand pages feature bolder type. 'This not only signals a change in mood for our target audience, it also allows us more space with a lighter font to write longer, more elaborate headlines,' said Gary.

He stresses that the significance design is given on the *Daily Post* does not mean it overrides the importance of the copy: 'Pages must project the stories in the best possible way. The best page design should be indiscernible to the reader.'

Nevertheless, Gary ensures he takes full responsibility for laying out and subbing the front page, called the splash. Despite the limitations on space and time, Gary feels this is one of the most creative exercises. 'Headlines on inside pages are always modular, but we break that rule on page one. The headline is always the most important thing, unless there is a particularly spectacular picture.'

Having a strong notion of the target readership which is communicated through highly researched design solutions means that the *Liverpool Daily Post* and its sister paper the *Liverpool Echo* are trying to redefine what the term 'tabloid' means. It can be argued that they are doing this more creatively and radically than the nationals, despite the controversial shift to compact format of the *Independent* and *The Times.* Gary said:

> If you think about it in football terms, lower league players may often have aspiration to play like Beckham or Rooney. But why should tabloid regional newspapers try to ape the *Sun* or the *Star*? By thinking more creatively, we can try to redefine what tabloid actually is. It certainly isn't about dumbing down or simplification. Popular journalism is what we are striving for. It's immediate and says what it's trying to say simply and clearly without having to wade through too many words.

Retargeting the Daily Post

Targeting research done by Funsworth and Owler in 2003 in a report commissioned by the *Liverpool Daily Post* produced a careful analysis of the profile and lifestyle of the groups that were to be targeted by the rebrand. The biggest concern in the report was twofold. First: 'only 56% of its readers are in the ABC1 target group, which advertisers are now questioning. Two-thirds of the potential "quality" audience does not currently read our daily titles, presenting an enormous opportunity' (2003: 3). Second was the concern that these readers were unable to recognise the brand. Therefore there was need for 'greater awareness of brand values'. The report also stated that: 'Brand research undertaken with both readers and target non-readers in July 2002 . . . indicated a strong perception of the title as dull and old fashioned' (2003: 6). Previously the newspaper had emphasised reliability and tradition. To reach the target groups the report recommended a move towards intellect/analysis;

indulgence; social awareness; success. Gary's job was to redesign the look of the newspaper in order to change these perceptions. In other words the newspaper had to visually communicate the kinds of values associated with a particular lifestyle. This group, as described in detail in terms of their psychographic characteristics, would not be in favour of tradition and reliability.

One major change was to include supplements. These had titles like 'Box Office' , 'Retail Therapy' and 'Day Six', a home, gardening and night-life Saturday supplement. These were themselves to signify a move away from tradition to lifestyle. Whilst being popular with advertisers the supplements could also be a visual representation of shared consumer behaviours (shared taste), shared patterns of leisure time activities (e.g. an interest in similar sports, or tourist destinations), and shared attitudes to key social issues which are so important in lifestyle.

Centrally the rebranding involved some basic adjustments in the look of the cover of the newspaper. Changes were made to fonts, layout, colours and images. For inspiration for the redesign Gary drew on a number of sources. In the US the Poynter Institute had carried out extensive consumer research for newspapers. This had included layout, the way the eye travels around the page and analysis of fonts and colours. The Ascender Corporation specifically produced fonts for brand consistency, again involving market research. The Pantone Institute specialised in market research for colour in branding. Much of this research and theory has been put into practice in the US and Latin America in the process of rebranding and targeting of newspapers. Gary was able to consult these rebrands where they had applied to his own target audience. In the US harmony between newspaper design and advertiser target groups has traditionally been of much greater importance.

In the following section we analyse Gary's choices in font, layout, colour and images. The reasons given for the choices made in the rebrand were generally aesthetic, although market research offered some basic rules of thumb. For example, lower socio-economic groups would prefer newspaper or magazine covers that were busy and lively, whereas higher socio-economic groups would prefer newspaper or magazine covers that were more spacious and conceptual. We can see that the older demographic research is still strong in marketing assumptions.

Font

One important communicative tool is font. Considerable market research is put into the fonts, for example of brands or of movie titles. The kind of font used, its boldness, its curvature, its colour, must signify something about the brand or the movie. On a promotional poster for an action movie, we will find very different fonts than we would on a poster for a romantic comedy. The action movie would use a much broader, heavier font with straight edges, whereas the romantic comedy may use more curves and a slimmer font. Gary emphasised that changes to fonts were not made on purely arbitrary, aesthetic grounds – it was about capturing a new Europeanness sweeping this maritime city. Gary explained: 'It's more cosmopolitan, like Bilbao or Barcelona. The docks are still thriving, but there's been the introduction of service industries, especially media and new media. We have to reflect this, plus we try to make it a little younger, starting to target the 35s to 55s.'

Gary specified that bolder fonts imply stability and solidity, whereas a slimmer font can appear more elegant, curved fonts appear more feminine and flowing. Van Leeuwen (2005) has placed such observations into categories. We can use these to analyse the font changes from the older *Post* in 2002 and the redesign in 2005. Font itself can be one important signifier of lifestyle categories and can be systematically analysed. Van Leeuwen draws on Halliday's (1978) view that language always fulfils three three communicative functions. These are to convey ideas and attitudes and to give coherence. The same can be said of images, colours, and, Van Leeuwen (2005) argues, of typography. Here we draw on his model of analysis. Using the example of typography, we can say that the three functions are:

- *to represent ideas* – for example a metallic font could represent the idea of durability
- *to offer attitudes* – by being bold and standing out a font can be a warning
- *to give coherence* – the same font can be used throughout a document to signify something is of the same order.

We can draw on Van Leeuwen's categories for analysing the meaning potential of fonts in terms of their shapes and weights. This kind of analysis relies very much on the metaphorical associations of font styles. Here we compare the *Daily Post* title fonts from 2002 to 2005.

2002: **DAILY POST**

Weight

The letters have a thick and blockish appearance. Van Leeuwen (2005) and Gary tell us that increased weight means solid and substantial, so realising idea- and attitude-giving functions. Of course solid can have both positive and negative connotations such as bossy. In our example, the font gives a sense of reliability through its solidity.

Expansion

Letters can be narrow or expanded: in other words, they take up different amounts of space. The *Daily Post* font is quite expanded. It fills its space.

We might see this as signifying confidence, or being comfortable. This of course will go along with what is communicated by the weight.

Curvature

The font has little curvature. The emphasis is on blockiness. Van Leeuwen suggests that straightness communicates control and certainty, whereas roundedness is smooth, natural, less technical. Curvature is classically used to connote femininity. The film *Cinderella*'s title is written not in blocks, with straight lines, but with lots of curves.

Orientation

This describes whether the font is tall or flattened. In the case of the *Daily Post* the combination of the width and height of the font gives the impression that they are slightly squat. Of course this is similar to weight as more squat fonts give a sense of being less elegant, heavier and therefore perhaps more stable.

Connectivity

This describes how close together the letters in a font are. Where a font has letters that are joined they might connote intimacy or collectiveness. In the film title *Cinderella* the letters are connected as in joined-up writing, suggesting some kind of informality and approachability. Van Leeuwen suggests that letters that are unconnected and well spaced might connote independence.

Flourishes

Fonts often have flourishes, such as serifs which are the 'feet' on letters. We find them at the bottom of the letter 'l' and the top of the letter 'w' in the font in which I am writing. Some fonts have flourishes that might indicate flamboyance, or represent an object. For example the word Dog could be written in a font so that the tail of the letter 'g' resembled the tail of a dog. The font for the *Daily Post* carries serifs which generally connote tradition.

In summary the 2002 *Daily Post* title denotes tradition, certainty, comfort, confidence.

2005: LIVERPOOL DAILY POST

Size

The new font takes up much greater space proportionally on the page. This was important for increasing the brand, but simply increasing the size of the older font would not have signified the right kinds of values.

Weight

The font is not heavy at all. We might argue that there has been a move away from tradition. The font is very slim. In this case we might say that it has the meaning potential of elegance rather than reliability.

Expansion

The 'Liverpool' letters take up very little space individually due to their slender form. This font is not about taking up space and confidence. The '*Daily Post*' is slightly heavier but uses a font where the letters are slimmer on the horizontal plane. In this way they can combine a degree of expansion without becoming too solid. On the whole the two fonts take up more space on the page than the older font but give a sense of much greater lightness and space. This is in accord with the general principle of higher socio-economic groups favouring spacious layouts.

Curvature

The slimmer vertical lines, as on the 'D' and 'O', for example, help to emphasise the curvature, and the overall sense of design of the fonts. The angularity of the older font has disappeared. As Van Leeuwen suggests roundness can connote smoothness and femininity. He also suggests that postmodernity has brought back round forms in design after the angularity of modernism. Here the fonts combine with the 'Liverpool' font being very angular.

Orientation

Is the font flattened or tall? There is a greater sense of height than with the older fonts, although letters remain broad. Height is brought in the use of slightly taller first letters in 'Daily' and 'Post', used to accommodate the word 'Liverpool'.

Connectivity

The 'Liverpool' letters stand apart from each other. The metaphoric potential of this could be about space itself. Important in the design culture at the time was empty spaces, with very little clutter, found in designer stores, cafés and corporate spaces. Space is found in advertising shots and stock photography used in promotions and brochures, along with high key lighting as part of a clean, professional modernity. The *Daily Post* font has more space in proportion to its width than the older font.

Flourishes

The 'Liverpool' font has no flourishes but is simple and clean. The *Daily Post* retains serifs and their connotations of tradition.

Summary

The new title fonts carry meaning potentials for elegance and modernity, along with the sophistication of postmodernity. There is a lightness and sense of space but also a connotation of tradition through the serifs.

Fonts elsewhere on the front pages

The new fonts in the main body of the text also combine tradition and modernity. The font in 'Fears for Future of Littlewoods' HQ' retains serifs, yet the flourishes are quite expressive and unpredictable. This adds a sense of playfulness and unexpectedness, an important move away from tradition.

Overall the new fonts are intended to signify a kind of newspaper brand that targets readers who do not associate with the values of tradition and reliability, but with clean designer space, with creativity, with the combination of the modern and traditional. Not all signifiers of tradition are removed as news itself as a concept leans heavily on tradition. Fonts are also given a textual/organisational function on the new page. On the left-hand side of the page we have a list of items inside, creating a sense of choice, important in lifestyle, but also copying both the broadsheet nationals and web page design, connoting sophistication. The fonts have different weights alternatively for presentation. Finally Gary told us that in the new design fewer fonts were used on the cover, to convey streamlined simplicity.

Colour

As with fonts Kress and Van Leeuwen (2002) argue that colour can communicate on the three levels used by Halliday (1978) to describe the functions of language. Colour can communicate ideas, attitudes and can be used to organise.

- *Ideas* – colours can be used to represent political parties. Red is socialist.
- *Attitudes* – a bright red might also mean danger.
- *Textual organisational* – red might be used both in an image and in a font used for a heading for that image, in some ways suggesting that they are the same.

There have been two changes in colour between the old and the new version of the newspaper.

Header

The older version used blue for the letters '*Daily Post*', whereas the rebrand uses a blue band where the title is written in white. The decision to retain the blue was never in doubt as it carefully distinguishes the *Liverpool Daily Post* from sister title the *Liverpool Echo*, which traditionally had a masthead of bold white letters on a red background with a thin blue line above it. There are a number of analytical categories that we can draw on from Kress and Van Leeuwen (2002) which employ semiotics and historical analysis of colours (Gage 1993, 1999).

Hue

This describes the scale from red to blue. The red end of the scale, they suggest, is associated with warmth, energy and salience, and blue with distance and coolness. Of course these potentials will depend on other aspects of the colour such as saturation. Therefore the distinction between red to blue in the sister titles could be thought of as a move away from warmth or salience to something cooler. In fact blues have become very popular in corporate logos and also most television news opens with sequences using blues. The cool detachment can also signify truth and science.

Saturation

Colours can be soft and diluted or intensely saturated. Historically saturation has been associated with emotive temperatures and exuberance. Advertising and stock photography often uses high saturation colours to emphasise the sensory. The blue of the older version is much more saturated than the newer blue. This is less sensory, more subtle and tender.

Modulation

This describes the way that colours are flat and uniform or contain textures and shades as they do when we see colours in the real world. Kress and Van Leeuwen (2002) say that flatter unmodulated colours are characteristic of modernity and certainty. Also they say that flat colours are less realistic, expressing the essential colour of things, as in cartoons, rather than real colours. The blue is of low modulation. This represents modernity and certainty, we might say.

Paper

The other colour change is in the colour of the paper used: the new version is a much purer white. Purity is also characteristic of the modernist painters such as Mondrian, but this white is highly saturated in its intensity and gives the impression of low modulation. The white saturation is related to the cleanness of advertising photos.

In summary, in the redesign colour has been used to move towards corporate blues of coolness and truth and a saturated white. Both are clean and uncluttered. This reflects changes in photography, design and page layout.

Layout

There are two changes to the front page: increased spacing of elements and a switch away from traditional positioning of the elements

Space

The redesigned page uses much more white space. There are bigger gaps between items, between columns and between lines of text. This does the metaphorical work of creating a sense of room and openness and is the kind of space that we find in advertising and stock photography where for example a woman sits in a large open space diffused with high-key lighting where all is slightly over-lit or over-exposed, giving the feel of brilliant yet soft brightness. In the room is only the woman and a chair. She sits working on a laptop. This is the world of design which is optimally clean and free of dirt and clutter. In the photograph the women would wear clothes that are of a saturated white, co-ordinated with the chair in which she sits. The same work of connotation is at work in the white saturated space of the newspaper cover. In this ad world of corporate office spaces, professional people are shown to work, drink coffee and bring up their children. The news on the page is located in the same clean space. Gary said:

> Paradoxically, while I'd bumped headline size initially to make it look mid-market, now I reduced headline size. It also apes an Internet front page, with hyperlinks. The thing that goes most against the grain is setting everything left. When you justify, you increase letter spacing. Everyone's got access to word processing software, and they tend to justify text just because you can. But I want consistency throughout and better use of space.

Arrangement of elements

Kress and Van Leeuwen (1996) discuss the way that a composition on a page is made up of elements. The way these are positioned as regards each other creates meanings and gives the elements values in relation to each other. What is particularly interesting for our analysis is their discussion of left to right positioning. They argue that in Western culture that which is positioned on the right is 'the given' and that on the left 'the new'. So we will often find things like photographs on the right-hand side of the page as this is where we are invited to identify with or consider the person, place or object in the image. On the left we will be given information that we already know. So on the left a headline on 'Politician in scandal', on the right a picture of a politician. We read from left to right. The information on the left is of concepts we are used to, the particular image is not. The given and new can also apply from top to bottom of a page.

The old design of the *Daily Post* did generally follow this rule, but the new layout is different. The image can occupy a central role: text can appear at either side of the image and often circulates around it. This is much more fluid than left to right, or top to bottom. The eye is encouraged to move around, as on a web page. The amount of white space on the new design also seems to make this happen much more easily. The layout, space and font give out just as much information about the meaning of the newspaper as the news 'information' that it carries. This new layout is much more dynamic, rather than linear. Like the fonts, it has energy. This is combined with the modern design space, the saturated white and flat corporate blue.

Images

The final redesign decision has been to change the kinds of photographs carried on the front page. Formerly industry convention held that images should be tightly descriptive and preferably have the subject looking towards the frame. Research by the Poynter Institute has suggested that there is room for photographs to be much more evocative when used as part of layout. Machin (2004) in his analysis of the Getty Image bank looked at the way that stock photographs – technically high quality designer photographs intended to be multi-purpose, to use in promotions, advertising and magazines – were now becoming dominant in world media, replacing the use of the photograph as witness. In advertising and promotional material we find these images, generally with blurred backgrounds and flat, saturated colours. They often show people in empty, modernist museum/ corporate spaces. Such photographs do not record a single moment in time but signify concepts such as 'happiness', 'freedom', 'work', etc. These images are used with increasing frequency in global media and their design-friendly style has seen them find their way into and influence photography in the news media. This is especially so because news media are now more and more concerned with design and layout. Gary told us that there was a decision to move towards images of this style: de-contextualised, out of focus backgrounds to draw attention to single details such as a person or object. There would be an emphasis on the iconic and on space. In a photograph on the rebranded version of the *Daily Post* the subject cannot be clearly seen as a specific individual. His face is hidden and he is not recorded in any specific place. This is a particular style of photography, like that dominating image banks.

Conclusion

Our aims in this chapter were to twofold. First, we wished to illuminate some of the gaps in academic interrogation of visual journalism. Here we have shown the way that lifestyle categories are used to shape news into a format which signifies a particular set of values and attitudes. Studies of visual journalism have traditionally taken a semiotic approach which has foregrounded text and the verbal as the dominant factor in meaning-making. By adopting a multimodal approach, we have shown that visuals can be independent and foregrounded in their own right. Furthermore, we have demonstrated through this methodology that the multiple modes of communication present in visual journalism texts are interwoven, rather than essentially hierarchical. Different communicative modes are used to realise discourses of modern, urban, corporate, commercial, chic. The look of the paper and the content is intended to align itself and readers alongside a new business/professional vision of Liverpool which replaced the former industrial culture. Writers on the changing nature of our cities (Zukin 1995; Sorkin 1992) have observed the way that urban planning and the purposes of cities are now inseparable from marketing and consumerism. Cities are now about cultural consumption of food, tourism, art, fashion and heritage. As Zukin states, the design of buildings and spaces in cities symbolises who belongs and who doesn't (1995: 1). The *Liverpool Daily Post* reflects these changes, away from the traditional and the reliable, to the slightly creative, energetic, confidence of design know-how. In the lifestyle society attitude and opinion merge with consumption. The newspaper places itself in one such lifestyle constellation, one such market-generated category of person in this consumer world. The *Liverpool Daily Post* is primarily produced to be symbolic of a set of core values. These core values are part of the discourses of the new professional, self-conscious consumerist, city dweller, with all the attributes and opinions that were mentioned earlier in the market research by Funsworth and Owler. The formula is very successful and has boosted circulations. Figures from the Audit Bureau of Circulations for January to June 2004 put daily circulations at just under 20,000, an immediate increase on previous figures, even though the paper was only relaunched in March of that year. By 2005, the paper had seen an increase in sales of more than four per cent, the biggest growth in this sector in the UK.

The second and more pressing aim of the chapter was to go further than evaluating academic approaches. By entering into a close dialogue with a visual journalist, we have identified and illuminated a raft of previously uncharted territory concerning the reflexive nature of contemporary journalism. The culture and history of UK regional production desks means that there may not be a great deal of outward discussion of creativity. Yet it is most evident from our ethnography that a tremendous amount of research, reflection and artistry takes place on the part of journalistic staff. It is evident from our study that there is a need for new journalists to become immersed in creative, visual approaches to storytelling if they are to successfully navigate the rapidly changing terrain of contemporary journalism, given the ebbs and flows of reader loyalties and lifestyles. This tells a very different story from that of academic approaches which insist that journalists are in some way trying to impede information uptake or conceal and distort the real meanings of news events. From our observations, the case is quite the opposite.

8 'The best job in the world'

The socialisation of the news journalist

For the new journalist in their first news job, fitting into the social context of newsroom culture is a primary concern. They wish to make a positive impression, rapidly gaining the confidence of colleagues and editors by doing a good job. The new reporter might be fresh out of university or college, where they have invested time, energy and considerable funds in pursuing their elusive dream career in journalism. Those first tentative steps into paid journalism employment hold tremendous resonance for the trainee or junior reporter. They know from work experience, from the mythology of journalism and from the on-screen depictions of journalists in popular cinema that editorial staff not only need to deliver the goods, they need to do so with a certain degree of confidence and aplomb. In an ideal situation, the reporter will be able to commence a successful career in news journalism that satisfies personal aspirations, ethical drives and also ensures financial security and career progression. But how realistic is this? However well-educated the new entrant might be, are they fully prepared for the barrage of personal and professional compromises they may face? Will they achieve their goal of being an autonomous, independent, authoritative roving reporter, or does a successful career in journalism mean abandoning those thoughts as mere idealism?

Certainly, if we reflect on the experiences of the journalists we have featured, compromise would seem to be needed on a regular basis as news organisations strive to keep ahead of their competition and hang onto an ever more demanding and diverse audience or readership. We have seen how everyone on the news floor, from reporter to chief sub-editor, from photographer to editor, has to have a much more acutely sharpened business and marketplace awareness than they might have necessarily had when many of the original theories of journalism were coined. Working under tight deadlines with pressure of space and staffing numbers, it comes as no surprise that there is little opportunity for journalists to follow their own agendas, or to creatively explore their own avenues. Rather than creativity, individuality and investigation, despite what the mastheads and advertising slogans might claim, it is in fact continuity, consistency and speed that are very much the bywords of the contemporary digital news operation.

It is evident from our study that the new reporter needs to have a broad range of skills and knowledge if they are to successfully navigate the challenges of a dynamic, fast-moving industry. It sounds like a cliché, but it is the best way to describe how news journalism is constantly evolving, subject to a range of internal and external forces as we outlined in the first chapter. While the fundamental skills of news-gathering seem to be consistently lauded (Randall 1996: 2), there is no doubt with the advent of citizen journalism and user-generated content that even they might be under threat.

It has been a concern of journalism academics for some time that the organisational structures and processes within newsrooms are indeed in conflict with the tenets of journalism to be independent watchdogs on the world. The emphasis on audience volume and revenue means that staff no longer have the security of continuous employment. Instead they must navigate short-term rolling contracts, performance-related pay and in many cases the uncertainty of freelance employment. In this context, a young journalist may feel under even greater pressure to conform to newsroom policy even if that policy goes against their own ethical concerns. Aldridge and Evetts (2003) pose this as a dilemma when they say 'recent changes in the occupation's social composition and training may mean that journalists, who have always cherished a self-image as socially marginal, will aspire to conventional professional respectability' (2003: 547).

This chapter will examine concerns that have been expressed about newsroom culture by academics in the field of media sociology and organisational theory. In varying ways, they have identified a pattern of journalists absorbing the editorial policy, instead of remaining independent and autonomous. Furthermore, that policy has been internalised in such a way as to make oppositional action in the workplace highly unlikely. These processes have serious implications for the role of the news media in a democratic society, say theorists, because they operate primarily for the benefit of senior managers and proprietors rather than for readers and audiences who should be viewed as the reporter's real clients. We go on to interview new entrants to journalism about their experiences of newsroom culture and policy during the early days of their career. In the course of these interviews, and through broader research, we gain insights into the recruitment of new journalists and their subsequent mentoring which both confirm and contradict the earlier theoretical studies. We find that whilst journalists may be inspired by their experiences and introduced to new career possibilities, they will not necessary lose their sense of self-direction and autonomy.

The socialisation of the journalist

How new journalists adapt to workplace culture has been a keen area of research interest since the middle of the twentieth century. The organisational structure of the newsroom has been accused of constraining consensual notions about news production. By operating as a hierarchy, newsroom management is said to cultivate professional standards for organisational benefit rather than in the public interest (Breed 1955; Sigelman 1973; Roshco 1975; Schlesinger 1978; Tuchman 1978; Gans 1980; Soloski 1989; Shoemaker and Reese 1991). In this way, journalists have little editorial independence, constrained as they are by professional norms and practices. Thus far journalism studies has only explored what is meant by the 'professionalisation' of journalism to a limited extent. There has been an unresolved debate within journalism over whether it is a profession or a craft or trade, with the opponents to the 'profession' approach arguing journalism should not be institution-focused. Jeremy Tunstall has noted the shifts, nonetheless: 'In the consensual 1960s British journalism was far from being an established profession: but it was moving in a "professionalizing" direction' (1996: 141). This debate has been embodied in the differing principles of two current representative groups in the UK – the National Union of Journalists (NUJ) and the Institute of Journalists (IOJ). Aldridge and Evetts (2003) argue that these bodies represent the two different models of occupational control, through the union of the dominant collective, as opposed to 'professional' voice. While the NUJ sets out to enable a shared, wage-based identity, the IOJ is about raising the profile and status of journalists by fostering a professional identity. Either way, there is a sense among academics that professional policies lurk very close to the surface of mainstream news organisations.

Warren Breed, a former journalist turned sociologist, was one of the pioneers of the scientific study of news production. His professional experience of journalism led him to query how staff get to know and follow newsroom 'policy', which is rarely if ever written down. His 1955 study 'Social Control in the Newsroom' was one of the first to acknowledge that the everyday practical role of the journalist can often be in conflict with public expectation or individual intention. For Breed, policy is the unwritten editorial standard that governs news selection and editing. This suggests, he acknowledged, that in a professional context, news is not always dictated by news values criteria but also by internal factors such as proprietor attitudes.

> Every newspaper has a policy, admitted or not. The central question will be: How is policy maintained, despite the fact that it often contravenes journalistic norms, that staffers often personally disagree with it, and that executives cannot legitimately command that it be followed?
> (cited in Tumber 1999: 79)

Drawing on theories of the organisation, Breed's study cuts to the quick of this conflict, in a way that continues to resonate in the ever-more business- and market-led newsroom culture of today.

> When the new reporter starts work he is not told what policy is. Nor is he ever told. Yet all but the newest staffers know what policy is. On being asked they say that they learn it 'by osmosis'. Sociologically this means they become socialised and 'learn the ropes' like a neophyte in any subculture. Basically the learning of policy is a process by which the recruit discovers and internalises the rights and obligations of his status and its norms and values.
>
> (Breed 1955: 79–80)

The ways the journalists might identify policy are as follows (Breed 1955):

- By reading their own paper
- By observing the way their stories are edited
- From praise and criticism
- From casual conversations with colleagues and editors
- Internal meetings
- Internal communications
- Observing executive feedback and decision-making.

Having addressed how journalists come to learn the policy, Breed then tackles how they come to comply with its tenets. The new entrant becomes socialised by conforming to the norms of policy rather than to personal beliefs. Breed says there are six key ways for the new entrant to conform to newsroom policy. These are:

1. Institutional authority and sanctions – the journalist feels they must obey their employer. The employer can also edit or spike stories that deviate from policy, though they will more than likely blame pressures of time and/or space.
2. Feelings of obligation and esteem for superiors – the journalist may respect older staffers who have schooled him or her.
3. Mobility aspirations – getting big stories on page one is good for a journalist's career.
4. Absence of conflicting group allegiance – it is very rare for groups of journalists to confront or complain about a newspaper's policy.
5. The pleasant nature of the activity – colleagues get on congenially, in a non-hierarchical way – it's a shared club
6. News becomes a value – news and filling space is a continuous challenge and journalists get rewarded for producing as much of it as they can. 'Newsmen do talk about ethics, objectivity, and the relative worth of various papers, but not when there is news to get. They are not rewarded for analysing the social structure, but for getting news' (Breed 1955: 82).

Breed explains that the process of learning policy 'crystallises into a process of social control', in which deviations may be gently but resolutely punished by reprimand or by cutting a story (ibid.: 83). He concludes his study by commenting that

> The newsman's source of rewards is located not among the readers, who are manifestly his clients, but among his colleagues and superiors. Instead of adhering to societal and professional ideals, he redefines his values to the more pragmatic level of the newsroom group.
>
> (Breed 1955: 84)

Breed's conclusions are reinforced in a similar study by Lee Sigelman, 'Reporting the news: an organisational analysis' (1973) first published in the *American Journal of Sociology*. This paper, which focuses on political reporters at two newspapers in a US city, explores recruitment, socialisation and the control process to shed light on the implications for bias in content. Sigelman draws on Herbert Simon's (1957) study of organisational behaviour which asserts that employers imbue employees with attitudes and approaches that suit the needs of the organisation. Applying this thesis to journalism, Sigelman proposes that news policy is disseminated from the top down through two methods: attitude promotion and organisational control (Tumber 1999: 87). Attitude promotion requires newspapers to recruit new staff who are known to be in accord with the organisation's policies. Thereafter the organisation invests energy and resources to further socialise reporters' favourable attitudes. More recently, McNair (1998) supports this view in his study of proprietiorial controls 'exercised, as in any other capitalistic organisation, through the appointment of like-minded personnel in key management positions who are delegated to carry out the boss's will' (1998: 107). Sigelman observed that the recruitment of journalists was frequently through word of mouth, or through potential employees making ad hoc approaches to editors, who would keep them on file should a vacancy arise. It was rare for posts to be formally advertised.

One example of this process at play is one of the authors' experience of being recruited by a major regional evening newspaper. During the course of the interview, it transpired that in addition to seeking traditional references, the newsdesk team had approached a number of regular beat sources, such as the police press office, for an account of professional conduct. In terms of socialisation, Sigelman says this is often hard to pin down specifically: 'the newspapers make no formal provisions for inculcating job or policy norms. Rather, the socialization process is highly diffuse and extremely informal. . . . Reporters felt that learning policy is simply "a process that takes place over time"' (1973: 88–9). Some of the understated mechanisms employed are young reporters attempting to emulate senior staffers, editorial revisions and the regular editorial conference.

One trainee journalist we spoke to, Jon Brooker, discovered this when he undertook a two-week placement at his local paper, the *Stratford Upon Avon Herald*. As a first year journalism undergraduate, he had had some training in the basics of news-writing and was using the placement to consolidate and refine his style. He said:

> Being quite early in the morning I was asked by the editor to go through the other local papers and regionals looking for Stratford-related stories. When the rest of the editorial team came in I was introduced to the news editor who asked me what journalistic experience I had and whether I was familiar with the *Herald*. I told him I was in my first year at City studying journalism and that I was familiar with the paper. He straight away said I should be fine and gave me some press releases to write up as fillers.
>
> I found that at first I was using the rules I had been taught which gave me a great foundation but when I forwarded them to the sub he asked me to go over and have a quick chat. He explained he wanted me to give the stories a little more of my own style or slant, really to write them as 'stories' not just information pieces. I got on with doing this more and found I grew more in confidence the more I wrote. A lot of what I'd been taught started making more sense, just through repeatedly writing stories. Confidence seemed a big point. Just backing myself that I had the right angle and style, and with a sub that was prepared to pull me up when he didn't like a piece, it worked well. The news editor liked the fillers and by the third day they were letting me effectively be a reporter. Confidence again grew, on the phone, especially in front of everyone in the newsroom. I just realised I had to get on with the job in hand and not worry about the results of what I was doing so much. I felt my news sense was growing and that the structure of reporting for that paper just made sense. Though topics varied greatly for reports, I still appreciated what each story needed through the structure. I ended up with almost 20 bylines, being sent out to get a story, to inquests, two press conferences (one about the sale of Coventry airport) and I think the confidence they showed in me gave me the confidence to work to the standard they wanted. I am still doing pieces for the *Herald* now and have been asked back to do paid work for them in the summer. The whole experience has really given me a passion for news reporting when I had felt my capability for reporting was perhaps not great and my enthusiasm was dwindling.

Jon's experience is interesting in the way his work placement encounters with journalists brought alive his passion for news. The sheer pleasure of seeing stories reach the page, along with positive affirmations from senior staff, seems to emulate the first process.

In terms of the second process, organisational control, or hierarchical authority, we might see this manifested in the way that senior journalists make decisions about what should be covered and who should be assigned the story. Sigelman also draws attention to the editing and revising process once a story is submitted by the journalists. 'Surely the ability to change the emphasis and direction of a news story is a substantial mechanism of control . . . the newsman operates within the constraining boundaries of a fairly elaborate set of organisational control structures and processes' (1973: 92). Sigelman stresses, in contrast with Breed, that this control rarely causes conflict in the newsroom.

This criticism is not confined to newspapers: in broadcast journalism it has already been shown in Chapter 3 that a seamless quality to continuity is necessary in order to deliver a well-targeted product that coheres with audience expectations. Philip Schlesinger, in a study of the BBC (1978), described how editors were entrusted with producing news output that is indistinguishable from that of fellow editors. Quoting from an editor he had observed: 'It mustn't be too obvious that someone else is doing every shift'; Schlesinger concludes that editorial consistency is a marker of its 'soundness' (1978: 149). The rapid growth in journalism education and training means that many new entrants to the career already have a grounding in the fundamental skills. Soloski (1989) suggests this may be a reason why newsrooms do not need to invest in inductions and training for new reporters (1989: 212). Rather, professional norms can serve as a more effective and cost-effective way of directing and controlling behaviour.

The question of the extent to which individual journalists are content with this hierarchical control remains. Journalists independently define and describe what they do. For example, Gans' study (1980: 234–5) discovered that journalists see themselves as professionals working for a predominantly lay clientele, the audience to which the journalist gives what it needs rather than what it wants. Hence, the journalists' individual professional norms may be seen to be in conflict with the norms of the business they work in, directed by the market and advertisers and the political inflections of the proprietor. The model of social control also strongly contradicts the fundamental tenets of journalism, for instance as articulated by David Randall (1996). In his book *The Universal Journalist*, Randall argues that journalists have a 'fraternity', a shared sense of identity, because wherever they work, or whoever they work for, they are all trying to do the same thing: 'intelligent fact-based journalism, honest in intent and effect, serving no cause but the discernible truth, and written clearly for its readers whoever they may be'.

Is this conflict felt by individual journalists and, if so, how is it manifested? One way is through competition. This competition is with other rival news outputs or with fellow journalists, which may be seen to override any internal conflicts within the organisation. Bantz (1999: 139) observed:

> This conflict is intensified by business norms that often characterise the competition between organisations as warfare (the prevalence of military and war metaphors in organisations has often been commented on . . .). In addition to the professional competition between reporters, news competition may escalate into inter-organisational conflict where the television stations compete for stories, news workers, prestige, and ratings as well as advertisers' dollars.

Bantz surmises that conflict becomes seen as useful and part of the dynamic, thus socialising journalists into accepting it as a useful and necessary tension in the news-making process.

Journalism occupational identity as socialisation

These accounts of social control in the newsroom have not gone uncontested, at least in terms of their need to embrace the diversity of news media personnel. One criticism of these accounts has been that they do not address the ever-changing nature of the news media, and the nature and drives of the individuals who seek to work within it. To what extent might an individual's background, which may encompass socio-economic context, gender and ethnicity, impact upon their sense of identity in the workplace? And in turn, what impact might this have upon their output? We have only to look at the changing profile of new entrants to see that their threshold skills and attributes have changed since Breed and others began to explore organisational control. Until the 1970s, almost no journalism training took place in the higher education sector. By the time of writing this chapter, journalism was becoming a graduate entry profession (Aldridge and Evetts 2003). A report by the Publishing National Training Organisation in 2002 observes that as a consequence and despite widening participation from diverse backgrounds in higher education, new entrants to journalism tend to have parents in professional/managerial employment (2002: 25).

The lack of diversity within UK newsrooms is something that has aroused concerns over several decades (Ainley 1998; Delano and Henningham 1995). At the time of writing, a row has erupted after the head of London's Metropolitan Police, Sir Ian Blair, attacked the media for its prioritising of white victims over those from other racial backgrounds, prompting angry responses from media professionals. Research undertaken by the website Chronicle World (www.chronicleworld.org) levels some of the blame for this on recruitment:

> Issues of race go straight to the heart of the UK media. Britain's newsrooms – in print, radio, television and on the Internet – lag far behind in recruitment of black staff at every level. Yet, racial disadvantage in hiring and promotion is patently obvious in newsrooms and in the

journalism schools that feed the industry. This 'blind-to-blacks' syndrome threatens to undermine claims of objectivity in the nation's press corps.

The so-called blind-to-blacks approach refers to the fact that editors often state that they hire the best candidate regardless of ethnicity and say they wish more black and other ethnic minority candidates would apply for positions. Many counter news organisations should be more transparent about their recruitment as it may impact on the objectivity of the reporting. *The Journalist*, the NUJ's own magazine, stated in an issue on race that 'the media have for months been reporting the Stephen Lawrence inquiry and the under-representation of black people in the police. They fail to report that they employ even fewer black people than the police'. We have mentioned race as but one factor in a candidate's background that may impact upon their opportunities to progress within the news industry. In a similar way, theories of newsroom organisation and socialisation should find tools to account for gender, disability and even socio-economic background. The rules cited by media sociologists may be neither universal not exhaustive.

There is also the fact that journalism has had to respond to wider cultural expectations about what a job or career should constitute, amidst widely circulated literature on 'job satisfaction', 'mentoring' and 'working hours directives'. The long working hours culture of journalism and the extent to which editors can push their staff have come under great scrutiny. Though even senior editors and journalists might reject any notion of being part of a profession, it has been observed that the journalism industry may still invoke a discourse of professionalism towards its workers. Fournier (1999) identifies how the discourse of professionalism – an occupational badge or marker – appeals to customers and to staff. In this sense, to become a journalist can be seen as to adopt a symbolically powerful identity associated with high standards. The National Council for the Training of Journalists encapsulates aspects of that identity in its promotional literature as such.

Want to be a Journalist?

Newspaper journalism is often seen as glamorous and exciting but, as with any occupation, success comes only after much hard work and routine activity. However, each day in newspapers is different and the training you receive will give you the flexibility to cover a wide range of news stories and features.

Newspaper journalism draws on all the knowledge and skills you have acquired and can give you a tremendous sense of achievement. If you've got what it takes, journalism could be the career for you!

What qualities do newspaper editors look for?

To convince an editor you are worth appointing you will need to be able to demonstrate the following:

- An interest in current affairs at all levels
- A lively interest in people, places and events
- An ability to write in a style which is easy to understand
- Good spelling, grammar and punctuation
- An appreciation of the part a local newspaper plays in the community
- A willingness to accept irregular hours
- An ability to work under pressure to meet deadlines
- Determination and persistence

Nctj.com

There is a wealth of autobiographies and training manuals that reinforce the notion of a journalistic identity (McKane 2004; Randall 1996) to sustain the occupational culture. Yet we have shown in many different contexts how the limitless pressures on the day-to-day practices of working journalists make the work increasingly desk-based and routine, very different from the ideal notion of the roving and autonomous beat reporter. Aldridge (1998) has gone so far as to argue that the occupational identity of journalists is clung onto even more as a response to the erosion of traditional news-gathering processes.

We spent time with Lou Thomas and Zoe Smith, both 25, three months into a year-long contract with the UK journalism trade paper, *Press Gazette*. Lou and Zoe were both graduates from the City University Bachelor of Arts programme in Journalism and a Social Science. Lou graduated shortly before joining the *Press Gazette*, while Zoe had graduated a year earlier and had freelanced for a range of titles in the UK and abroad, including *The Observer* Sunday newspaper, and *Rolling Stone* in Italy. It was a good time to reflect on their early days with the title, they said, as they would be going in for appraisal with their managers the following week. The pair had had to compete for six weeks against eight other candidates to 'win' the contracts, which were sponsored by Camelot, organisers of the National Lottery. Each week during the recruitment process, each potential candidate had to undertake a journalism task, and each week two candidates were eliminated. This process was reported week by week in the host publication.

The *Press Gazette* is a weekly paid-for colour magazine/newspaper hybrid edited by Ian Reeves. It is owned by the former *Mirror* editor Piers Morgan and public relations guru Matthew Freud, and since their takeover had relocated from its old base in Croydon, outside London, to offices close to the original home of the UK's national press, Fleet Street. It was first launched in 1965. The first editorial, by Fleet Street veteran Colin Valdar, proclaimed: 'We're here to provide journalists with a weekly newspaper devoted exclusively to the problems, personalities and practice of our craft.'

In its early days, it covered such stories as how *The Times* had made the historic decision to put stories on its front page. The publication's media pack clearly states the visionary aims of its editorial policy, and contains motivational insights into what it perceived as a united community of journalists:

> Now *Press Gazette* is the only place that brings all journalists together, regardless of the medium they work in. It champions their causes, reports on their successes and their failings, understands their concerns, helps them do their jobs and influences their thinking. It is the only publication that can guarantee to have been read by every editor of every national newspaper, regional newspaper, consumer magazine, business magazine, website and broadcast bulletin by Friday lunchtime. That means their bosses read it too, as do the key decision-makers in media law, PR, printing and press technology. Every self-respecting newsdesk has at least one (increasingly dog-eared as the day goes on) copy circulating. Since these journalists collectively reach audiences running into the tens of millions, *Press Gazette*'s readership is arguably the most influential group of people in the country.
>
> For the next 40 years, and beyond, *Press Gazette* will continue to do the work that Colin Valdar started: to inform, illuminate, influence, enlighten and entertain the people doing the best job in the world. Journalism.

According to the Audit Bureau of Circulations, it has a circulation of 5,600, though *Press Gazette's* publishers say the actual readership is four times this number each week. The majority of its readership are subscribers, who work in national and regional newsrooms across all media. A quarter of its readers are based in the regional press, closely followed by the national and then the consumer sector of the magazine industry.

Zoe and Lou first saw the contest for the contract advertised on *Press Gazette*'s web site. They were asked initially to submit a CV, their best cutting and a statement about why they wanted to be a journalist. Lou submitted an interview with the pop band Bloc Party that he had written for City University's student magazine *Massive*, while Zoe sent in a news focus piece she had written for *The Observer*. Zoe recalls that unlike traditional job applications, 'there wasn't an interview for the whole process. We saw the editor and features editor for a meeting, but that was the only impression they had of us face-to-face'. Lou adds: 'That was the strangest thing.' The short-listed candidates came from a diverse range of backgrounds but each had a demonstrable background in mainstream journalism, so were short-listed on the basis of their proven suitability rather than their individuality as such. In a similar way, university journalism departments selecting undergraduate or postgraduate students will sometimes require demonstrable newsroom experience, as a marker of the applicants' commitment to journalism, but also of their understanding and acceptance of newsroom culture.

Each week during the elimination process, the candidates were briefed on journalism tasks they had to complete to tight deadlines. These included all attending the same music concert then writing a review of it suitable for the *NME*, a weekly youth music magazine. In addition to the review, they had to supply headlines and other page furniture to ascertain whether they also had subbing skills. With two candidates eliminated, their next task was to study the weekly populist *Take a Break* magazine, establish 10 differences between it and another magazine, then sub-edit a reader's letter to style and length. Lou explained: 'The third task was the most interesting. There was a Hogarth wood cutting from his *Gin Lane* series. We had to write something based on this. That was pretty cool, I really enjoyed doing that.'

Applicants then spent time in the newsroom at *Five News*, based at the Sky headquarters in west London, and at the *Telegraph* newspaper in London's Docklands. Zoe said that 'they didn't explain what they were looking for. There was no real job description but they said they were looking for someone versatile who could best represent the aims of the company'. Zoe and Lou's experience in the earlier stages of the exercise would seem to correspond with the process of socialisation depicted by Breed but especially the attitude promotion witnessed by Sigelman (1973) and supported by McNair (1998). Both already had some experience in journalism, and they were being tested less for their personal attributes and more for their ability to adapt to a range of journalism contexts. Each of these journalism contexts was also highly targeted, suggesting the selection panel were prioritising news selection and writing skills that would adhere closest to a given brief. However, the Hogarth exercise was highly abstract and was looking for a different set of skills that were less normative and more creative and personal. This suggests that the selection process was more sophisticated than simply finding candidates who would conform to the brief. This is not so easily explained by the theoretical accounts.

For both Zoe and Lou, attaining the one-year contract was an ambition achieved. Zoe was delighted and also relieved at getting through. 'I had freelanced for a while and wondered if I would ever get a job. I had even contemplated going into advertising.' Lou's job started a day or two before Zoe, and appears to have been an induction of sorts into *Press Gazette* policy. Although he says that the only formalities were the welcome introductions to his new colleagues and superiors ('nothing formal, usual handshakes') he was immediately given a task to complete over a few days that would ground him in policy. He said:

> The very first thing I did was to go through old issues, scanning front covers of newsy events. That was very useful, and I had a good idea of what the PG was about. What was also good about that is that

> I came into contact with people I wouldn't normally deal with much on a day to day basis, such as the art editor.

After a few days of meeting new colleagues and learning about the editorial structure, both Lou and Zoe quickly became aware of the availability of promotion routes within the organization. 'Most of the people who edit pages now started off as editorial assistant,' said Lou. 'Our editor was once features editor, for instance.' The pair were assigned respective mentors, though it quickly became apparent that this arrangement would be informal. Zoe said: 'They keep an eye on us a little bit. Mine gives me advice as and when it is needed, but there is nothing formal such as a meeting each week.' They say there is constant interaction in the newsroom between junior and senior editorial staff, which is not perceived to be top-down. Lou is aware that he is being gently and informally coached, but adds:

> It's difficult to describe. I will go to my news or features editors and say 'I've seen this what do you think?' and they'll say 'that looks OK, give them a call', and I'll say 'I was thinking of asking them this, this and this.' Then I'll write the story. Sometimes they'll say maybe 'you could add this in or ask them this', and sometimes they won't. It's the perfect way of doing things but at this stage in my career I wouldn't feel I could do everything by myself.

This type of exchange is interesting in light of Breed's formulation of how the new entrant is socialised. Lou and Zoe both express feelings of obligation and esteem for superiors, though it must be stressed that the nature of their contract means that the emphasis is expressed more as esteem and respect than as obligation. Neither in any way begrudge their superiors – rather they enjoy the learning curve that ensues. As a consequence, both Lou and Zoe are thoroughly enjoying their work, and would be keen to work for the *Press Gazette* for longer if permanent vacancies were to arise.

In accordance with Breed, both Lou and Zoe are driven by the pleasures of their tasks. The work is varied and will often take them out of the office to social events or bring them into contact with interesting people. Zoe also relishes opportunities to generate her own stories, and feels she is allowed a fair degree of autonomy and independence. She said:

> Most of the stories I've done so far are ones I've suggested myself. I find it more interesting to suggest my own stuff. There isn't an expectation as such that I should do, but that's the way I like to work and I am able to do that here.

Lou agrees that he derives the most pleasure from seeing his byline next to a story he has generated by himself: 'There is more satisfaction with seeing something you've written that you've originated on your own rather than being told to do it. That's the most rewarding part of news for me.' In Lou's particular case, his pleasure is tangible because a self-generated story is due to appear in a prominent position in the next issue.

While there is a lack of conflict within the newsroom, and very real pleasures for each of the junior staff, there is a drive to compete reflecting Bantz's observations that competition can often be manifested through rivalry. The pair are already keenly aware of their main print and online competitors and support editorial policy to try to gain exclusives or at least different takes on stories to maintain a clear editorial identity for *Press Gazette*. Lou said jokingly: '*Media Guardian* are the enemy.' He added:

> Seriously, the Hold The Front Page web site and *Media Guardian* are our big rivals but if we end up doing a similar story we'll have our own angle and own quotes and do something totally different from them. By the same token when we go through the national newspapers we see something that might make a story and dig around to get an interesting take on it. The whole process helps you to think for yourself and think laterally.

The following exchange between Lou and Zoe reveals they know that they must have a strong brand awareness, but that it is more revered if it appears to be instinctive rather than learnt or strategic:

Zoe: I wish we'd had more on who their reader is and what sort of angle we should take. Sometimes I think I don't understand how a *Press Gazette* story should be different from a *Media Guardian* story or a *Broadcast* story.

Interviewer: Do they explain that?

Zoe: The subs are in the same room as us, so we hear them say whether something is awful. But there hasn't been a mission as such.

Lou: It hasn't even crossed my mind whether *Media Guardian* or *Broadcast* would do it a certain way. I don't know whether that's naive – I just know . . .

Zoe: No you are getting it, sometimes I am not sure explicitly of what distinguishes a *Press Gazette* story.

Lou: Well you seem to be getting it right! There are little bits and pieces the subs change in terms of syntax and so on, but that's what you would expect a sub-editor to do anyway. Comparatively they don't touch our copy. I've met people on national newspapers with horrendous stories. But we would know if we were doing badly by now, three months in. My one thing that I didn't get – and after three months the penny must have dropped because I understand it now – is that when you write a news story there is always a certain amount of background context you have to write. Now I totally,

totally, get it. I know instinctively how much to put in. If I miss a little bit out, the news editor will put it in and will tell me as such.

The sub-editors are senior members of the editorial team at *Press Gazette* and Zoe and Lou both view them with esteem. There is a feeling that changes and decisions are made consensually rather than over their heads. They say there is 'always constant dialogue about editing – when subs bring through the page proofs we'll all have a copy and work together on it'. Bantz's (1985) observations about conflict are further illustrated by their apprehensions about what they have heard and experienced of practices on the national titles. They express this as a professional ethical concern even more than a personal worry. 'They'll totally re-write your copy. It's only when you read a newspaper every day and really know about the stories that you can see how subs get it wrong.'

So it is the pleasant nature of the job, and increasing concern about practices at rivals which makes them loyal to their present employers. There are a few perks to be had, such as invitations to media awards and other events where food and drink will be served and there will be the chance to network. Zoe and Lou appreciate that these are distributed democratically around the office rather than being dominated by more senior staff. There is also no internal conflict over the placing of stories, as the magazine follows a similar format each week. National media stories are at the front, broadcast and magazine are further inside, and so on. Zoe explains: 'Because we know what goes on each page – so broadcast is always pages 9/10 – everything is obvious and structured so it avoids confrontation.' Once again, they compare their positive experiences at *Press Gazette* with what they have picked up about national newspapers. Lou says he has concerns about the nationals and the internal competition for stories.

In accordance with Breed, a key motivating factor has emerged as they have become more immersed in the *Press Gazette* newsroom. News has become a motivating value. They are both driven by the desire to find and write up stories, and it is a common bond that unites the whole operation. The emphasis is on reporting, rather than reflection. This is aided by the fact that they are encouraged to be part of the editorial decision-making.

Zoe: There is a Monday news conference, where we go through potential stories, and a features conference at end of week. We are encouraged to contribute to each.

Lou: In an average news meeting, there will be a dozen of us. The news editor will go through the prospects list and we will comment on it, then say Zoe will offer a story, and we'll throw our ideas in.

Interviewer: Have you had any front-page bylines yet?

Lou: I have a big story appearing this week on page five and it is a page lead. It's on page five because it is a national newspaper story and the national newspaper pages are all always the first pages in the magazine. The exception is the front page which is, rather obviously, the biggest story of the week, regardless of it being a regional, national, magazine or broadcast story. The editor and the news editor usually decide what goes on the front.

Zoe: When I was at *The Observer* I got a front page byline which was exhilarating.

Lou: News is the toughest thing I've done. I want to have at least one decent byline each week or I am disappointed with myself. I don't know whether the editors would feel the same, but I do.

Mobility aspirations are also a motivating factor to do well in their current contracts, though it is interesting to see how Zoe and Lou diverge in their ambitions and how those ambitions are partly shaped by the experiences at *Press Gazette*.

Lou: I have learnt a great deal about what an editor does simply through observing our own editor at work. I have a range of ambitions, in print and in other media, but I would hope to be a section editor in the next five years or so.

Zoe: I have not really been interested in the managerial side of journalism so much. I am much more driven by the ability to work flexibly, and I would love to also be able to work abroad. If you work it well you could be in a varied role, so you do one thing for a couple of days per week and another on the other days. At the end of the day, if you want to do your job well you need to really enjoy it, so I am looking to create a career that's varied and satisfying. The ideal job in journalism is where you say what you want to do and you don't fit into any specific category.

Both Zoe and Lou are keen to develop their careers in journalism but still retain a keen sense of their individuality, and the need for their career to be ultimately personally fulfilling. Zoe in particular articulates her desire to fit her journalism outputs around her personal drives and interests rather than necessarily follow a traditional promotional route within one organisation.

Conclusion

This is but a small snapshot update of contemporary practices since Breed (1955) and others wrote of their concerns, but it nonetheless illuminates a number of confirmations and contradictions that need further scrutiny and research. Overall, it would appear that their observations have been supported over time, rather than refuted. Our study confirms that new staff will swiftly identify the goals of management and do what they can to adhere to them in a newsroom context. The question that remains hard to answer is to what extent this is a bad thing. We can start by reviewing the evidence that socialisation does indeed occur, then reflect on the possible implications.

Breed's six key criteria for ensuring the reinforcement of policy do seem to be evidenced in Zoe and Lou's early experiences of working life at the *Press Gazette*. For a start, they identified policy in the ways predicted by Breed, although there is also one main key addition that could be added to his list – that of awareness of rival outputs. Lou expressed confidence in being able to identify a *Press Gazette* angle or story, in a way that had become almost second nature. Zoe agreed that this was important and something to aspire to. It seems that an important sense of collective identity within the newsroom might be achieved by defining the group against what it is not. This is certainly this writer's experience in national and regional newsrooms, where often the newspaper or magazine was defined in comparison to other rival media. As in the other news operations we have studied, an awareness of brand position and approach is ever more present in contemporary newsrooms. *Press Gazette* is in the same situation, and is attempting to grow its readership and identity under its new leadership.

Breed emphasises that in his observations at least five of his six key criteria for journalists complying with policy were present. In this study, we were also aware of five; Lou and Zoe felt esteem for their line managers and mentors, had mobility aspirations, enjoyed the pleasant nature of the work, saw an absence of internal dissent and shared their mission to find stories. Their descriptions of newsroom interactions suggest the combined goal of the team is to make the next edition the best ever and to keep one step ahead of their rivals. Institutional authority and sanctions do not seem to be especially relevant to their experience, though Zoe draws on her past experience to show that this does take place. 'When I worked for one newspaper, the then news editor told me that I would never have a career as a news journalist.' Their reflections and fears about other publications, especially the national press, also seem to fulfill this category.

Sigelman's observations about the way young staff are encouraged to emulate their superiors are apparent at *Press Gazette*, for example in the way the entire staff are given page proofs to edit collectively. While Sigelman might read this as a desire on the part of management to coach junior staff into conforming, from another perspective it might be seen as democratising, though the lack of any apparent conflict or dissent from colleagues as regards editorial decision-making is perhaps cause for concern. The journalistic media are under incredible scrutiny over their practices, and one might expect a drive from staff to wish to break free from the norms of covering regular items to address these debates more forcefully.

Scholars have emphasised professionalism in newsrooms as a key influence on journalistic production practices. The enforcement of a hierarchy minimises the opportunity for personal style, non-conformity and independence. These views would seem to be largely supported by our limited research. But there remains a significant gap in scholarly understanding of the socialisation of young journalists – and that is understanding both their individual backgrounds and the overall industry and cultural context within which they must operate. Media sociology models are not well placed to examine the individual factors within a young journalists' own background that may determine whether or not they accede wholeheartedly to newsroom policy. Lou and Zoe are very much individuals in their own right with some common background characteristics but also many that diverge. These may have a great deal of impact in shaping their responses to their experiences at *Press Gazette*. They have differing ambitions, and it would seem that they are learning news skills and knowledge from their current roles to enable them to progress more swiftly. In this sense they display autonomy and self-reflexivity.

There is undoubtedly an absence of how audiences and wider cultural conventions may also play a role in shaping these practices. How can journalism studies measure the impact of wider developments in professionalising the workplace on news production? In this way, the hierarchical structure of the newsroom is part of a wider continuum, rather than being part of an institutional conspiracy to hoodwink its staff. It reflects broader cultural and political economy issues that have developed through modernisation, that journalism like other seemingly 'marginal' occupations such as higher education, have found impossible to resist. This may be problematic on some levels, as has been illustrated in terms of constraining autonomy and independence. But some of the processes may also be democratising, such as in illuminating issues like workplace bullying that had previously been excused as part and parcel of editorial pressures.

9 Conclusion

This reflexive journey through the theory and practice of news journalism has illuminated the complexity and sophistication of the news industry, and the need for theories of journalism to move and develop alongside it. It has also highlighted how mutually beneficial a closer alliance and shared vocabulary between journalism academe and practice could be. The clear message that we have received in the research for this book is that journalism is in no way inherently averse to engaging with theoretical discourse about itself – it views theory as any other piece of information with the necessary scepticism and scrutiny that you would expect from this industry. The experience has actually brought into sharp focus many of the problems with theories of journalism and academic rigidity. That is not to say that journalism studies should not be robust and rigorous in its explorations, but it does mean that theory must be flexible enough and dynamic to account for an industry that is constantly changing. In this conclusion we come back to our first point – news journalism is at the nexus of a range of factors that are external and internal and is very much subject to them as a craft and process. But there is no doubt that journalists themselves recognise this and seek to navigate these factors in order to produce high-quality output. To go back to Schon, there is reflection-in-action. There needs to be compromise and development on both sides of this theory–practice debate.

We began by describing some of the most abiding theoretical approaches to journalism, and how the idea of news developed out of a particular social and cultural climate. Underlying the ensuing commentary and case studies has been the essential premise – shared by the academy and many in the industry – that the fundamental practices of news journalism are under threat. Study of the political economy of journalism reveals that news organisations are often huge enterprises, frequently part of even larger corporations with cross-media interests and full control over the entire distribution process. This urgent commercial imperative of news has always been there, but in the contemporary context, news output is intertwined with advertising and marketing to a greater extent that permeates the lower rungs of the newsroom. Media studies and media sociology have shown that what makes news is not a neutral reflection of the world but rather events that are selected because they fit preordained criteria. The idea of the news instinct of the journalists is the internalisation of these. News-gathering is part of established routines where journalists gather predictably processed events from regular sources, frequently people or institutions with authority.

We explored theoretical approaches to war reporting that claim audiences and readers get little contextualisation of events, largely due to journalists' increasing lack of access to first-hand verifiable information. The same concerns appear in studies of humanitarian reporting. It is said that there is too little context to the events described, which use simplified news frames through which to mediate. Yet this type of reporting can have a huge impact on the allocation of resources. Young people are attracted to journalism on a range of romantic notions. Yet on entry they are covertly tutored in the acceptable culture of the newsroom, which is becoming much faster-paced, dependent on press releases with reduced staff. In summary, this gloss of journalism theory has presented a very pessimistic and worrying depiction of standards in contemporary news journalism – one of an industry that is image-led, exploiting emotive and sensational reporting to maximise readers, listeners, viewers and profits for shareholders. At the same time news outlets deprive audiences of thorough contextual reporting of matters of real human interest, rather than interest-to-humans. We beg to differ with these accounts.

Whilst many theoretical models derived from media sociology and media studies have robustly critiqued the institutions and products of journalism, they have been unable to account for the sensibilities of the news practitioners themselves. To put it simply and crudely, they have not managed to witness or get inside the hearts and minds of journalists doing their job. They have not had to sit at a newsdesk at deadline time, they have not had to make split-second judgements. Academics have time, and lots of it, to reflect and analyse and hypothesise. We do not think for one moment that we have managed to unpack this debate in its entirety, but it has caused us to reflect carefully on our role as journalism and media researchers and educators. What is emerging is recognition of the parallel aims and motivations of journalists and academics that we should build on:

- The desire to step out of 'society' in order to scrutinise its foundations and practices;
- The desire to provide fresh insights and generate original material;
- The desire to challenge the status quo;
- The desire to conduct research that is accurate, balanced and ethical.

In short, journalists and academics are united in a mission to improve upon practice – it is what needs improving and how that needs bringing together.

The journalists we have spoken to have been far from dismissive about that theory – many are keenly aware of the criticisms made of their trade. But it has been clearly evident that those theories have so far been unable to rigorously and accurately unpack the sheer complexity of factors that impact upon news editorial decision-making. The vocabulary and working methods of the academic study of journalism have been delimited by foreclosed methodologies and, at worst, an inbuilt mistrust of the news industry. Practitioners feel frustrated about academic work and dismiss its validity to working life in a pressured environment. How can an academic know what it is like to work in some of the situations we have described in this book? The academic world could be accused of being as self-protective as any newsroom, always wishing to defend its systems and methods. It is no surprise that the area of journalism scholarship causes friction both between academe and the industry and within university journalism departments themselves.

In this book we have examined real-life case studies, comparing and contrasting them with the associated theories. We saw that some theoretical approaches remain highly perceptive and relevant in their critical description of the forces that drive and shape contemporary news practice. The most notable approaches have been those that steer very close to the industry practices and processes in their data gathering, such as the ethnographies of Fishman and others, and the observations of Breed on newsroom culture. These approaches have stood the test of time. This may be because journalism itself has a continuing vision of its underlying motives and responsibilities, so that certain practices remain embedded while others need modifying. Other analytical models clearly need modification and updating. This study has shown that inflexible theories that can neither account for contextual change nor practitioner autonomy tend to make blanket judgements, which are not in the interests of bettering practice. Journalism practices, processes and contexts change faster than academic studies can always embrace. For instance, during the research for this book the structure of IRN changed. As we explored war reporting, new developments broke regarding the status of foreign stringers. As we examined newspaper design, many leading national broadsheets changed format, so we can no longer make easy distinctions between tabloid and broadsheet. We started this book by stating that journalism is at the nexus of a range of factors that are external and internal. As such it is necessarily organic and changing, subject to changes in technology, culture, audience expectations, legislation, economy and globalisation. That is before we even start to consider what the individuals who work within journalism bring to their trade.

In undertaking this analysis and encouraging journalists to reflect-on-action, we believe that we have shown that news journalism needs to address some of these issues as recent changes in this ever-evolving industry are putting the status of the profession under threat. This is crucial as democratic society relies on journalism to be its watchdog, to make sure that its citizens are informed. In the case of IRN, we worked with the journalists to illuminate the use of marketing criteria as the basis for choice and form of news output. This was not a case of dumbing down but rather a sophisticated process of selection and modelling. Journalists themselves do express concern about this. They still maintain the desire to inform and understand the social responsibility of their trade, but reflection revealed that they realise they need to find ways to work with the restrictions caused by the fast pace of what they do.

The sociological work on journalism reveals that the beat and sourcing are the basis of sound practice, yet financial pressures and massive staff cuts have put these under threat. There is now less time to develop the kinds of stories once routinely discovered and developed through close working with a range of sources. Instead there is a reliance on official statements and press releases. Here the reflections by journalists on changes over time were far bleaker. Yet in the context of reporting war and conflict, journalists felt more positive. War and conflict is where journalism is most often judged. There is often pressure from government to reflect the national interest, and correspondents themselves may feel support for the soldiers they spend time with. Journalists accept that there has been a lack of context and there has been much simplification of issues. There is also the need to meet with production cycles which may demand 24-hour rolling news with no new information coming in, and the impetus to report action over context when military activity is underway. Journalists are mindful of this, though, and it was particularly gratifying to receive such robust feedback from many of our case studies on our analysis of this area. It is here more than anywhere that journalism theory finds it hard to account for the rapidity of change and split-second decision-making that is essential in conflict coverage.

This crystallises the sheer complexity and unpredictability of the working lives of journalists in war zones, and the resourcefulness required to deliver information. This is quite a different account from the myth of the gung-ho ego-driven war reporter, and highlights the delicacy of their work against a backdrop of tight resources, deadlines and ever-present dangers.

The experiences of the humanitarian and post-conflict journalist once again indicate how much individual journalists must navigate the often conflicting pressures of access, editorial pressures and resources as well as trying to impart highly complex and difficult scenarios. Caught up with the routine nature of editorial production, news tends to give audiences a distorted view of the world in the context of humanitarian aid. There is a tendency to repeat typical themes and there is a concern that audiences will not tolerate in-depth analyses of situations. Reporters are aware that they must work hard to persuade news outlets to allow them to create quality stories that do not disappear into cliché or do a disservice to the immeasurable courage of the subjects they encounter.

What has been absolutely evident throughout this study is the way that journalists are not only having to produce a vast stream of output, but are doing this in such a rapidly changing environment. We have witnessed rapid change while working with our case studies. Journalistic practices have expanded and changed. Newspapers have changed format and targeted new markets. A new breed of visually literate and design-savvy sub-editor has emerged in newsrooms that were formerly very distrustful of anything that might detract from the content of a story, which must now appeal to target market groups visually and in terms of content. The design editor we spoke to was aware of how the seamless presentation of news must be carried over into the copy. This is not necessarily a negative development, and could be seen as one way that news must modernise to reach new audiences. It was clear in all these case studies that journalists are committed to delivering the best stories, in keeping with the highest standards of ethics, accuracy and balance, and they do so in often stressful and highly pressured circumstances. The crux of this study is that journalism scholarship and research must have as its core aim the encouragement of the very best standards of practice, which means it must support journalistic endeavour rather than seeing it as forever delimited.

The key themes that have emerged from this work, and that point towards a need for further analysis, include the following:

- Journalism media convergence – how will news journalists navigate the ever-changing nature of their media, given that process drives content?
- Ethics – how do journalists apply ethical decision-making to this evolving media landscape?
- Changing editorial priorities – in an increasingly market-led and targeted news environment, how will journalists negotiate the ensuing shift in their news judgement and prioritising?
- Trust – against this context, how will journalists work to maintain the trust of their public(s) in what they produce and the way in which they produce it?
- Employment issues – how will journalists' careers be affected by change and how will employers and educators respond and prepare the next generation of news journalists accordingly?

This research has nonetheless proved problematic in a number of ways. First, it is not driven in many ways by accepted research methodologies. It does not fit easily within either media studies approaches or sociology. Second, it is not responding directly to any given pieces of academic research in the way that, say, a new approach to science or engineering might. This gives greater weight, in the first case, to the need for journalism studies to develop reflexive methodologies of its own. In response to the second, this is one of its strengths as it illuminates the sheer non-linear interdisciplinarity of journalism practice and its related academic study.

Journalism studies requires a more effective interdisciplinary vocabulary for describing and interrogating news production, and for the betterment of practice. This is particularly important if journalism research is to have relevance for the news journalism industry and for policy-makers in areas such as regulation. One way this book has attempted to move this debate forward is to connect with those who do journalism, and to encourage them to reflect upon their own practical experience and decision-making. It is this that makes journalism studies so very immediate and contemporary, more so than perhaps other traditional media research paradigms that will often examine media artefacts retrospectively. Now that so many journalism educators have moved into academe straight from the industry, they have the advantage over media studies and media sociology of greater access to newsroom personnel. Additionally, by thoroughly engaging and identifying with the working lives of their subjects, the journalism academic is able to produce influential and accessible work that will be read not only by other academics and students, but also journalists themselves and the public. In this way, we can widen and deepen the public's understanding of the news industry, and beckon more of a debate with the practitioners themselves.

But journalism research is changing. At the time of writing, journalism studies scholars in higher education departments are forging a collective identity that prioritises engagement with practitioners. There is a burning desire to develop new approaches to the study of journalism that brings the discipline in line with cutting edge research in, say, science or engineering. In these spheres, the industry is led by pioneering scholarship and development aimed at the betterment of practice. This is also the way forward for journalism – for practitioners and journalism academics to work in unison to ensure the very best standards are set in the industry and in training and education. This book is part of that dialogue. There is the new breed of journalist-scholar who is trying to bring the two of these together. Theory and practice should not be separated.

References

Ainley, B. (1998) *Black Journalists, White Media*, Stoke on Trent: Trentham Books.

Aldridge, M. (1998) 'The Tentative Hell-raisers: Identity and Mythology in Contemporary UK Press Journalism', *Media, Culture & Society* 20, 109–27.

Aldridge, M. and Evetts, J. (2003) 'Rethinking the concept of professionalism: the case of journalism', *The British Journal of Sociology*, 54(4): 547.

Arback, J. (1999) 'Unscripted Television Programs and Corporate/State Concerns: The View from Nilesa', Business Research International. http://nmit George town.edu/papers/jarback.htm.

Bailey, W. and Peterson, R. (1989) 'Murder and Capital Punishment: A Monthly Time-series Analysis of Execution Publicity', *American Sociological Review* 54(5).

Bantz, C. (1999) 'News Organizations: Conflict as a Crafted Cultural Norm,' *Communications* 8, (1985): 225–44.

Barthes, R. (1977) *Image – Music – Text*, London: Fontana.

Bauman, Z. (2001) *Community: Seeking Safety in an Insecure World*, Cambridge: Polity.

Bell, A. (1991) *The Language of News Media*, Oxford: Blackwell.

Bennett, W. L. (2005) *News: the Politics of Illusion*, 6th edn, London and New York: Longman, Pearson.

Benthall, J. (1993) *Disasters, Relief and the Media*, London: I. B. Tauris.

Blumler, J. G. (1969), 'Producers' Attitudes Towards Television Coverage of an Election Campaign', in Halmos P., *The Sociology of Mass Media Communicators*, pp. 85–115. Keele: University of Keele.

Boorstin, D. (1973) *The Image*, New York: Athenaeum.

Bourdieu, P. (1998) *Television and Journalism*, London: Pluto.

Boyd, A. (1988) *Broadcast Journalism: Techniques of Radio and TV News*, Oxford: Heinemann.

Boyd-Barrett, O. (1980) *The International News Agencies*, London: Constable.

Boyd-Barrett, O. and Rantanen, T. (eds) (1998) *The Globalisation of News*, London: Sage.

Breed, W. (1955) *Social Control in the Newsroom: A Functional Analysis*, Social Forces, University of North Carolina Press. Available at http://www.jstor.org/journals/uncpress.html.

Bromley, M. (1997) 'The End of Journalism? Changes in Workplace Practices in the Press and Broadcasting in the 1990s', in Bromley, M. and O'Malley, T. (eds) *A Journalism Reader*, pp. 330–50, London: Routledge.

Carruthers, S. L. (2000) *The Media at War: Communication and Conflict in the Twentieth Century*. London: Macmillan.

Cate, F. H. (ed.) (1994) *International Disaster Communications: Harnessing the Power of Communications to Avert Disasters and Save Lives*, Washington, DC: The Annenberg Washington Program in Communications Policy Studies of Northwestern University.

Chan, J. (1996) 'Television in Greater China: Structure, Exports, and Market Formation', in Sinclair, J., Jacka, E. and Cunningham, S. (eds) *New Patterns in Global Television: Peripheral Vision*, pp. 126–60, Oxford: Oxford University Press.

Chaney, D. (1996) *Lifestyles*, London: Routledge.

Chen, C. Y. (2003) 'CLEAR CHANNEL: Not the Bad Boys of Radio', *Fortune*, 18 February. Available at http://www.fortune.com/fortune/ceo/articles/0,15114,423802,00.html.

Chopra, S. (2005) 'Role of Media in Covering Humanitarian Conflict', South Asian Women's Forum, available at http://www.fritzinstitute.org/PDFs/Media-Coverage/SAWF_121001.pdf.

Chronicle World (accessed online 2006) 'What colour is the news? Minority Journalists hold key to media's role in multi-cultural Britain'. Available at http://www.thechronicle.demon.co.uk/archive/colnews.htm.

Cohen, A., Levy, M., Roeh, I. and Gurevitch, M. (1996) *Global Newsrooms, Local Audiences: A Study of the Eurovision News Exchange*, London: John Libbey.

Cohen, S. (1973) *Folk Devils and Moral Panics*, London: Paladin.

Cohen, S. and Young, J. (eds) (1981) *The Manufacture of News: Social Problems, Deviance and the Mass Media*, London: Constable.

Competition Commission (2003) Available at http://www.competition-commission.org.uk/rep.

Connell, I. (1991) 'Tales of Tellyland: The Popular Press and TV in the UK' in Dahlgren, P. and Sparks, C. (eds) *Communication and Citizenship: Journalism and the Public Sphere*, pp. 236–53, London: Routledge.

Content wire (2002) Syndication News: Syndicated Content for Affiliates, 21 February 2002. Available at http://www.content-wire.com/online/Syndication.cfm?ccs=111&cs=1423.

Coward, R. (1989) *The Whole Truth: Myth of Alternative Health*, London: Faber and Faber.

Coward, R. (2004) *Diana: The Portrait*, London: Harper Collins Entertainment.

Cronkite, W. and Snow, J. (1997) 'More Bad News', *Guardian* 27 January.

Cunningham, B. (2003) 'Rethinking Objectivity', *Columbia Journalism Review* available at http://www.archives.cjr.org/year/03/4/cunningham.asp.

Curran, J. (1991) 'Mass Media and Democracy: A Reappraisal', in Curran, J. and Gurevitch, M. (eds) *Mass Media and Society*, London: Routledge.

Deacon, D. (2004) 'Journalists and Quasi-government in the UK: Conflict, Co-operation or Co-option?', *Journalism Studies* 5: 339–52.

Delano, A., Henningham, J. (1995) *The News Breed: British Journalists in the 1990s*, London: School of Media, London College of Printing and Distributive Trades.

Delano Brown, J., Bybee, C. R. Wearden, S. T. and Murdock, D. (1987) 'Invisible Power: Newspaper Sources and the Limits of Diversity' *Journalism Quarterly* 64: 45–54.

Dewey, J. (1989) *The Public and Its Problems*, Ohio University Press (originally published 1927).

Donald, J. and Kaplan, C. (eds) *Formations of Fantasy*, pp. 167–99, London and New York: Methuen.

Drayton, H. (2005) 'My doubts over the Barclay sale', *Guardian*, 5 December. Available at http://media.guardian.co.uk/site/story/0,14173,1657945,00.html.

Ebo, B. (1992) 'American Media and African Culture', in Hawk, B.G. *Africa's Media Image*, pp. 15–22, New York: Praeger.

Edelman, M. (1977) *Political Language: Words That Succeed, Policies That Fail*, New York: Academic Press.

Edwards, D. (2002) 'Hide The Looking Glass: *The Observer*, ITV, Channel 4, *The New York Times*, *The Washington Post*', Znet media lens, September. Available at http://www.zmag.org/content/showarticle.cfm?SectionID=22&ItemID=2387.

Ekstrom, M. (2000) 'Information, Story Telling and Attractions: TV Journalism in 3 Modes of Communication', *Media, Culture & Society* 22: 465–96.

Ericson, R. V., Baranek, P. M. and Chan, J. B. L. (1987) *Visualising Deviance: A Study of News Organisation*, Toronto: University of Toronto Press.

Ericson, R., Baranek, P. M. and Chan J. B. L. (1989) *Negotiating Control: A Study of News Sources*, Toronto: University of Toronto Press.

European Journalism Centre Online (2005) See http://www.ejc.nl/jr/emland/index/html.

Evans, H. (1973) *Newspaper Design*, London: Heinemann.

Evans, H. (1974b) *News Headlines*, London: Butterworth-Heinemann Ltd.

Evans, H. (1972) *Editing and Design: A Five-Volume Manual of English, Typography and Layout*, London: Heinemann.

Evans, H. (1974a) *Handling Newspaper Text*, New York: Henry Holt & Company, Inc.

Evans. H. (1986) *Editing and Design: Book 2: Handling Newspaper Text,* London: Butterworth-Heinemann Ltd.

Ewen, S. (1996) *PR: A Social History of Spin*, New York: Basic Books.

Fair, J. E. (1989) 'Are we really the world? Coverage of US Food Aid in Africa 1980–1989', in Hawk, B. G. (ed.) *Africa's Media Image*, pp. 109–20, New York: Praeger.

Fishman, M. (1980) *Manufacturing the News*, Austin, TX and London: University of Texas Press.

Foucault, M. (1972) *The Archaeology of Knowledge*, trans. Smith, S., London: Tavistock.

Fournier, V. (1999) 'The Appeal to "Professionalism" as a Disciplinary Mechanism', *The Sociological Review*, 47(2), 280–307.

Fowler, R. (1991) *Language in the News: Discourse and Ideology in the Press.* London: Routledge.

Frankel, G. (2004) 'Off-the-Cuff Remark Sent The BBC Reeling' *Washington Post Foreign Service* Saturday, 31 January, C01. Available at http://www.washingtonpost.com/ac2/wp-dyn/A15–2004Jan30?language=printer.

Franklin, B. (1997) *Newszak And News Media*, London: Arnold.

Furedi, F. (1997) *Culture of Fear*, London: Continuum Books.

Furedi, F. (2003) *Therapy Culture*, London: Routledge.

Gage, J. (1993) *Colour and Culture – Practice and Meaning from Antiquity to Abstraction*, London: Thames and Hudson.

Gage, J. (1999) *Colour and Meaning – Art, Science and Symbolism*, London: Thames and Hudson.

Gallagher, M. and Von Euler, M. (1995) 'An Unfinished Story: Gender Patterns In Media Employment', Reports and Papers on Mass Communication, 110, Paris: UNESCO.

Galtung, J. and Ruge, M. H. (1965) 'The Structure of Foreign News', *Journal of International Peace Research* 1: 64–90.

Gans, H. J. (1980) *Deciding What's News: A Study of CBS Evening News, NBC Nightly News, Newsweek and Time*, London: Constable.

Garcia Aviles, J. A., Bienvenido, L., Sanders, K. and Harrison, J. (2004) 'Journalists at Digital Television Newsrooms in Britain and Spain: Workflow and Multi-skilling in a Competitive Environment', *Journalism Studies* 5: 87–100.

Garcia, M. (2005) 'March of the Tabloids', Poynter Online 27 April. Available at http://www.poynter.org/content/content_view.asp?id=81557&sid=11.

Gitlin, T. and Sylvain, O. (2005) 'Staff Cuts are a Disgrace to Journalism', available at Newsday.com/news/opinion/ny-opgit124549541dec12,0,7718222.story?coll=ny-viewpoints-headlines.

Glasgow University Media Group (1976) *Bad News*, London: Routledge.

Grade, M. (2005) Making the Important Interesting: BBC Journalism in the twenty-first Century. Cudlipp Lecture, London College of Communications 21 January 2005. Avaliable at http://www.bbc.co.uk/preswsoffice/speeches/stories/grade_cudlipp.shtml.

Graham, P., Keenan, T. and Dowd, A. (2004) 'A Call to Arms at the End of History: A Discourse–Historical Analysis of George W. Bush's Declaration of War on Terror', *Discourse & Society*, 15(2–3): 199–221.

Greenslade, R. (2004) *Press Gang: How Newspapers Make Profits From Propaganda*, London: Pan MacMillan.

Griffin, M. (2004) 'Picturing America's "War on Terrorism" in Afghanistan and Iraq: Photographic Motifs as News Frames', *Journalism* 5(4): 381–402.

Grossman, L. K. (1998) 'Does Local TV News Need a National Nanny?', *Columbia Journalism Review* May–June. Available at http://archives.cjr.org/year/98/3/grossman.asp.

Grossman, L. K. (1998) 'In the Public Interest. The Death of Radio Reporting: Will TV be Next?', *Columbia Journalism Review* September/October.

Gunther, B. and Funham, A. (1992) *Consumer Profiles: An Introduction to Psychographics*, London: Routledge.

Hall, S. (1973) 'The Determination of News Photographs', Working Papers in Cultural Studies, no.3. Reprinted in *The Manufacture of News* (1973), S. Cohen and J. Young, London: Constable.

Hall, S. (1980) 'Encoding/decoding', in Centre for Contemporary Cultural Studies (ed.) *Culture, Media, Language*, London: Hutchinson.

Hall, S., Critchern, C., Jefferson, T., Clarke, J. and Roberts, B. (1978) *Policing the Crisis: Mugging, the State and Law and Order*, London: Macmillan.

Halliday, F. (1996) *Islam and the Myth of Confrontation*, London: I. B. Taurus.

Halliday, M. A. K. (1978) *Language as Social Semiotics*, London: Edward Arnold.

Halliday, M. A. K. (1985) *Introduction to Functional Grammar*, London: Edward Arnold.

Hallin, D. (1996) 'Commercialism and Professionalism in the American News Media', in Curran, J. and Gurevitch, M. (eds) *Mass Media and Society*, 2nd edn, pp. 243–62, London: Arnold.

Hallin, D. C. and Gitlin, T. (1994) 'The Gulf War as Popular Culture and Television Drama', in Bennett, W. Lance and Paletz, David L. (eds) *Taken by Storm: The Media, Public Opinion, and U.S. Foreign Policy in the Gulf War*, pp. 149–63, Chicago, IL and London: University of Chicago Press.

Hanke, R. (1989) 'Mass Media and Lifestyle Differentiation: An Analysis of the Public Discourse about Food', *Communication* 11: 221–38.

Harcup, T. and O'Neill, D. (2001) 'What Is News? Galtung and Ruge revisited', *Journalism Studies* 2(2): 261–80.

Hartley, J. (1982) *Understanding News*, London: Routledge.

Herman, E. S. and Chomsky, N. (1988) *Manufacturing Consent: The Political Economy of the Mass Media*, New York: Pantheon Books.

Herman, E. S. and McChesney, R. W. (1997) *The Global Media: The New Missionaries of Corporate Capitalism*, Herndon, VA: Cassell.

Hold the Front Page (2004) Available at http://www/holdthefrontpage.co.uk/behind/analysis/040226liv.shtml.

Holleufer, G. (1996) 'Images of Humanitarian Crises: Ethical Implications', *International Review of the Red Cross* 315: 609–13.

Hollingsworth, M. (1986) *The Press and Political Dissent*, London: Pluto Press.

Hourani, A. (1991) *A History of the Arab Peoples*, New York: Warner Books.

Hoyer, W. D. and MacInnis, D. J. (1997) *Consumer Behaviour*, Boston, MA: Houghton Mifflin.

Ignatieff, M. (1998) *The Warrior's Honor: Ethnic War and the Modern Conscience*, London: Chatto & Windus.

INMA (2005) 'The Bottom Line of Broadsheet-to-Compact Format Change: Why Do It, How to Deal With Advertising, How Consumers React'. Available at http://www.inma.org/bookstore/2005-formatchange.cfm.

Just, M., Levine, R. and Regan, K. (2002) 'Investigative Journalism Against the Odds', *Columbia Journalism Review* November–December: 103.

Katovsky, B. and Carlson, T. (2003) *The Media at War in Iraq*, Guildford, CT: The Lyons Press.

Keeble, R. (ed.) (1998) *The Newspapers Handbook*, London: Routledge.

Keeble, R. (2001) *Ethics for Journalists*, London: Routledge.

Keeble, R. (ed.) (2005) *Print Journalism: A Critical Introduction*, London: Routledge.

Kellner, D. (2004) '9/11, Spectacles of Terror, and Media Manipulation: A Critique of Jihadist and Bush Media Politics', *Critical Discourse Studies* 1(1): 41–64.

Kimball, P. (1988) 'The Stab-in-the-Back Legend and the Vietnam War', *Armed Forces & Society* 14(3): 433–58.

Kirtley, J. (2001) 'Waving the flag', *American Journalism Review*, 23(9).

Kress, G. and Van Leeuwen, T. (1996) *Reading Images: the Grammar of Visual Design*, London: Routledge.

Kress, G. and Van Leeuwen, T. (2001) *Multimodal Discourse: The Modes and Media of Contemporary Communication*, London: Arnold.

Kress, G. and Van Leeuwen, T. (2002) 'Colour as a semiotic mode: notes for a grammar of colour', *Visual Communication* 1(3): 343–68.

Lefebvre, J. A. (1991) *Arms for The Horn: US Security Policy in Ethiopia and Somalia 1953–1991*, Pittsburgh, PA: University of Pittsburgh Press.

Levinas, E. (1961) *Totality and Infinity: An Essay on Exteriority*, New York: Springer-Verlag.

Lewis, B. (1998) *The Multiple Identities of the Middle East*, London: Phoenix.

Lewis, J. (2001) *Constructing Public Opinion: How Political Elites Do What They Like and Why We Seem to Go Along with It*, New York: Columbia University Press.

Lloyd, J. (2004) *What the Media are Doing to our Politics*, London: Constable and Robinson.

Lutz, C. A. and Collins, J. L. (1993) *Reading National Geographic*, Chicago, IL: University of Chicago Press.

Lynch, J. and McGoldrick, A. (2005) *Peace Journalism*, Stroud: Hawthorn Press.

MacArthur, John R. (1992) *Second Front: Censorship and Propaganda in the Gulf War*, New York: Hill and Wang.

Machin, D. (2004) 'Building the World's Visual Language: The Increasing Global Importance of Image Banks in Corporate Media', *Visual Communication* 13(3): 316–36.

Machin, D. (in press) 'Visual Discourses of War – A Multimodal Analysis of Photographs of the Iraq Occupation', in Adam Hodges, A. and Nilep, C. (eds) *Discourse, War and Terrorism*. London: John Benjemins.

Machin, D. and Thornborrow, J. (2003) 'Branding and Discourse: the Case of Cosmopolitan', *Discourse and Society* 14(4): 453–71.

Maren, M. (1997) *The Road to Hell: The Ravaging Effect of Foreign Aid and International Charity*, New York: Free Press.

McChesney, R. W. (2004) *The Problem with the Media: US Communication Politics in the twenty-first Century*. New York: Monthly Review Press.

McCombs, M. and Shaw, D. L. (1972) 'The Agenda-Setting Function of the Mass Media', *Public Opinion Quarterly*, 36, 176–87.

McManus, J. H. (1994) *Market-Driven Journalism: Let the Citizen be Aware*, London: Sage.

McNair, B. (1994) *The Sociology of Journalism*, London: Arnold.

McQuail, D. (1994) *Mass Communication Theory*, London: Sage.

McRobbie, A. (1982) 'The Politics of Feminist Research', *Feminist Review* 12(October): 46–57.

McRobbie, A. (1984) 'Dance and Social Fantasy', in McRobbie, A. and Nava, M. (eds) *Gender and Generation*, pp. 130–61, London: Macmillan.

Mehrotra, S. and Wells, D. (1979) 'Psychographics and Buyer Behaviour: Theory and Recent Empirical Findings', in Woodside, A. G., Sheth, J. N. and Bennett, P. D. (eds) *Consumer Behavior and Industrial Buying Behaviour*, pp. 49–65, New York: North Holland.

Miller, J. (1992) 'But Can You Dance To It? MTV Turns to News', *New York Times Magazine*, 11 October, A17.

Mitchell, A. (1978) *Consumer Values: A Typology*, Menlo Park, CA: Stanford Research Institute.

Moeller, S. D. (1999) *Compassion Fatigue: How the Media Sell Disease, Famine, War and Death*, London: Routledge.

Murdock, G. and Golding, P. (1977) 'Capitalism, Communication and Class relations', in Curran, J., Gurevitch, M. and Woollacott, J. (eds) *Mass Communication and Society*, London: Arnold.

Newspaper Society website at www.newspapersoc.org.uk.

Niblock, S. (1996) *Inside Journalism*, London: Blueprint.

Niblock, S. (2005) 'Practice and theory: what is news?' in Keeble, R. (ed.) *Print Journalism: A Critical Introduction*, pp. 73–82, London: Routledge.
Niblock, S. and Machin, D. (2006) 'News Values for Consumer Groups: The Case of Independent Radio News', *Journalism: Theory and Practice* (in press).
Nielsonmedia (2006) Citing http://www.stateofthenewsmedia.org/2006/narrative_networktv_audience.asp?cat=3&media=5.
Ochs, M. (1986) *The African Press*, Cairo: The American University.
Olsen, G. M., Carstensen, N. and Høyen K. (2003) 'What Determines the Level of Emergency Assistance? Media Coverage, Donor Interests, and the Aid Business', *Disasters* 27(2): 109–26.
Orr, C. J. (1980) 'Reporters Confront the President: Sustaining a Counterpoised Situation', *Quarterly Journal of Speech* 66: 17–32.
Parenti, M. (2002) *The Terrorism Trap: Sept 11th and Beyond*, San Francisco, CA: City Light Books.
Park, R. E. and Burgess, E. W. (1927) *The City*, Chicago, IL: University of Chicago Press.
Parker, T. (1995) *Mixed Signals: The Prospects for Global TV News*, New York: Twentieth Century Fund Press.
Paterson, C. (1998) 'Global Battlefields', in Boyd-Barret, O. and Rantanen, T. *The Globalisation of News*, London: Sage.
Patterson, P. and Wilkins, L. (1994) *Media Ethics*, Dubuque, IA: Brown & Benchmark.
PEJ (2002) Local TV News Project available at http://www.stateofthemedia.org/2005/narrative_localtv_contentanalysis.asp?cat=2&media=6.
Pilger, J. (1999) 'We Helped Them Descend Into Hell', *New Statesman*, 13 September.
Pooley, J. (1999) 'Tricks of the trade: Hamburger Helper for Newscasters', *Brill's Content* December 1998–January 1999: 49.
Postman, M. (1986) *Amusing Ourselves to Death: Public Discourse in the Age of Show Business*, London: Penguin.
Potter, D. and Gantz, W. (2004) Bringing viewers back to local TV: What could reverse the ratings slide? Available at Newslab.org.
Prior, D. (1996) 'Working the Network': Local Authority Strategies in the Reticulated Local State', in Davis, H. (ed.) *Quangos and Local Government: A Changing World*, pp. 26–38, London: Frank Cass.
Quinn, S. (2002) *Knowledge Management in the Digital Newsroom*, Oxford: Focal Press.
Rampton, S. and Stauber, J. (2000) *Trust Us, We're Experts: How Industry Manipulates Science and Gambles With Your Future*, New York: Tarcher.
Randall, D. (1996) *The Universal Journalist*, London: Pluto Press.
Ray, M. and Jacka, E. (1996) 'Indian Television: An Emerging Regional Force', in Sinclair, J., Jacka, E. and Cunningham, S. (eds) *New Patterns in Global Television: Peripheral Vision*, pp. 83–100, Oxford: Oxford University Press.
Rieff, D. (1997) 'Charity on the Rampage; The Business of Foreign Aid', review section, Council on Foreign Relations, Inc. Available at http://www.princeton.edu/~amimages/rieff.html.
Robinson, P. (2002) *The CNN Effect: The Myth of News, Foreign Policy and Intervention*, London: Routledge.

Roshco, B. (1975) *Newsmaking*, Chicago, IL and London: University of Chicago Press.

Ross, S. (2004) 'Toward New Understandings: Journalists and Humanitarian Relief Coverage', *Civic Society Observer* 1(2). http://www.un-ngls.org/cso/cso2/toward.html.

Rusbridger, A. (2005) 'The Shape of Things to Come', *Guardian* 12 September. Available at http://www.guardian.co.uk/theguardian/story/0,16391,1568006,00.html.

Schlesinger, P. (1978) *Putting 'Reality' Together*, London: Routledge.

Schon, D. A. (1983) *The Reflective Practitioner: How Professionals Think in Action*, London: Basic Books.

Schraeder, P. J. (1990) 'The Horn of Africa: US foreign Policy in an Altered Cold War Environment', *Middle East Journal* 46(4): 573–74.

Schudson, M. (1978) *Discovering the News: A Social History of American Newspapers*, New York: Basic Books.

Sergeant, J. (2001) *Give Me Ten Seconds*, London: Macmillan.

Seymour, M. H. (1983) *The Price of Power: Kissinger in the Nixon White House*, New York: Summit Books.

Seymour-Ure, C. (1968) *The Press, Politics and the Public: An Essay on the Role of the National Press in the British Political System*, London: Methuen.

Shoemaker, P. J. and Reese, S. D. (1991) *Mediating the Message: Theories of Influences on Mass Media Content*, New York: Longman Publishing Group.

Siebert, F. S. (1963) *Four Theories of the Press*, University of Illinois Press. (Originally published 1956.).

Sigal, L. V. (1973) *Reporters and Officials: The Organisation and Politics of News Reporting*, Lexington, MA: Heath.

Sigelman, L. (1973) 'Reporting the News: An Organisational Analysis', *American Journal of Sociology*, 79(1): 132–51.

Simon, H. A. (1957) *Models of Man – Social and Rational*, New York: John Wiley and Son.

Simpson, J. (2000) *A Mad World, My Masters: Tales From a Traveller's Life*, London: Macmillan.

Soloski, J. (1989) 'New reporting and professionalism: some constraints on the reporting of the news', *Media, Culture and Society*, 11: 207–28.

Sontag, S. (2004) *Regarding the Pain of Others*, New York: Farrar Straus & Giroux.

Sorkin, M. (ed.) (1992) *Variations on a Theme Park*, New York: Hill and Wang.

Sparks, C. (1992) 'Popular Journalism: Theories and Practice', in Dahlgren, P. and Sparks, C. (eds) *Journalism and Popular Culture*, pp. 22–44, London: Sage.

Stoff, M. (1980) *Oil War and American Security: The Search for a National Policy on Foreign Oil, 1941–1947*, New Haven, CT: Yale University Press.

Tanguy, J. (1999) 'The Media and the Cycle of Humanitarian Crisis', *Tikkun* 14(1): 48.

Taylor, P. (1992) *War and the Media: Propaganda and Persuasion in the Gulf War*, Manchester: Manchester University Press.

Temporal, P. (2002) *Advanced Brand Management: From Vision to Valuation*, New York: John Wiley & Sons.

Tompkins, A. (2001) 'Tragedies Create a Lifetime of Memories', available at http://www.dartcenter.org/articles/books/tragedies_00.html.

Tuchman, G. (1973) 'Making News by Doing Work: Routinizing the Unexpected', *The American Journal of Sociology* 79(1): 110–31.

Tuchman, G. (1978) *Making News*, New York: Free Press.

Tucker, R. W. (1980–81) 'The purpose of American Power' *Foreign Affairs* 59(2): 253.

Tumber, H. (1999) *News: A Reader*, Oxford: Oxford University Press.

Tumber, H. and Palmer, J. (2004) *The Media at War: The Iraq Crisis*, London: Sage.

Tumber, H. and Webster, F. (2006) *Journalists Under Fire: Information War and Journalistic Practice*, London: Sage.

Tunstall, J. (ed.) (1970) *Media Sociology*, London: Constable.

Tunstall, J. (1971) *Journalists at Work*, London: Constable.

Tunstall, J. (1996) *Newspaper Power: The New National Press in Britain*, Oxford: Oxford University Press.

Tunstall, J. and Machin, D. (1999) *The Anglo American Media Connection*, Oxford: Oxford University Press.

Tunstall, J. and Palmer, M. (1991) *Media Moguls*, London: Routledge.

Underwood, D. (1995) *When MBAs Rule the Newsroom: How the Marketers and Managers Are Reshaping Today's Media*, New York: Columbia University Press.

United States Government (1945) *Foreign Relations of the United States*, Washington, DC: Government Printing Office, 8: 45.

Ursell, G. (2001) 'Dumbing Down or Shaping Up? New Technologies, New Media, New Journalism', *Journalism* 2(2): 175–96.

Usher, R., Bryant, I. and Johnstone, R. (1997) *Adult Education and the Postmodern Challenge*, London: Routledge.

Van Leeuwen, T. (2005) 'Towards a Semiotics of Typography', Unpublished paper.

Walkerdine, V. (1986) 'Video Replay: Families, Films and Fantasy' in Burgin, V.,

Walkerdine, V., Lucey, H. and Melody, J. (2001) *Growing up Girl: Psycho-social Explorations of Gender and Class*, London: Palgrave Macmillan.

Wasko, J. (1982) *Movies and Money: Financing the American Film Industry*, Norwood, NJ: Ablex.

Weaver, D. H. (ed.) (1997) *The Global Journalist: News People Around the World*, New Jersey: Hampton Press.

White, David Manning (1950). 'The "Gatekeeper": A Case Study in the Selection of News', *Journalism Quarterly* 27(4): 383–90.

Young, K. (2001) 'UNHCR and ICRC in the Former Yugoslavia: Bosnia-Herzegovina', *RICR* 83(843): 781–805.

Zelizer, B., Park, D. and Gudelunas, D. (2002) 'How Bias Shapes the News: Challenging The *New York Times*' Status as a Newspaper of Record on the Middle East', *Journalism* 3(3): 283–307.

Zukin, S. (1995) *The Cultures of Cities*, London: Blackwell.

Index